Learn React with TypeScript

A beginner's guide to reactive web development with React 18 and TypeScript

Carl Rippon

BIRMINGHAM—MUMBAI

Learn React with TypeScript

Group Product Manager: Pavan Ramchandani
Publishing Product Manager: Jane D'Souza
Senior Editor: Hayden Edwards
Technical Editor: Joseph Aloocaran
Copy Editor: Safis Editing
Project Coordinator: Sonam Pandey
Proofreader: Safis Editing
Indexer: Rekha Nair
Production Designer: Aparna Bhagat
Marketing Coordinator: Anamika Singh

First published: November 2018

Second edition: March 2023

Production reference: 1010223

Published by Packt Publishing Ltd.
Livery Place
35 Livery Street
Birmingham
B3 2PB, UK.

ISBN 978-1-80461-420-4

www.packtpub.com

Contributors

About the author

Carl Rippon has been in the software industry for over 20 years, developing complex line-of-business applications in various sectors. He has spent the last 8 years building single-page applications using a wide range of JavaScript technologies, including Angular, ReactJS, and TypeScript. He has also written over 100 blog posts on various technologies.

I'd like to thank Sarah, Ellie-Jayne, Lilly-Rose, Fudge, and Arlo for all the support and encouragement they've given me while writing this book. A special thanks to everyone on the Packt editorial team for their hard work and great feedback, especially Hayden Edwards.

About the reviewer

Andrew Baisden is a software developer with a passion for helping others succeed in the tech industry. He has made a name for himself as a skilled programmer and a valuable resource for those looking to enter or advance in the field. Proficient in both JavaScript and Python, Andrew has a diverse skill set and a track record of delivering high-quality work. In addition to his technical expertise, Andrew is also a gifted technical writer and content creator. He regularly posts articles and resources on social media to assist others in their programming journey and career growth. Whether through code or written words, Andrew is dedicated to empowering and supporting the community in the tech world.

Table of Contents

2

Introducing TypeScript 37

3

Setting Up React and TypeScript 75

4

Using React Hooks   107

Part 2: App Fundamentals

5

Approaches to Styling React Frontends   147

6

Routing with React Router   179

7

Working with Forms   227

Part 3: Data

8

State Management   265

9

Interacting with RESTful APIs   295

10

Part 4: Advanced React

11

12

Unit Testing with Jest and React Testing Library   413

Preface

React was built by Meta to provide more structure to its code base and allow it to scale much better. React worked so well for Facebook that they eventually made it open source. Today, React is the dominant technology for building the frontend of an application; it allows us to build small, isolated, and highly reusable components that can be composed together to create complex frontends.

TypeScript was built by Microsoft to help developers more easily develop large JavaScript-based programs. It is a superset of JavaScript that brings a rich type system to it. This type system helps developers to catch bugs early and allows tools to be created to robustly navigate and refactor code.

This book will teach you how to use both of these technologies to create large, sophisticated frontends that are easy to maintain.

Who this book is for

If you are a developer who wants to create large and complex frontends with React and TypeScript, this book is for you. The book doesn't assume you have any previous knowledge of React or TypeScript – however, basic knowledge of JavaScript, HTML, and CSS will help you get to grips with the concepts covered.

What this book covers

Chapter 1, Introducing React, covers the fundamentals of building React components. This includes defining component output using JSX, making a component configurable using props, and making a component interactive using states.

Chapter 2, Introducing TypeScript, is all about the fundamentals of TypeScript and its type system. This includes using inbuilt types, as well as creating new types.

Chapter 3, Setting Up React and TypeScript, explains how to create a project for React and TypeScript development. The chapter then moves on to how to create React components that use TypeScript to make props and states type-safe.

Chapter 4, Using React Hooks, details the common React hooks and their typical use cases. The chapter also covers how to use the hooks with TypeScript to make them type-safe.

Chapter 5, Approaches to Styling React Frontends, walks through how to style React components using several different approaches. The benefits of each approach are also explored.

Chapter 6, Routing with React Router, introduces a popular library that provides client-side routing for applications with multiple pages. It covers how to declare the paths for the pages and how to create links between them. It also covers how to implement page parameters for highly dynamic pages.

Chapter 7, Working with Forms, explores how forms can be implemented using several different approaches, including the use of a popular library. The benefits of each approach are also included.

Chapter 8, State Management, walks through how states can be shared between different components. Several approaches are explored, along with their benefits.

Chapter 9, Interacting with RESTful APIs, demonstrates how React components can interact with a REST API. The chapter steps through an approach using core React and then an alternative approach using a popular library.

Chapter 10, Interacting with GraphQL APIs, shows how React components can interact with a GraphQL API. The chapter details how this can be done using two different popular libraries.

Chapter 11, Reusable Components, brings in several patterns for making React components highly reusable but still type-safe.

Chapter 12, Unit Testing with Jest and React Testing Library, first delves into how functions can be tested with Jest. The chapter then moves on to how React components can be tested with the help of the React Testing Library.

To get the most out of this book

To get the most out of this book, you need to know the basics of JavaScript, including the following:

- An understanding of some of the primitive JavaScript types, such as `string`, `number`, `boolean`, `null`, and `undefined`
- An understanding of how to create variables and reference them, including arrays and objects
- An understanding of how to create functions and call them
- An understanding of how to create conditional statements with the `if` and `else` keywords

You also need to know the basics of HTML, including the following:

- An understanding of basic HTML elements such as `div`, `ul`, `a`, and `h1`
- An understanding of how to reference a CSS class to style an HTML element

An understanding of basic CSS is also helpful, including the following:

- How to size elements and include margins and padding
- How to position elements
- How to color elements

To follow along with this book, you will need the following technologies installed on your computer:

- A modern browser such as **Google Chrome**, which can be installed from `https://www.google.com/chrome/`
- **Node.js** and **npm**: You can install them from `https://nodejs.org/en/download/`
- **Visual Studio Code**: You can install it from: `https://code.visualstudio.com/`

Software/hardware covered in the book
React 18.0 or later
TypeScript 4.7 or later

If you are using the digital version of this book, we advise you to type the code yourself or access the code from the book's GitHub repository (a link is available in the next section). Doing so will help you avoid any potential errors related to the copying and pasting of code.

Download the example code files

You can download the example code files for this book from GitHub at `https://github.com/PacktPublishing/Learn-React-with-TypeScript-2nd-Edition`. If there's an update to the code, it will be updated in the GitHub repository.

We also have other code bundles from our rich catalog of books and videos available at `https://github.com/PacktPublishing/`. Check them out!

Download the color images

We also provide a PDF file that has color images of the screenshots and diagrams used in this book. You can download it here: `https://packt.link/5CvU5`.

Conventions used

There are a number of text conventions used throughout this book.

`Code in text`: Indicates code words in text, database table names, folder names, filenames, file extensions, pathnames, dummy URLs, user input, and Twitter handles. Here is an example: "Here, `null` is passed because there are no properties."

A block of code is set as follows:

```
<div className="title">
  <span>Oh no!</span>
</div>
```

When we wish to draw your attention to a particular part of a code block, the relevant lines or items are set in bold:

```
React.createElement(
  'span',
  null,
  title ? title : 'Something important'
);
```

Any command-line input or output is written as follows:

```
$ mkdir css
$ cd css
```

Bold: Indicates a new term, an important word, or words that you see onscreen. For instance, words in menus or dialog boxes appear in **bold**. Here is an example: "Select **System info** from the **Administration** panel."

> **Tips or important notes**
> Appear like this.

Get in touch

Feedback from our readers is always welcome.

General feedback: If you have questions about any aspect of this book, email us at customercare@ packtpub.com and mention the book title in the subject of your message.

Errata: Although we have taken every care to ensure the accuracy of our content, mistakes do happen. If you have found a mistake in this book, we would be grateful if you would report this to us. Please visit www.packtpub.com/support/errata and fill in the form.

Piracy: If you come across any illegal copies of our works in any form on the internet, we would be grateful if you would provide us with the location address or website name. Please contact us at copyright@packt.com with a link to the material.

If you are interested in becoming an author: If there is a topic that you have expertise in and you are interested in either writing or contributing to a book, please visit authors.packtpub.com.

Share Your Thoughts

Once you've read *Learn React with TypeScript (Second Edition)*, we'd love to hear your thoughts! Scan the QR code below to go straight to the Amazon review page for this book and share your feedback.

https://packt.link/r/1-804-61420-3

Your review is important to us and the tech community and will help us make sure we're delivering excellent quality content.

Download a free PDF copy of this book

Thanks for purchasing this book!

Do you like to read on the go but are unable to carry your print books everywhere? Is your eBook purchase not compatible with the device of your choice?

Don't worry, now with every Packt book you get a DRM-free PDF version of that book at no cost.

Read anywhere, any place, on any device. Search, copy, and paste code from your favorite technical books directly into your application.

The perks don't stop there, you can get exclusive access to discounts, newsletters, and great free content in your inbox daily

Follow these simple steps to get the benefits:

1. Scan the QR code or visit the link below

https://packt.link/free-ebook/9781804614204

2. Submit your proof of purchase

3. That's it! We'll send your free PDF and other benefits to your email directly

Part 1:
Introduction

This part will get you started with both React and TypeScript, learning about the fundamentals of both technologies separately. We will then start to use these technologies together to enable us to create powerful type-safe components. We will also learn about React's common hooks in detail and the cases in which they are used in applications.

This part includes the following chapters:

- *Chapter 1, Introducing React*
- *Chapter 2, Introducing TypeScript*
- *Chapter 3, Setting Up React and TypeScript*
- *Chapter 4, Using React Hooks*

1
Introducing React

Facebook has become an incredibly popular app. As its popularity has grown, so has the demand for new features. **React** is Facebook's answer to helping more people work on the code base and deliver features more quickly. React has worked so well for Facebook that Meta eventually made it open source. Today, React is a mature library for building component-based frontends that is extremely popular and has a massive community and ecosystem.

TypeScript is also a popular, mature library maintained by another big company, Microsoft. It allows users to add a rich type system to their JavaScript code, helping them be more productive, particularly in large code bases.

This book will teach you how to use both of these awesome libraries to build robust frontends that are easy to maintain. The first two chapters in the book will introduce React and TypeScript separately. You'll then learn how to use React and TypeScript together to compose robust components with strong typing. The book covers key topics you'll need to build a web frontend, such as styling, forms, and data fetching.

In this chapter, we will introduce React and understand the benefits it brings. We will then build a simple React component, learning about the JSX syntax and component props. After that, we will learn how to make a component interactive using component state and events. Along the way, we will also learn how to structure code in JavaScript modules.

By the end of this first chapter, you'll be able to create simple React components and will be ready to learn how to strongly type them with TypeScript.

In this chapter, we'll cover the following topics:

- Understanding the benefits of React
- Understanding JSX
- Creating a component
- Understanding imports and exports
- Using props

- Using state
- Using events

Technical requirements

We use the following tools in this chapter:

- **Browser**: A modern browser such as Google Chrome.
- **Babel REPL**: We'll use this online tool to briefly explore JSX. It can be found at `https://babeljs.io/repl`.
- **CodeSandbox**: We'll use this online tool to build a React component. This can be found at `https://codesandbox.io/`.

All the code snippets in this chapter can be found online at `https://github.com/PacktPublishing/Learn-React-with-TypeScript-2nd-Edition/tree/main/Chapter1/`.

Understanding the benefits of React

Before we start creating our first React component, in this section, we will understand what React is and explore some of its benefits.

React is incredibly popular. We have already mentioned that Meta uses React for Facebook, but many other famous companies use it, too, such as Netflix, Uber, and Airbnb. React's popularity has resulted in a huge ecosystem surrounding it that includes great tools, popular libraries, and many experienced developers.

A reason for React's popularity is that it is simple. This is because it focuses on doing one thing very well – providing a powerful mechanism for building UI components. Components are pieces of the UI that can be composed together to create a frontend. Furthermore, components can be reusable so that they can be used on different screens or even in other apps.

React's narrow focus means it can be incorporated into an existing app, even if it uses a different framework. This is because it doesn't need to take over the whole app to run; it is happy to run as part of an app's frontend.

React components are displayed performantly using a **virtual DOM (Document Object Model)**. You may be familiar with the real DOM – it provides the structure for a web page. However, changes to the real DOM can be costly, leading to performance problems in an interactive app. React solves this performance problem by using an in-memory representation of the real DOM called a virtual DOM. Before React changes the real DOM, it produces a new virtual DOM and compares it against the current virtual DOM to calculate the minimum amount of changes required to the real DOM. The real DOM is then updated with those minimum changes.

The fact that Meta uses React for Facebook is a major benefit because it ensures that it is of the highest quality – React breaking Facebook is not good for Meta! It also means a lot of thought and care goes into ensuring new versions of React are cheap to adopt, which helps reduce the maintenance costs of an app.

React's simplicity means it is easy and quick to learn. There are many great learning resources, such as this book. There is also a range of tools that make it very easy to scaffold a React app – one such tool is called **Create React App**, which we will learn about in *Chapter 3, Setting up React and TypeScript*.

Now that we are starting to understand React, let's dig deeper in the next section to understand how a React component defines what to display.

Understanding JSX

JSX is the syntax we use in a React component to define what the component should display. JSX stands for **JavaScript XML**, which starts to give us a clue as to what it is. We will start to learn about JSX in this section and write some JSX in an online playground.

The following code snippet is a React component with its JSX highlighted:

```
function App() {
  return (
    <div className="App">
      <Alert type="information" heading="Success">
        Everything is really good!
      </Alert>
    </div>
  );
}
```

You can see that JSX looks a bit like HTML. However, it isn't HTML because an HTML `div` element doesn't contain a `className` attribute, and there is no such element name as `Alert`. The JSX is also embedded directly within a JavaScript function, which is a little strange because a `script` element is normally used to place JavaScript inside HTML.

JSX is a JavaScript syntax extension. This means that it doesn't execute directly in the browser – it needs to be transpiled to JavaScript first. A popular tool that can transpile JSX is called Babel.

Carry out the following steps to write your first piece of JSX in the Babel playground:

1. Open a browser, go to `https://babeljs.io/repl`, and enter the following JSX in the left-hand pane:

    ```
    <span>Oh no!</span>
    ```

The following appears in the right-hand pane, which is what our JSX has compiled down to:

```
React.createElement("span", null, "Oh no!");
```

We can see that it compiles down to a `React.createElement` function call, which has three parameters:

- The element type can be an HTML element name (such as `"span"`), a React component type, or a React fragment type.

- An object containing the properties to be applied to the element. Here, `null` is passed because there are no properties.

- The content of the element. Note that the element's content is often referred to as **children** in React.

> **Note**
>
> The right-hand panel may also contain a `"use strict"` statement at the top to specify that the JavaScript will be run in **strict mode**. Strict mode is where the JavaScript engine throws an error when it encounters problematic code rather than ignoring it. See the following link for more information on the strict mode in JavaScript: `https://developer.mozilla.org/en-US/docs/Web/JavaScript/Reference/Strict_mode`.
>
> You may also see `/*#__PURE__*/` comments in the right-hand panel. These comments help bundlers such as webpack remove redundant code in the bundling process. We will learn about webpack in *Chapter 3*, *Setting up React and TypeScript*.

2. Let's expand our example by putting a `div` element around the `span` element, as shown in the following code snippet:

```
<div className="title">
  <span>Oh no!</span>
</div>
```

This now transpiles to two function calls to `React.createElement`, with `span` being passed in as a child to `div`:

```
React.createElement("div", {
  className: "title"
}, React.createElement("span", null, "Oh no!"));
```

We can also see a `className` property, with the `"title"` value passed with the `div` element.

> **Note**
>
> We have seen that React uses a `className` attribute rather than `class` for CSS class references. This is because `class` is a keyword in JavaScript, and using that would cause an error.

3. Let's do something really interesting now. Let's embed some JavaScript within the JSX. So, make the following highlighted changes:

```
const title = "Oh no!";
<div className="title">
  <span>{title}</span>
</div>
```

We declared a `title` JavaScript variable, assigned it `"Oh no!"`, and embedded it within the `span` element.

Notice that the `title` variable is placed in curly braces inside the element. Any piece of JavaScript can be embedded within JSX by surrounding it in curly braces.

Our code now transpiles to the following:

```
const title = "Oh no!";
React.createElement("div", {
  className: "title"
}, React.createElement("span", null, title));
```

4. To further illustrate the use of JavaScript in JSX, let's use a JavaScript ternary expression inside the `span` element. Add the following ternary expression:

```
const title = "Oh no!";
<div className="title">
  <span>{title ? title : "Something important"}</span>
</div>
```

A ternary expression is an inline conditional statement in JavaScript. The expression starts with the condition followed by ?, then what returns when the condition is true followed by :, and finally, what returns when the condition is false. For more information on ternary expressions, see the following link: `https://developer.mozilla.org/en-US/docs/Web/JavaScript/Reference/Operators/Conditional_Operator`.

We see that the nested call to `React.createElement` uses the ternary expression as the child of `span`:

```
React.createElement(
  "span",
  null,
  title ? title : "Something important"
);
```

This completes our exploration of JSX in the Babel playground.

In summary, JSX can be thought of as a mix of HTML and JavaScript to specify the output of a React component. JSX needs to be transpiled into JavaScript using a tool such as Babel. For more information on JSX, see the following link: `https://reactjs.org/docs/introducing-jsx.html`.

Now that we understand a little more about JSX, we will create our first React component in the next section.

Creating a component

In this section, we will create a React project using an online tool called CodeSandbox. We will take time to understand the entry point of a React app and how components are structured in a project before creating a basic React component.

Creating a CodeSandbox project

The great thing about CodeSandbox is that we can create a React project at the click of a button in a web browser and then focus on how to create a React component. Note that we will learn how to create React projects in a code editor on your local computer in *Chapter 3, Setting up React and TypeScript*. Our focus is learning about the React fundamentals in this chapter.

For now, let's carry out the following steps to create a React component in CodeSandbox:

1.   Go to `https://codesandbox.io/` in a browser and click the **Create Sandbox** button found on the right hand side of the page.

> **Note**
>
> You can create a CodeSandbox account if you want, but you can also create a React project as an anonymous user.

2.   A list of project templates appears. Click the **React** template (don't choose the **React TypeScript** template because we are focusing solely on React in this chapter).

In a few seconds, a React project will be created:

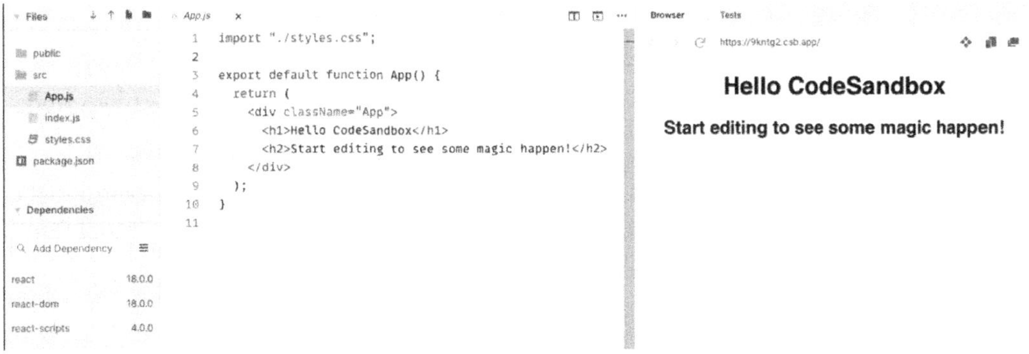

Figure 1.1 – React project in CodeSandbox

There are three main panels in the CodeSandbox editor:

- The **Files** panel: This is usually on the left-hand side and contains all the files in the project.

- The **Code editor** panel: This is usually the middle panel, and it contains the code. This is where we will write our React component code. Clicking a file in the **Files** panel will open it in the code editor panel.

- The **Browser** panel: This displays a preview of the running app and is usually on the right-hand side.

Now that we have created a React project, we will take some time to understand the app's entry point.

Understanding the React entry point

The entry point of this React app is in the index.js file. Open this file by clicking on it in the **Files** panel and inspect its contents:

```
import { StrictMode } from 'react';
import { createRoot } from 'react-dom/client';

import App from './App';

const rootElement = document.getElementById('root');
const root = createRoot(rootElement);

root.render(
  <StrictMode>
```

```
    <App />
  </StrictMode>
);
```

There is quite a lot going on in this code. Here's an explanation of each line of the code (don't worry if you don't fully understand it all at this point in the book, you will soon!):

- The first statement imports a `StrictMode` component from React. This means that the `StrictMode` component from the `react` library will be used later in the code in this file. We will cover import statements in detail in the next section.

- The second statement imports a `createRoot` function from React.

- The third import statement imports an App component from the `App.js` file in our project.

- A `rootElement` variable is then assigned to a DOM element with an `id` of `"root"`.

- React's `createRoot` function takes in a DOM element and returns a variable that can be used to display a React component tree. The `rootElement` variable is then passed into `createRoot`, and the result is assigned to a `root` variable.

- The render function is called on the `root` variable, passing in JSX containing the `StrictMode` component with the App component nested inside. The `render` function displays the React components on the page. This process is often referred to as **rendering**.

> **Note**
>
> The `StrictMode` component will check the content inside it for potential problems and report them in the browser's console. This is often referred to as React's strict mode. The strict mode in React is different from the strict mode in JavaScript, but their purpose of eliminating bad code is the same.

In summary, the code in `index.js` renders the App component in React's strict mode in a DOM element with an `id` of `"root"`.

Next, we will take some time to understand the React component tree and the App component that is referenced in `index.js`.

Understanding the React component tree

A React app is structured in a tree of components and DOM elements. The root component is the component at the top of the tree. In our CodeSandbox project, the root component is the `StrictMode` component.

React components can be nested inside another React component. The App component is nested inside the `StrictMode` component in the CodeSandbox project. This is a powerful way of putting components together because any component can be placed inside `StrictMode` – it doesn't necessarily need to be `App`.

React components can reference one or more other components, and even DOM elements, in their JSX. Open the `App.js` file and observe that it references DOM elements `div`, `h1`, and `h2`:

```
<div className="App">
  <h1>Hello CodeSandbox</h1>
  <h2>Start editing to see some magic happen!</h2>
</div>
```

The component tree in the CodeSandbox project is constructed as follows:

```
StrictMode
└── App
      └── div
            └── h1
                  └── h2
```

In summary, a React app is structured in a tree of React components and DOM elements.

Next, it is time to create a React component.

Creating a basic alert component

Now, we are going to create a component that displays an alert, which we will simply call `Alert`. It will consist of an icon, a heading, and a message.

> **Important note**
>
> A React component name must start with a capital letter. If a component name starts with a lowercase letter, it is treated as a DOM element and won't render properly. See the following link in the React documentation for more information: `https://reactjs.org/docs/jsx-in-depth.html#user-defined-components-must-be-capitalized`.

Carry out the following steps to create the component in the CodeSandbox project:

1. In the **Files** panel, right-click on the `src` folder and choose **Create File** in the menu that appears.

2. The cursor is placed in a new file, ready for you to enter the component filename. Enter `Alert.js` as the filename and press *Enter*.

> **Note**
>
> The filename for component files isn't important to React or the React transpiler. It is common practice to use the same name as the component, either in Pascal or snake case. However, the file extension must be `.js` or `.jsx` for React transpilers to recognize these as React components.

3. The `Alert.js` file automatically opens in the code editor panel. Enter the following code into this file:

```
function Alert() {
  return (
    <div>
      <div>
        <span role="img" aria-label="Warning">⚠</span>
        <span>Oh no!</span>
      </div>
      <div>Something isn't quite right ...</div>
    </div>
  );
}
```

Remember that the code snippets are available online to copy. The link to the preceding snippet can be found at `https://github.com/PacktPublishing/Learn-React-with-TypeScript-2nd-Edition/blob/main/Chapter1/Section3-Creating-a-component/Alert.js`.

The component renders the following items:

- A warning icon (note that this is a warning emoji).

- A title, *Oh no!*.

- A message, *Something isn't quite right ....*

> **Note**
>
> The `role` and `aria-label` attributes have been added to the `span` element containing the warning icons to help screen readers understand that this is an image with a title of warning.
>
> For more information on the `img` role, see `https://developer.mozilla.org/en-US/docs/Web/Accessibility/ARIA/Roles/img_role`.
>
> For more information on the `aria-label` attribute, see `https://developer.mozilla.org/en-US/docs/Web/Accessibility/ARIA/Attributes/aria-label`.

Alternatively, a React component can be implemented using arrow function syntax. The following code snippet is an arrow syntax version of the `Alert` component:

```
const Alert = () => {
  return (
    <div>
      <div>
        <span role="img" aria-label="Warning">
          ⚠
        </span>
        <span>Oh no!</span>
      </div>
      <div>Something isn't quite right ...</div>
    </div>
  );
};
```

> **Note**
>
> There aren't any significant differences between arrow functions and normal functions in the context of React function components. So, it is down to personal preference which one you choose. This book generally uses regular function syntax because it has fewer characters to type, however, if you wish, you can find more information on JavaScript arrow functions here: `https://developer.mozilla.org/en-US/docs/Web/JavaScript/Reference/Functions/Arrow_functions`.

Congratulations, you have created your first React component. Let's quickly recap the key points in this section:

- The entry point in a React app is usually `index.js`.

- React's `createRoot` function allows a React component tree to be rendered inside a DOM element.

- A React component is a JavaScript function whose name starts with a capital letter. The function returns what should be displayed using JSX syntax.

You may have noticed that the alert component doesn't appear in the **Browser** panel. This is because it hasn't been added to the React component tree yet. We will do this in the next section after we have learned about the `import` and `export` statements.

Understanding imports and exports

import and export statements allow JavaScript to be structured into modules.

This section will start by covering why JavaScript modules are important and then how to define and use them using import and export statements. We will then use that knowledge to add the alert component to the React component tree in the CodeSandbox project.

Understanding the importance of modules

By default, JavaScript code executes in what is called the **global scope**. This means code from one file is automatically available in another file. Unfortunately, this means that the functions we implement can overwrite functions in other files if the names are the same. You can imagine how this structure quickly becomes challenging and risky to maintain.

Thankfully, JavaScript has a modules feature. A module's functions and variables are isolated, so functions with the same name in different modules won't collide. This is a much safer way to structure code and is common practice when structuring React apps.

Next, we will learn about how to define modules.

Using export statements

A module is a file with at least one export statement. An export statement references members that are available to other modules. Think of this as making members publically available. A member can be a function, a class, or a variable within the file. Members not contained within the export statement are private and not available outside the module.

The following code statement is an example of a module with its export statement highlighted. This is called a **named export statement** because the public members are explicitly named:

```
function myFunc1() {
  ...
}

function myFunc2() {
  ...
}

function myFunc3() {
  ...
```

```
   }

export { myFunc1, myFunc3 };
```

In the example, the myFunc1 and myFunc3 functions are public, and myFunc2 is private.

Alternatively, the export keyword can be added before the function keyword on the public functions:

```
export function myFunc1() {
   ...
}

function myFunc2() {
   ...
}

export function myFunc3() {
   ...
}
```

We will use the export keyword approach in this book because it is immediately apparent which function is public. With the single export statement at the bottom of the file, you have to keep going to the bottom of the file to find out whether a function is public.

A **default export statement** can be used to export a single public member. Like named exports, this comes in two variants. The first variant is where the export statement is defined at the bottom of the module:

```
export default myFunc1;
```

The default keyword signifies that the export is a default export statement.

The second variant is where the export and default keywords are added in front of the member:

```
export default function myFunc1() {
   ...
}
```

This book will generally use named exports rather than default exports.

Next, we will learn about import statements.

Using import statements

Using an `import` statement allows public members from a module to be used. Like an `export` statement, there are **named** and **default** `import` statements. A default `import` statement can only be used to reference a default `export` statement.

Here is an example of a default `import` statement:

```
import myFunc1 from './myModule';
```

The default exported member from the `myModule.js` file is imported and named `myFunc1`.

> **Note**
>
> The name of an imported default member doesn't necessarily need to match the name of the default exported member, but it is common practice to do so.

Here is an example of a named `import` statement:

```
import { myFunc1, myFunc3 } from './myModule';
```

Here, the `myFunc1` and `myFunc3` named exported members from the `myModule.js` file are imported.

> **Note**
>
> Unlike default imports, the names of imported members must match the exported members.

Now that we understand how to structure JavaScript code into modules, we will use this knowledge to add the alert component in the CodeSandbox project to the React component tree.

Adding Alert to the App component

Going back to the `Alert` component in our CodeSandbox project, we will reference `Alert` in the App component. To do this, carry out the following steps:

1. First, we need to export the `Alert` component. Open `Alert.js` and add the `export` keyword before the `Alert` function:

    ```
    export function Alert() {
      ...
    }
    ```

> **Note**
> It is common practice to have each React component in a separate file and, therefore, a separate module. This prevents files from becoming too large and helps the readability of the code base.

2. Now we can import `Alert` into the `App.js` file. Open `App.js` and add the highlighted `import` statement at the top of the file:

```
import { Alert } from './Alert';
import "./styles.css";

export default function App() {
  ...
}
```

3. We can now reference `Alert` in the App component's JSX. Add the highlighted line inside the `div` element, replacing its existing content:

```
export default function App() {
  return (
    <div className="App">
      <Alert />
    </div>
  );
}
```

The component will display the following in the **Browser** panel:

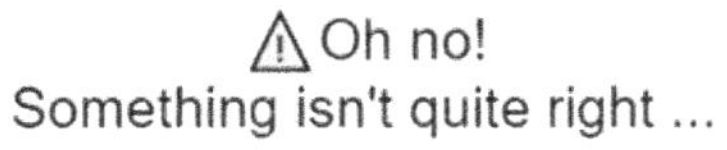

⚠Oh no!
Something isn't quite right ...

Figure 1.2 – The alert component in the Browser panel

Nice! If you have noticed that the alert component isn't styled nicely, don't worry – we will learn how to style it in *Chapter 4, Approaches to Styling React Frontends*.

Here's a recap of a couple of key points in this section:

- React apps are structured using JavaScript modules to help the code base be maintainable.
- Generally, a React component is structured in its own module and so needs to be exported and imported before being referenced in another React component.

Next, we will learn how to make the alert component a little more flexible.

Using props

Currently, the alert component is pretty inflexible. For example, the alert consumer can't change the heading or the message. At the moment, the heading or the message needs to be changed within `Alert` itself. **Props** solve this problem, and we will learn about them in this section.

> **Note**
>
> Props is short for *properties*. The React community often refers to them as props, so we will do so in this book.

Understanding props

`props` is an optional parameter that is passed into a React component. This parameter is an object containing the properties of our choice. The following code snippet shows a `props` parameter in a `ContactDetails` component:

```
function ContactDetails(props) {
   console.log(props.name);
   console.log(props.email);

   ...

}
```

The `props` parameter contains the `name` and `email` properties in the preceding code snippet.

> **Note**
> The parameter doesn't have to be named `props`, but it is common practice.

Props are passed into a component in JSX as attributes. The prop names must match what is defined in the component. Here is an example of passing props into the preceding `ContactDetails` component:

```
<ContactDetails name="Fred" email="fred@somewhere.com" />
```

So, props make the component output flexible. Consumers of the component can pass appropriate props into the component to get the desired output.

Next, we will add some props to the alert component we have been working on.

Adding props to the alert component

In the CodeSandbox project, carry out the following steps to add props to the alert component to make it more flexible:

1. Open `alert.js` and add a `props` parameter to the function:

   ```
   export function Alert(props) {
     ...
   }
   ```

2. We will define the following properties for the alert:

   - `type`: This will either be `"information"` or `"warning"` and will determine the icon in the alert.

   - `heading`: This will determine the heading of the alert.

   - `children`: This will determine the content of the alert. The `children` prop is actually a special prop used for the main content of components.

   Update the alert component's JSX to use the props as follows:

   ```
   export function Alert(props) {
     return (
       <div>
         <div>
           <span
             role="img"
             aria-label={
               props.type === "warning"
                 ? "Warning"
                 : "Information"
             }
           >
             {props.type === "warning" ? "⚠️" : "i"}
           </span>
           <span>{props.heading}</span>
   ```

```
      </div>
      <div>{props.children}</div>
    </div>
  );
}
```

Notice that the **Browser** panel now displays nothing other than an information icon (this is an information emoji); this is because the App component isn't passing any props to Alert yet:

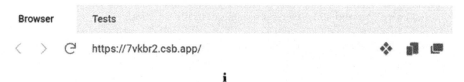

Figure 1.3 – The alert component only showing the information icon

3. Open App.js and update the Alert component in the JSX to pass in props as follows:

```
export default function App() {
  return (
    <div className="App">
      <Alert type="information" heading="Success">
        Everything is really good!
      </Alert>
    </div>
  );
}
```

Notice that the Alert component is no longer self-closing so that Everything is really good! can be passed into its content. The content is passed to the children prop.

The **Browser** panel now displays the configured alert component:

iSuccess
Everything is really good!

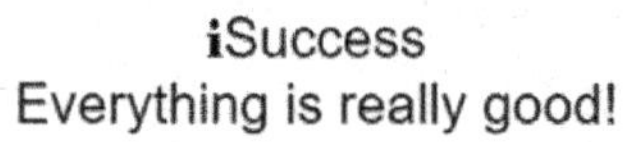

Figure 1.4 – The configured alert component in the browser panel

4. We can clean up the alert component code a little by destructuring the props parameter.

> **Note**
>
> Destructuring is a JavaScript feature that allows properties to be unpacked from an object. For more information, see the following link: `https://developer.mozilla.org/en-US/docs/Web/JavaScript/Reference/Operators/Destructuring_assignment`.

Open `Alert.js` again, destructure the `function` parameter, and use the unpacked props as follows:

```
export function Alert({ type, heading, children }) {
  return (
    <div>
      <div>
        <span
          role="img"
          aria-label={
            type === "warning" ? "Warning" :
              "Information"
          }
        >
          {type === "warning" ? "⚠" : "i"}
        </span>
        <span>{heading}</span>
      </div>
      <div>{children}</div>
    </div>
  );
}
```

This is a little cleaner because we use the unpacked props directly rather than having to reference them through the `props` parameter.

5. We want the `type` prop to default to `"information"`. Define this default as follows:

```
export function Alert({
  type = "information",
  heading,
  children
}) {
  ...
}
```

That completes the implementation of the props in the alert component for now. Here's a quick recap on props:

- Props allow a component to be configured by the consuming JSX and are passed as JSX attributes
- Props are received in the component definition in an object parameter and can then be used in its JSX

Next, we will continue to make the alert component more sophisticated by allowing it to be closed by the user.

Using state

The component **state** is a special variable containing information about the component's current situation. For example, a component may be in a *loading* state or an *error* state.

In this section, we'll learn about state and use it within our alert component in the CodeSandbox project. We will use state to allow the alert to be closed by the user.

Understanding state

There isn't a predefined list of states; we define what's appropriate for a given component. Some components won't even need any state; for example, the `App` and `Alert` components in our CodeSandbox project haven't required state for the requirements so far.

However, state is a key part of making a component interactive. When a user interacts with a component, the component's output may need to change. For example, clicking on a component may need to make an element in the component invisible. A change to a component state causes the component to refresh, more often referred to as **re-rendering**. So, a user could click on a component causing a state change, resulting in an element in the component becoming invisible.

State is defined using a `useState` function from React. The `useState` function is one of React's **hooks**. React hooks were introduced to React in version 16.8 and give function components powerful capabilities such as state. There is a whole chapter on React hooks in *Chapter 4, Using React Hooks*.

The syntax for `useState` is as follows:

```
const [state, setState] = useState(initialState);
```

Here are the key points:

- The initial state value is passed into `useState`. If no value is passed, it will initially be `undefined`.
- `useState` returns a tuple containing the current state value and a function to update the state value. The tuple is destructured in the preceding code snippet.

- The state variable name is state in the preceding code snippet, but we can choose any meaningful name.

- We can also choose the state setter function name, but it is common practice to use the same name as the state variable preceded by set.

- Multiple states can be defined by defining multiple instances of useState. For example, here are definitions for loading and error states:

```
const [loading, setLoading] = useState(true);
const [error, setError] = useState();
```

Next, we will implement state in the alert component to determine whether it is visible or not.

Implementing a visible state in the alert component

We will begin by implementing a feature in the alert component that allows the user to close it. A key part of that feature is controlling the alert's visibility, which we will do with a visible state. This state will either be true or false and it will initially be set to true.

Follow these steps to implement a visible state in Alert:

1. Open Alert.js in the CodeSandbox project.

2. Add the following import statement at the top of the file to import the useState hook from React:

```
import { useState } from 'react';
```

3. Define the visible state as follows in the component definition:

```
export function Alert(...) {
  const [visible, setVisible] = useState(true);
  return (
    ...
  );
}
```

4. After the state declaration, add a condition that returns null if the visible state is false. This means nothing will be rendered:

```
export function Alert(...) {
  const [visible, setVisible] = useState(true);
  if (!visible) {
    return null;
```

```
  }
  return (
    ...
  );
}
```

The component will render in the **Browser** panel the same as before because the `visible` state is `true`. Try changing the initial state value to `false`, and you will see it disappear in the **Browser** panel.

Currently, the alert component is making use of the `visible` state's value by not rendering anything if it is `false`. However, the component isn't updating the `visible` state yet – that is, `setVisible` is unused at the moment. We will update the `visible` state after implementing a `close` button, which we will do next.

Adding a close button to Alert

We will add a close button to the alert component to allow the user to close it. We will make this configurable so that the alert consumer can choose whether the close button is rendered.

Carry out the following steps:

1. Start by opening `Alert.js` and add a `closable` prop:

    ```
    export function Alert({
      type = "information",
      heading,
      children,
      closable
    }) {
      ...
    }
    ```

    The consumer of the alert component will use the `closable` prop to specify whether the close button appears.

2. Add a close button between the heading and content as follows:

    ```
    export function Alert(...) {
      ...
      return (
        <div>
          <div>
    ```

```
    . . .
    <span>{heading}</span>
  </div>
  <button aria-label="Close">
    <span role="img" aria-label="Close"> X </span>
  </button>
  <div>{children}</div>
 </div>
);
}
```

Notice that the span element that contains the close icon is given an "img" role and a "Close" label to help screen readers. Likewise, the button is also given a "Close" label to help screen readers.

The close button appears in the alert component as follows:

iSuccess

Everything is really good!

Figure 1.5 – The close button in the alert component

3. At the moment, the close button will always render rather than just when the closable prop is true. We can use a JavaScript logical AND short circuit expression (represented by the && characters) to render the close button conditionally. To do this, make the following highlighted changes:

```
import { useState } from 'react';

export function Alert(...) {
  . . .
  return (
    <div>
      <div>
        . . .
        <span>{heading}</span>
      </div>
      {closable && (
        <button aria-label="Close">
          <span role="img" aria-label="Close">
```

```
          ✖
        </span>
      </button>
    )}
    <div>{children}</div>
  </div>
);
}
```

If `closable` is a **falsy** value, the expression will **short-circuit** and consequently not render the button. However, if `closable` is **truthy**, the button will be rendered.

> **Note**
>
> See the following link for more information about logical AND short-circuit expressions: `https://developer.mozilla.org/en-US/docs/Web/JavaScript/Reference/Operators/Logical_AND`.
>
> See the following link for JavaScript's falsy values, `https://developer.mozilla.org/en-US/docs/Glossary/Falsy`, and `https://developer.mozilla.org/en-US/docs/Glossary/Truthy` for truthy values.

4. Open `App.js` and pass the `closable` prop into `Alert`:

```
export default function App() {
  return (
    <div className="App">
      <Alert type="information" heading="Success"
        closable>
        Everything is really good!
      </Alert>
    </div>
  );
}
```

Notice that a value hasn't been explicitly defined on the `closable` attribute. We could have passed the value as follows:

```
closable={true}
```

However, there is no need to pass the value on a boolean attribute. If the boolean attribute is present on an element, its value is automatically `true`.

When the `closable` attribute is specified, the `close` button appears in the alert component as it did before in *Figure 1.5*. But when the `closable` attribute isn't specified, the close button doesn't appear:

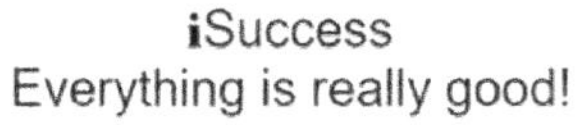

iSuccess
Everything is really good!

Figure 1.6 – The close button not in the alert component when closable is not specified

Excellent!

A quick recap of what we have learned so far about React state:

- State is defined using React's `useState` hook

- The initial value of the state can be passed into the `useState` hook

- `useState` returns a state variable that can be used to render elements conditionally

- `useState` also returns a function that can be used to update the value of the state

You may have noticed that the `close` button doesn't actually close the alert. In the next section, we will rectify this as we learn about events in React.

Using events

Events are another key part of allowing a component to be interactive. In this section, we will understand what React events are and how to use events on DOM elements. We will also learn how to create our own React events.

We will continue to expand the alert component's functionality as we learn about events. We will start by finishing the close button implementation before creating an event for when the alert has been closed.

Understanding events

Browser events happen as the user interacts with DOM elements. For example, clicking a button raises a `click` event from that button.

Logic can be executed when an event is raised. For example, an alert can be closed when its close button is clicked. A function called an **event handler** (sometimes referred to as an **event listener**) can be registered for an element event that contains the logic to execute when that event happens.

> **Note**
> See the following link for more information on browser events: `https://developer.mozilla.org/en-US/docs/Learn/JavaScript/Building_blocks/Events`.

Events in React events are very similar to browser native events. In fact, React events are a wrapper on top of the browser's native events.

Event handlers in React are generally registered to an element in JSX using an attribute. The following code snippet registers a `click` event handler called `handleClick` on a `button` element:

```
<button onClick={handleClick}>...</button>
```

Next, we will return to our alert component and implement a `click` handler on the close button that closes the alert.

Implementing a close button click handler in the alert

At the moment, our alert component contains a close button, but nothing happens when it is clicked. The alert also contains a `visible` state that dictates whether the alert is shown. So, to finish the close button implementation, we need to add an event handler when it is clicked that sets the `visible` state to `false`. Carry out the following steps to do this:

1. Open `Alert.js` and register a `click` handler on the close button as follows:

    ```
    <button aria-label="Close" onClick={handleCloseClick}>
    ```

    We have registered a `click` handler called `handleCloseClick` on the close button.

2. We then need to implement the `handleCloseClick` function in the component. Create an empty function to start with, just above the `return` statement:

    ```
    export function Alert(...) {
      const [visible, setVisible] = useState(true);
      if (!visible) {
        return null;
      }
      function handleCloseClick() {}
      return (
    
        ...
    
      );
    }
    ```

This may seem a little strange because we have put the `handleCloseClick` function inside another function, `Alert`. The handler needs to be inside the `Alert` function; otherwise, the alert component won't have access to it.

Arrow function syntax can be used for event handlers if preferred. An arrow function version of the handler is as follows:

```
export function Alert(...) {
  const [visible, setVisible] = useState(true);
  if (!visible) {
    return null;
  }
  const handleCloseClick = () => {}
  return (
    ...
  );
}
```

Event handlers can also be added directly to the element in JSX as follows:

```
<button aria-label="Close" onClick={() => {}}>
```

In the alert component, we will stick to the named `handleCloseClick` event handler function.

3. Now we can use the `visible` state setter function to make the `visible` state `false` in the event handler:

```
function handleCloseClick() {
  setVisible(false);
}
```

If you click the close button in the **Browser** panel, the alert disappears. Nice!

The refresh icon can be clicked to make the component reappear in the **Browser** panel:

Figure 1.7 – The Browser panel refresh option

Next, we will extend the close button to raise an event when the alert closes.

Implementing an alert close event

We will now create a custom event in the alert component. The event will be raised when the alert is closed so that consumers can execute logic when this happens.

A custom event in a component is implemented by implementing a prop. The prop is a function that is called to raise the event.

To implement an alert close event, follow these steps:

1. Start by opening `Alert.js` and add a prop for the event:

    ```
    export function Alert({
        type = "information",
        heading,
        children,
        closable,
        onClose
    }) {}
    ```

    We have called the prop `onClose`.

> **Note**
>
> It is common practice to start an event prop name with on.

---

2. In the `handleCloseClick` event handler, raise the close event after the `visible` state is set to `false`:

    ```
    function handleCloseClick() {
        setVisible(false);
        if (onClose) {
            onClose();
        }
    }
    ```

    Notice that we only invoke `onClose` if it is defined and passed as a prop by the consumer. This means that we aren't forcing the consumer to handle this event.

3. We can now handle when an alert is closed in the `App` component. Open `App.js` and add the following event handler to `Alert` in the JSX:

    ```
    <Alert
        type="information"
        heading="Success"
        closable
        onClose={() => console.log("closed")}
    >
    ```

```
    Everything is really good!
  </Alert>;
```

We have used an inline event handler this time.

In the **Browser** panel, if you click the close button and look at the console, you will see that **closed** has been output:

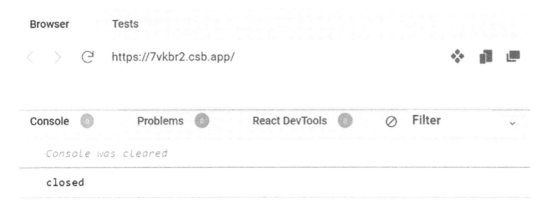

Figure 1.8 – The Browser panel closed console output

That completes the close event and the implementation of the alert for this chapter.

Here's what we have learned about React events:

- Events, along with state, allow a component to be interactive
- Event handlers are functions that are registered on elements in JSX
- A custom event can be created by implementing a function prop and invoking it to raise the event

The component we created in this chapter is a function component. You can also create components using classes. For example, a class component version of the alert component is at `https://github.com/PacktPublishing/Learn-React-with-TypeScript-2nd-Edition/blob/main/Chapter1/Class-component/Alert.js`. However, function components are dominant in the React community because of the following reasons:

- Generally, they require less code to implement
- Logic inside the component can be more easily reused
- The implementation is very different

For these reasons, we will focus solely on function components in this book.

Next, we will summarize what we have learned in this chapter.

Summary

We now understand that React is a popular library for creating component-based frontends. In this chapter, we created an alert component using React.

Component output is declared using a mix of HTML and JavaScript called JSX. JSX needs to be transpiled into JavaScript before it can be executed in a browser.

Props can be passed into a component as JSX attributes. This allows consumers of the component to control its output and behavior. A component receives props as an object parameter. The JSX attribute names form the object parameter property names. We implemented a range of props in this chapter in the alert component.

Events can be handled to execute logic when the user interacts with the component. We created an event handler for the close button click event in the alert component.

State can be used to re-render a component and update its output. State is defined using the useState hook. State is often updated in event handlers. We have created state for whether the alert is visible.

Custom events can be implemented as a function prop. This allows consumers of the component to execute logic as the user interacts with it. We implemented a close event on the alert component.

In the next chapter, we will introduce ourselves to TypeScript.

Questions

Answer the following questions to reinforce what you have learned in this chapter:

1. What is wrong with the following component definition?

    ```
    export function important() {
      return <div>This is really important!</div>;
    }
    ```

2. A component with a prop is defined as follows:

    ```
    export function Name({ name }) {
      return <div>name</div>;
    }
    ```

    The value of the prop isn't output though. What is the problem?

3. Component props are passed into a component as follows:

    ```
    <ContactDetails name="Fred" email="fred@somewhere.com" />
    ```

The component is then defined as follows:

```
export function ContactDetails({ firstName, email }) {
  return (
    <div>
      <div>{firstName}</div>
      <div>{email}</div>
    </div>
  );
}
```

The name `Fred` isn't output though. What is the problem?

4. What is wrong with how the `click` event is handled in the following JSX:

```
<button click={() => console.log("clicked")}>
  Click me
</button>;
```

5. What is the initial value of the `loading` state defined here?

```
const [loading, setLoading] = useState(true);
```

6. What is wrong with how the state is set in the following component?

```
export function Agree() {
  const [agree, setAgree] = useState();
  return (
    <button onClick={() => agree = true}>
      Click to agree
    </button>
  );
}
```

7. The following component implements an optional `Agree` event. What is wrong with this implementation?

```
export function Agree({ onAgree }) {
  function handleClick() {
    onAgree();
  }
  return (
```

```
        <button onClick={handleClick}>
          Click to agree
        </button>
      );
    }
```

Answers

Here are the answers to the questions on what you have learned in this chapter:

1. The problem with the component definition is that its name is lowercase. React functions must be named with an uppercase first character:

    ```
    export function Important() {
      ...
    }
    ```

2. The problem is that the name variable inside the div element isn't enclosed in curly brackets. So, the word name will be output rather than the value of the name prop. Here's the corrected version of the component:

    ```
    export function Name({ name }) {
      return <div>{name}</div>;
    }
    ```

3. The problem is that a name prop is passed rather than firstName. Here's the corrected JSX:

    ```
    <ContactDetails firstName="Fred" email="fred@somewhere.
    com" />
    ```

4. The problem is that a click prop is passed rather than onClick. Here's the corrected JSX:

    ```
    <button onClick={() => console.log("clicked")}>
      Click me
    </button>;
    ```

5. The initial value of the loading state is true.

6. The state isn't updated using the state setter function. Here's the corrected version of the state being set:

```
export function Agree() {
  const [agree, setAgree] = useState();
  return (
    <button onClick={() => setAgree(true)}>
      Click to agree
    </button>
  );
}
```

7. The problem is that clicking the button will cause an error if onAgree isn't passed because it will be undefined. Here's the corrected version of the component:

```
export function Agree({ onAgree }) {
  function handleClick() {
    if (onAgree) {
      onAgree();
    }
  }
  return (
    <button onClick={handleClick}>
      Click to agree
    </button>
  );
}
```

2

Introducing TypeScript

In this chapter, we will start by understanding what TypeScript is and how it provides a much richer type system on top of JavaScript. We will learn about the basic types in TypeScript, such as numbers and strings, and then learn how to create our own types to represent objects and arrays using different TypeScript features. Finally, we will finish the chapter by understanding the TypeScript compiler and its key options in a React app.

By the end of the chapter, you'll be ready to learn how to use TypeScript to build frontends with React.

In this chapter, we'll cover the following topics:

- Understanding the benefits of TypeScript
- Understanding JavaScript types
- Using basic TypeScript types
- Creating TypeScript types
- Using the TypeScript compiler

Technical requirements

We will use the following technologies in this chapter:

- **Browser**: A modern browser such as Google Chrome.
- **TypeScript Playground**: This is a website at https://www.typescriptlang.org/play/ that allows you to play around with and understand the features of TypeScript without installing it.
- **CodeSandbox**: We'll briefly use this online tool to explore JavaScript's type system. This can be found at https://codesandbox.io/.

- **Visual Studio Code**: We'll need an editor to experience TypeScript's benefits and explore the TypeScript compiler. This one can be installed from `https://code.visualstudio.com/`. Other editors that could be used can be found at `https://github.com/Microsoft/TypeScript/wiki/TypeScript-Editor-Support`.

- **Node.js** and **npm**: TypeScript is dependent on these pieces of software. You can install them from `https://nodejs.org/en/download/`.

All the code snippets in this chapter can be found online at `https://github.com/PacktPublishing/Learn-React-with-TypeScript-2nd-Edition/tree/main/Chapter2`.

Understanding the benefits of TypeScript

In this section, we will start by understanding what TypeScript is, how it relates to JavaScript, and how TypeScript enables teams to be more productive.

Understanding TypeScript

TypeScript was first released in 2012 and is still being developed, with new releases happening every few months. But what is TypeScript, and what are its benefits?

TypeScript is often referred to as a superset or extension of JavaScript because any feature in JavaScript is available in TypeScript. Unlike JavaScript, TypeScript can't be executed directly in a browser – it must be transpiled into JavaScript first.

> **Note**
>
> It is worth being aware that a proposal is being considered that *would* allow TypeScript to be executed directly in a browser without transpilation. See the following link for more information: `https://github.com/tc39/proposal-type-annotations`.

TypeScript adds a rich type system to JavaScript. It is generally used with frontend frameworks such as Angular, Vue, and React. TypeScript can also be used to build a backend with Node.js. This demonstrates how flexible TypeScript's type system is.

When a JavaScript codebase grows, it can become hard to read and maintain. TypeScript's type system solves this problem. TypeScript uses the type system to allow code editors to catch type errors as developers write problematic code. Code editors also use the type system to provide productivity features such as robust code navigation and code refactoring.

Next, we will step through an example of how TypeScript catches an error that JavaScript can't.

Catching type errors early

The type information helps the TypeScript compiler catch type errors. In code editors such as Visual Studio Code, a type error is underlined in red immediately after the developer has made a type mistake. Carry out the following steps to experience an example of TypeScript catching a type error:

1. Open Visual Studio Code in a folder of your choice.

2. Create a new file called `calculateTotalPrice.js` by choosing the **New File** option in the **EXPLORER** panel.

Figure 2.1 – Creating a new file in Visual Studio Code

3. Enter the following code into the file:

    ```
    function calculateTotalPriceJS(product, quantity,
    discount) {
      const priceWithoutDiscount = product.price * quantity;
      const discountAmount = priceWithoutDiscount * discount;
      return priceWithoutDiscount - discountAmount;
    }
    ```

    Remember that the code snippets are available online to copy. The link to the previous snippet can be found at `https://github.com/PacktPublishing/Learn-React-with-TypeScript-2nd-Edition/blob/main/Chapter2/Section1-Understanding-TypeScript/calculateTotalPrice.js`.

    There is a bug in the code that might be difficult to spot, and the error won't be highlighted by Visual Studio Code.

4. Now create a copy of the file but with a `.ts` extension instead of `.js`. A file can be copied by right-clicking on the file in the **EXPLORER** panel and selecting the **Copy** option. Then right-click the **EXPLORER** panel again and select the **Paste** option to create the copied file.

Note

A `.ts` file extension denotes a TypeScript file. This means a TypeScript compiler will perform type checking on this file.

---

5. In the `calculateTotalPrice.ts` file, remove the JS from the end of the function name and make the following highlighted updates to the code:

```
function calculateTotalPrice(
  product: { name: string; unitPrice: number },
  quantity: number,
  discount: number
) {
  const priceWithoutDiscount = product.price * quantity;
  const discountAmount = priceWithoutDiscount * discount;
  return priceWithoutDiscount - discountAmount;
}
```

Here, we have added TypeScript **type annotations** to the `function` parameters. We will learn about type annotations in detail in the next section.

The key point is that the type error is now highlighted by a red squiggly underline:

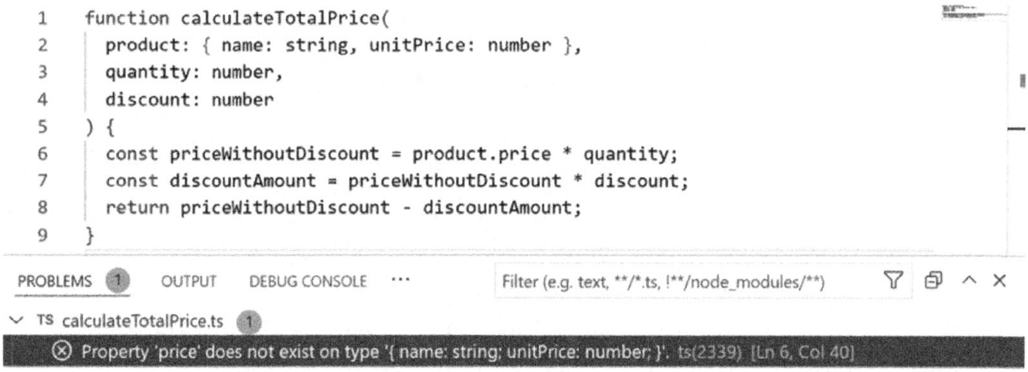

```
1    function calculateTotalPrice(
2      product: { name: string, unitPrice: number },
3      quantity: number,
4      discount: number
5    ) {
6      const priceWithoutDiscount = product.price * quantity;
7      const discountAmount = priceWithoutDiscount * discount;
8      return priceWithoutDiscount - discountAmount;
9    }
```

PROBLEMS ①   OUTPUT   DEBUG CONSOLE ⋯   Filter (e.g. text, **/*.ts, !**/node_modules/**)   ▽ 🗗 ∧ ✕

∨ TS calculateTotalPrice.ts ①

⊗ Property 'price' does not exist on type '{ name: string; unitPrice: number; }'. ts(2339) [Ln 6, Col 40]

Figure 2.2 – Highlighted type error

The bug is that the function references a `price` property in the product object that doesn't exist. The property that should be referenced is `unitPrice`.

Catching these problems early in the development process increases the team's throughput and is one less thing for quality assurance to catch. It could be worse – the bug could have gotten into the live app and given users a bad experience.

Keep these files open in Visual Studio Code because we will run through an example of TypeScript improving the developer experience next.

Improving developer experience and productivity with IntelliSense

IntelliSense is a feature in code editors that gives useful information about elements of code and allows code to be quickly completed. For example, IntelliSense can provide the list of properties available in an object.

Carry out the following steps to experience how TypeScript works better with IntelliSense than JavaScript and how this positively impacts productivity. As part of this exercise, we will fix the price bug from the previous section:

1. Open `calculateTotalPrice.js` and on line 2, where `product.price` is referenced, remove `price`. Then, with the cursor after the dot (.), click *Ctrl* + spacebar. This opens Visual Studio Code's IntelliSense:

```
function calculateTotalPriceJS(product, quantity, discount) {
  const priceWithoutDiscount = product. * quantity;
  const discountAmount = priceWithoutDi abc calculateTotalPriceJS
  return priceWithoutDiscount - discoun abc discount
}                                        abc discountAmount
                                         abc priceWithoutDiscount
                                         abc product
                                         abc quantity
                                         □ #endregion           Region End
                                         □ #region            Region Start
                                         □ define             define module
                                         □ dowhile         Do-While Statement
                                         □ error        Log error to console
                                         □ for                     For Loop
```

Figure 2.3 – IntelliSense in a JavaScript file

Visual Studio Code can only guess the potential property name, so it lists variable names and function names it has seen in the file. Unfortunately, IntelliSense doesn't help in this case because the correct property name, `unitPrice`, is not listed.

2. Now open `calculateTotalPrice.ts`, remove `price` from `product.price`, and press *Ctrl* + spacebar to open IntelliSense again:

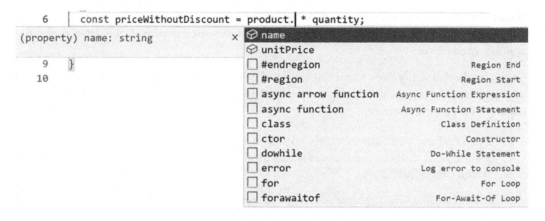

Figure 2.4 – IntelliSense in a TypeScript file

This time, Visual Studio Code lists the correct properties.

3. Select **unitPrice** from IntelliSense to resolve the type error.

IntelliSense is just one tool that TypeScript provides. It can also provide robust refactoring features, such as renaming React components, and helps with accurate code navigation, such as going to a function definition.

To recap what we learned in this section:

- TypeScript's type-checking feature helps catch problems earlier in the development process
- TypeScript enables code editors to offer productivity features such as IntelliSense
- These advantages provide significant benefits when working in larger codebases

Next, we will learn about the type system in JavaScript. This will further underline the need for TypeScript in a large codebase.

Understanding JavaScript types

Before understanding the type system in TypeScript, let's briefly explore the type system in JavaScript. To do this, open the CodeSandbox at `https://codesandbox.io/` and carry out the following steps:

1. Create a new plain JavaScript project by choosing the **Vanilla** option.

2. Open `index.js`, remove its content, and replace it with the following code:

```
let firstName = "Fred"
console.log("firstName", firstName, typeof firstName);
let score = 9
console.log("score", score, typeof score);
let date = new Date(2022, 10, 1);
console.log("date", date, typeof date);
```

The code assigns three variables to various values. The code also outputs the variable values to the console, along with their JavaScript type.

Here's the console output:

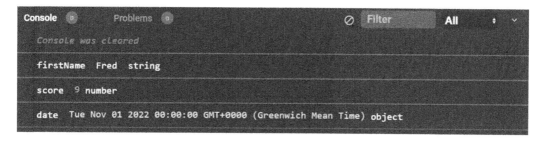

Figure 2.5 – Some JavaScript types

It isn't surprising that `firstName` is a string and `score` is a number. However, it is a little surprising that `date` is an object rather than something more specific such as a date.

3. Let's add another couple of lines of code after the existing code:

```
score = "ten"
console.log("score", score, typeof score);
```

Again, the console output is a little surprising:

Figure 2.6 – Variable changing type

The `score` variable has changed from a `number` type to a `string` type! This is because JavaScript is loosely typed.

A key point is that JavaScript only has a minimal set of types, such as `string`, `number`, and `boolean`. It is worth noting that all of the JavaScript types are available in TypeScript because Typescript is a superset of Javascript.

Also, JavaScript allows a variable to change its type – meaning that the JavaScript engine won't throw an error if a variable is changed to a completely different type. This loose typing makes it impossible for code editors to catch type errors.

> **Note**
>
> For more information on JavaScript types, see `https://developer.mozilla.org/en-US/docs/Web/JavaScript/Data_structures`.

Now that we understand the limitations of the type system in JavaScript, we will learn about TypeScript's type system, starting with basic types.

Using basic TypeScript types

In this section, we'll start by understanding how TypeScript types can be declared and how they are inferred from assigned values. We will then learn the basic types commonly used in TypeScript that aren't available in JavaScript and understand helpful use cases.

Using type annotations

TypeScript type annotations enable variables to be declared with specific types. These allow the TypeScript compiler to check that the code adheres to these types. In short, type annotations allow TypeScript to catch bugs where our code uses the wrong type much earlier than we would if we were writing our code in JavaScript.

Open the TypeScript Playground at `https://www.typescriptlang.org/play` and carry out the following steps to explore type annotations:

1. Remove any existing code in the left-hand pane and enter the following variable declaration:

   ```
   let unitPrice: number;
   ```

   The type annotation comes after the variable declaration. It starts with a colon followed by the type we want to assign to the variable. In this case, `unitPrice` is going to be a `number` type. Remember that `number` is a type in JavaScript, which means that it is available for us to use in TypeScript too.

   The transpiled JavaScript appears on the right-hand side as follows:

   ```
   let unitPrice;
   ```

However, notice that the type annotation has disappeared. This is because type annotations don't exist in JavaScript.

> **Note**
>
> You may also see `"use strict"`; at the top of the transpiled JavaScript. This means that the JavaScript will be executed in JavaScript strict mode, which will pick up more coding mistakes. For more information on JavaScript strict mode, see `https://developer.mozilla.org/en-US/docs/Web/JavaScript/Reference/Strict_mode`.

2. Add a second line to the program:

   ```
   unitPrice = "Table";
   ```

   Notice that a red line appears under `unitPrice` on this line. If you hover over the underlined `unitPrice`, a type error is described:

   ```
   let unitPrice: number

   Type 'string' is not assignable to type 'number'. (2322)

   View Problem (Alt+F8)    No quick fixes available
   unitPrice = "Table";
   ```

   Figure 2.7 – A type error being caught

3. You can also add type annotations to function parameters and a function's return value using the same syntax as annotating a variable. As an example, enter the following function in the TypeScript Playground:

   ```
   function getTotal(
     unitPrice: number,
     quantity: number,
     discount: number
   ): number {
     const priceWithoutDiscount = unitPrice * quantity;
     const discountAmount = priceWithoutDiscount * discount;
     return priceWithoutDiscount - discountAmount;
   }
   ```

We've declared the unitPrice, quantity, and discount parameters, all with a number type. The return type annotation comes after the function's parentheses, which is also a number type in the preceding example.

> **Note**
>
> We have used both const and let to declare variables in different examples. let allows the variable to change the value after the declaration, whereas const variables can't change. In the preceding function, priceWithoutDiscount and discountAmount never change the value after the initial assignment, so we have used const.

4. Add another line of code to call getTotal with an incorrect type for quantity. Assign the result of the call to getTotal to a variable with an incorrect type:

    ```
    let total: string = getTotal(500, "one", 0.1);
    ```

    Both errors are immediately detected and highlighted:

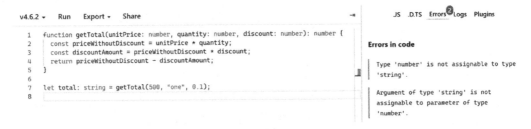

Figure 2.8 – Both type errors being caught

This strong type checking is something that we don't get in JavaScript, and it is very useful in large codebases because it helps us immediately detect type errors.

Next, we will learn how TypeScript doesn't always need type annotations in order to type-check code.

Using type inference

Type annotations are really valuable, but they require additional code to be written. This extra code takes time to write. Luckily, TypeScript's powerful **type inference** system means type annotations don't need to be specified all the time. TypeScript infers the type of a variable when it is assigned a value from that value.

Explore type inference by carrying out the following steps in the TypeScript Playground:

1. First, remove any previous code and then add the following line:

    ```
    let flag = false;
    ```

2. Hover over the `flag` variable. A tooltip will appear showing the type that `flag` has been inferred to:

```
let flag: boolean
let flag = false;
```

Figure 2.9 – Hovering over a variable reveals its type

3. Add another line beneath this to incorrectly set `flag` to an invalid value:

```
flag = "table";
```

A type error is immediately caught, just like when we used a type annotation to assign a type to a variable.

Type inference is an excellent feature of TypeScript and prevents code bloat that lots of type annotations would bring. Therefore, it is common practice to use type inference and only revert to using type annotations where inference isn't possible.

Next, we will look at the `Date` type in TypeScript.

Using the Date type

We are already aware that a `Date` type doesn't exist in JavaScript, but luckily, a `Date` type does exist in TypeScript. The TypeScript `Date` type is a representation of the JavaScript `Date` object.

> **Note**
>
> See the following link for more information on the JavaScript `Date` object: `https://developer.mozilla.org/en-US/docs/Web/JavaScript/Reference/Global_Objects/Date`.

To explore the TypeScript `Date` type, carry out the following steps in the TypeScript Playground:

1. First, remove any previous code and then add the following lines:

```
let today: Date;
today = new Date();
```

A `today` variable is declared that is assigned a `Date` type and set to today's date.

2. Refactor these two lines into the following single line that uses type inference rather than a type annotation:

```
let today = new Date();
```

3. Check that today has been assigned the Date type by hovering over it and checking the tooltip:

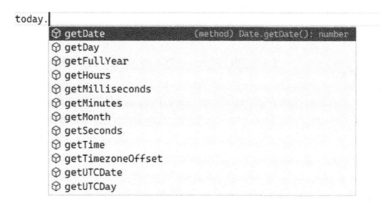

```
let today: Date
let today = new Date();
```

Figure 2.10 – Confirmation that today has inferred the Date type

4. Now, check IntelliSense is working by adding today. on a new line:

```
today.
    🔷 getDate                    (method) Date.getDate(): number
    🔷 getDay
    🔷 getFullYear
    🔷 getHours
    🔷 getMilliseconds
    🔷 getMinutes
    🔷 getMonth
    🔷 getSeconds
    🔷 getTime
    🔷 getTimezoneOffset
    🔷 getUTCDate
    🔷 getUTCDay
```

Figure 2.11 – IntelliSense working nicely on a date

5. Remove this line and add a slightly different line of code:

```
today.addMonths(2);
```

An addMonths function doesn't exist in the Date object, so a type error is raised:

```
v4.6.2 ▾   Run   Export ▾   Share   ⇥      JS  .D.TS  Errors ❶Logs  Plugins

1   let today = new Date();                  "use strict";
2   today.addMonths(2)                       let today = new Date();
3                                            today.addMonths(2);
4
5
```

Figure 2.12 – Type error caught on a date

In summary, the Date type has all the features we expect – inference, IntelliSense, and type checking – which are really useful when working with dates.

Next, we will learn about an escape hatch in TypeScript's type system.

Using the any type

What if we declare a variable with no type annotation and no value? What will TypeScript infer as the type? Let's find out by entering the following code in the TypeScript Playground:

```
let flag;
```

Now, hover the mouse over flag:

```
let flag: any
let flag
```

Figure 2.13 – Variable given the any type

So, TypeScript gives a variable with no type annotation and no immediately assigned value the any type. It is a way of opting out of performing type checking on a particular variable and is commonly used for dynamic content or values from third-party libraries. However, TypeScript's increasingly powerful type system means that we need to use any less often these days.

Instead, there is a better alternative: the unknown type.

Using the unknown type

unknown is a type we can use when we are unsure of the type but want to interact with it in a strongly-typed manner. Carry out the following steps to explore how this is a better alternative to the any type:

1. In the TypeScript Playground, remove any previous code, and enter the following:

```
fetch("https://swapi.dev/api/people/1")
  .then((response) => response.json())
  .then((data) => {
    console.log("firstName", data.firstName);
  });
```

The code fetches a Star Wars character from a web API. No type errors are raised, so the code appears okay.

2. Now click on the **Run** option to execute the code:

```
v4.6.2 ▾    Run    Export ▾    Share                    ⇥           .JS  .D.TS  Errors  Logs  Plugins

1    fetch("https://swapi.dev/api/people/1")
2      .then((response) => response.json())                  [LOG]: "firstName",  undefined
3      .then((data) => {
4        console.log("firstName", data.firstName);
5      });
6
```

Figure 2.14 – firstName property has an undefined value

The firstName property doesn't appear to be in the fetched data because it is undefined when it is output to the console.

Why wasn't a type error raised on line 4 where firstName was referenced? Well, data is of the type any, which means no type checking will occur on it. You can hover over data to confirm that it has been given the any type.

3. Give data the unknown type annotation:

```
fetch("https://swapi.dev/api/people/1")
  .then((response) => response.json())
  .then((data: unknown) => {
    console.log("firstName", data.firstName);
  });
```

A type error is now raised where firstName is referenced:

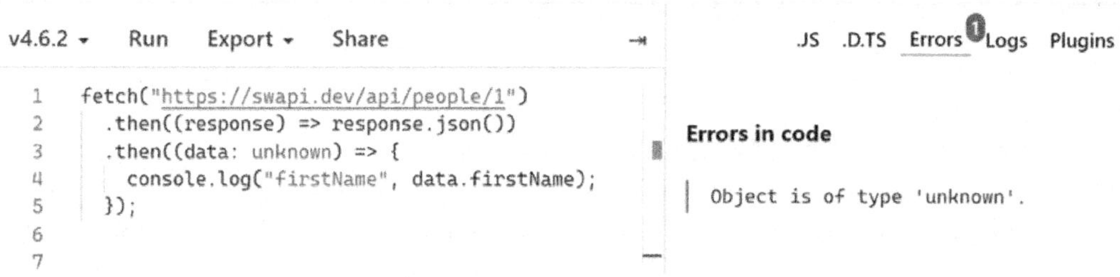

Figure 2.15 – Type error on unknown data parameter

The unknown type is the opposite of the any type, as it contains nothing within its type. A type that doesn't contain anything may seem useless. However, a variable's type can be widened if cheks are made to allow TypeScript to widen it.

4. Before we give TypeScript information to widen data, change the property referenced within it from firstName to name:

```
fetch("https://swapi.dev/api/people/1")
  .then((response) => response.json())
  .then((data: unknown) => {
    console.log("name", data.name);
  });
```

name is a valid property, but a type error is still occurring. This is because data is still unknown.

5. Now make the highlighted changes to the code to widen the data type:

```
fetch("https://swapi.dev/api/people/1")
  .then((response) => response.json())
```

```
  .then((data: unknown) => {
    if (isCharacter(data)) {
      console.log("name", data.name);
    }
  });


function isCharacter(
  character: any
): character is { name: string } {
  return "name" in character;
}
```

The code snippet can be copied from `https://github.com/PacktPublishing/Learn-React-with-TypeScript-2nd-Edition/blob/main/Chapter2/Section2-Basic-types/Using-the-unknown-type/code.ts`.

The `if` statement uses a function called `isCharacter` to verify that a `name` property is contained within the object. The result of this call is `true` in this example, so the logic will flow into the `if` branch.

Notice the return type of `isCharacter`, which is:

```
character is { name: string }
```

This is a **type predicate**. TypeScript will narrow or widen the type of `character` to `{ name: string }` if the function returns `true`. The type predicate is `true` in this example, so `character` is widened to an object with a `name` string property.

6. Hover over the `data` variable on each line where it is referenced. `data` starts off with the `unknown` type where it is assigned with a type annotation. Then, it is widened to `{name: string}` inside the `if` branch:

```
fetch("https://swapi.dev/a
  .then((response) => resp  (parameter) data: {
  .then((data: unknown) =>      name: string;
    if (isCharacter(data))  }
      console.log("name", data.name);
    }
  });
```

Figure 2.16 – Widened type given to data

Notice that the type error has also disappeared. Nice!

7. Next, run the code. You will see `Luke Skywalker` output to the console.

In summary, the unknown type is an excellent choice for data whose type you are unsure about. However, you can't interact with unknown variables – the variable must be widened to a different type before any interaction.

Next, we will learn about a type used for a function not returning a value.

Using the void type

The void type is used to represent a function's return type where the function doesn't return a value.

As an example, enter the following function in the TypeScript Playground:

```
function logText(text: string) {
  console.log(text);
}
```

Hovering over the function name confirms that the function return type is given a void type.

```
function logText(text: string): void
function logText(text: string) {
  console.log(text);
}
```

Figure 2.17 – Return type confirmed as void

You may think that you could use undefined as the return type for the preceding example:

```
function logText(text: string): undefined {
  console.log(text);
}
```

However, this raises a type error because a return type of undefined means that the function is expected to return a value (of type undefined). The example function doesn't return any value, so the return type is void.

In summary, void is a special type for a function's return type where the function doesn't have a return statement.

Next, we will learn about the never type.

Using the never type

The never type represents something that will never occur and is typically used to specify unreachable code areas. Let's explore an example in the TypeScript Playground:

1. Remove any existing code and enter the following code:

```
function foreverTask(taskName: string): never {
  while (true) {
    console.log(`Doing ${taskName} over and over again
      ...`);
  }
}
```

The function invokes an infinite loop, meaning the function is never exited. So, we have given the function a return type annotation of never because we don't expect the function to be exited. This is different from void because void means it *will* exit, but with no value.

> **Note**
>
> We used a JavaScript template literal to construct the string to output to the console in the preceding example. Template literals are enclosed by backticks (` `` `) and can include a JavaScript expression in curly braces prefixed with a dollar sign (${expression}). Template literals are great when we need to merge static text with variables. See this link for more information on template literals: https://developer.mozilla.org/en-US/docs/Web/JavaScript/Reference/Template_literals.

2. Change the foreverTask function to break out of the loop:

```
function foreverTask(taskName: string): never {
  while (true) {
    console.log(`Doing ${taskName} over and over again
      ...`);
    break;
  }
}
```

TypeScript quite rightly complains:

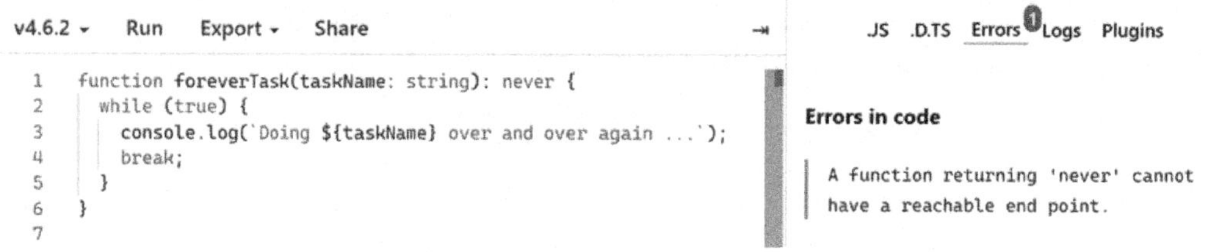

```
v4.6.2 ▾    Run    Export ▾    Share                          ⇥      JS  .D.TS  Errors ❶ Logs  Plugins
1   function foreverTask(taskName: string): never {
2     while (true) {                                          Errors in code
3       console.log(`Doing ${taskName} over and over again ...`);
4       break;                                                A function returning 'never' cannot
5     }                                                       have a reachable end point.
6   }
7
```

Figure 2.18 – Type error on the never return type

3. Remove the break statement and remove the never return type annotation:

```
function foreverTask(taskName: string) {
  while (true) {
    console.log(`Doing ${taskName} over and over again
...`);
  }
}
```

4. Hover over the foreverTask function name with your mouse. We can see that TypeScript has inferred the return type as void:

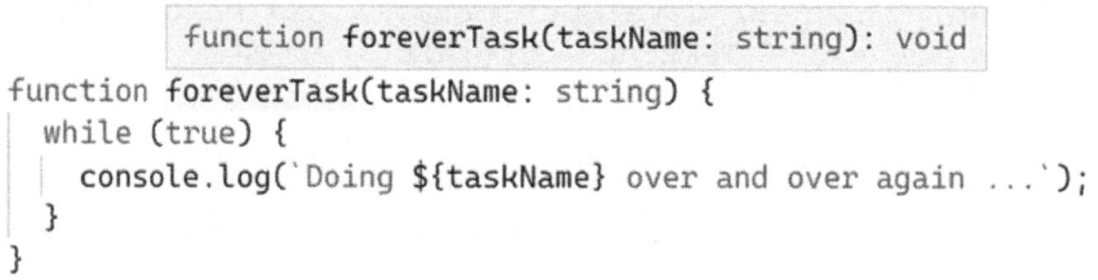

```
function foreverTask(taskName: string): void
function foreverTask(taskName: string) {
  while (true) {
    console.log(`Doing ${taskName} over and over again ...`);
  }
}
```

Figure 2.19 – Return type inferred as void

So, TypeScript is unable to infer the never type in this case. Instead, it infers the return type as void, which means the function will exit with no value, which isn't the case in this example. This is a reminder to always check the inferred type and resort to using a type annotation where appropriate.

In summary, the never type is used in places where code never reaches.

Next up, let's cover arrays.

Using arrays

Arrays are structures that TypeScript inherits from JavaScript. We add type annotations to arrays as usual, but with square brackets [] at the end to denote that this is an array type.

Let's explore an example in the TypeScript Playground:

1. Remove any existing code, and enter the following:

    ```
    const numbers: number[] = [];
    ```

    Alternatively, the Array generic type syntax can be used:

    ```
    const numbers: Array<number> = [];
    ```

    We will learn about generics in TypeScript in *Chapter 11, Reusable Components*.

2. Add 1 to the array by using the array's push function:

    ```
    numbers.push(1);
    ```

3. Now add a string to the array:

    ```
    numbers.push("two");
    ```

    A type error is raised as we would expect:

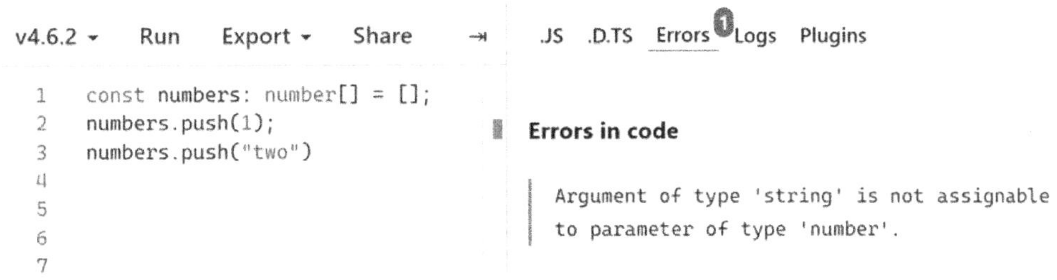

Figure 2.20 – Type error when adding a string type to a number array

4. Now replace all the code with the following:

    ```
    const numbers = [1, 2, 3];
    ```

5. Hover over numbers to verify that TypeScript has inferred its type to be number[].

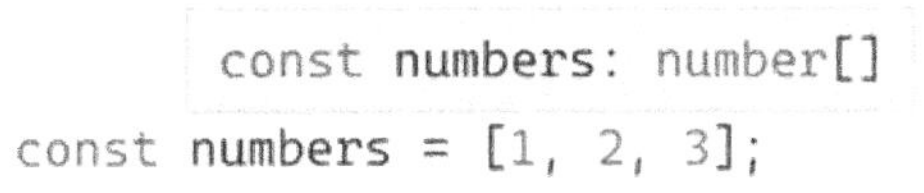

Figure 2.21 – Array type inference

Excellent – we can see that TypeScript's type inference works with arrays!

Arrays are one of the most common types used to structure data. In the preceding examples, we've only used an array with elements having a number type, but any type can be used for elements, including objects, which have their own properties.

Here's a recap of all the basic types we have learned in this section:

- TypeScript adds many useful types to JavaScripts types, such as Date, and is capable of representing arrays.

- TypeScript can infer a variable's type from its assigned value. A type annotation can be used where type inference doesn't give the desired type.

- No type checking occurs on variables with the any type, so this type should be avoided.

- The unknown type is a strongly-typed alternative to any, but unknown variables must be widened to be interacted with.

- void is a return type for a function that doesn't return a value.

- The never type can be used to mark unreachable areas of code.

- Array types can be defined using square brackets after the array item type.

In the next section, we will learn how to create our own types.

Creating TypeScript types

The last section showed that TypeScript has a great set of standard types. In this section, we will learn how to create our own types. We will start by learning three different methods for creating object types. We will then learn about strongly-typing JavaScript classes. Lastly, we will learn two different methods for creating types for variables that hold a range of values.

Using object types

Objects are very common in JavaScript programs, so learning how to represent them in TypeScript is really important. In fact, we have already used an object type earlier in this chapter for the product parameter in the calculateTotalPrice function. Here is a reminder of the product parameter's type annotation:

```
function calculateTotalPrice(
  product: { name: string; unitPrice: number },
    ...
) {
    ...
}
```

An object type in TypeScript is represented a bit like a JavaScript object literal. However, instead of property values, property types are specified instead. Properties in the object definitions can be separated by semicolons or commas, but using a semicolon is common practice.

Clear any existing code in the TypeScript Playground and follow this example to explore object types:

1. Enter the following variable assignment to an object:

    ```
    let table = {name: "Table", unitPrice: 450};
    ```

    If you hover over the `table` variable, you'll see it is inferred to be the following type:

    ```
    {
      name: string;
      unitPrice: number;
    }
    ```

    So, type inference works nicely for objects.

2. Now, on the next line, try to set a `discount` property to `10`:

    ```
    table.discount = 10;
    ```

    A `discount` property doesn't exist in the type, though – only the `name` and `unitPrice` properties exist. So, a type error occurs.

3. Let's say we want to represent a `product` object containing the `name` and `unitPrice` properties, but we want `unitPrice` to be optional. Remove the existing code and replace it with the following:

    ```
    const table: { name: string; unitPrice: number } = {
      name: "Table",
    };
    ```

4. This raises a type error because `unitPrice` is a required property in the type annotation. We can use a ? symbol as follows to make this optional rather than required:

    ```
    const table: { name: string; unitPrice?: number } = {
      name: "Table",
    };
    ```

    The type error disappears.

> **Note**
>
> The ? symbol can be used in functions for optional parameters. For example, `myFunction(requiredParam: string, optionalParam?: string)`.

Now, let's learn a way to streamline object type definitions.

Creating type aliases

The type annotation we used in the last example was quite lengthy and would be longer for more complex object structures. Also, having to write the same object structure to assign to different variables is a little frustrating:

```
const table: { name: string; unitPrice?: number } = ...;
const chair: { name: string; unitPrice?: number } = ...;
```

Type aliases solve these problems. As the name suggests, a type alias refers to another type, and the syntax is as follows:

```
type YourTypeAliasName = AnExistingType;
```

Open the TypeScript Playground and follow along to explore type aliases:

1. Start by creating a type alias for the product object structure we used in the last example:

    ```
    type Product = { name: string; unitPrice?: number };
    ```

2. Now assign two variables to this `Product` type:

    ```
    let table: Product = { name: "Table" };
    let chair: Product = { name: "Chair", unitPrice: 40 };
    ```

    That's much cleaner!

3. A type alias can extend another object using the & symbol. Create a second type for a discounted product by adding the following type alias:

    ```
    type DiscountedProduct = Product & { discount: number };
    ```

    `DiscountedProduct` represents an object containing `name`, `unitPrice` (optional), and `discount` properties.

> **Note**
>
> A type that extends another using the & symbol is referred to as an **intersection type**.

4. Add the following variable with the `DiscountedProduct` type as follows:

    ```
    let chairOnSale: DiscountedProduct = {
        name: "Chair on Sale",
        unitPrice: 30,
    ```

```
  discount: 5,
};
```

5. A type alias can also be used to represent a function. Add the following type alias to represent a function:

```
type Purchase = (quantity: number) => void;
```

The preceding type represents a function containing a `number` parameter and doesn't return anything.

6. Use the `Purchase` type to create a `purchase` function property in the `Product` type as follows:

```
type Purchase = (quantity: number) => void;
type Product = {
  name: string;
  unitPrice?: number;
  purchase: Purchase;
};
```

Type errors will be raised on the `table`, `chair`, and `chairOnSale` variable declarations because the `purchase` function property is required.

7. Add a `purchase` function property to the `table` variable declarations as follows:

```
let table: Product = {
  name: "Table",
  purchase: (quantity) =>
    console.log(`Purchased ${quantity} tables`),
};
table.purchase(4);
```

The type error is resolved on the `table` variable declaration.

8. A purchase property could be added in a similar way to the `chair` and `chairOnSale` variable declarations to resolve their type errors. However, ignore these type errors for this exploration and move on to the next step.

9. Click the **Run** option to run the code that purchases four tables. **"Purchased 4 tables"** is output to the console.

In summary, type aliases allow existing types to be composed together and improve the readability and reusability of types. We will use type aliases extensively in this book.

Next, we will explore an alternative method of creating types. Leave the TypeScript Playground open with the code intact – we'll use this in the next section.

Creating interfaces

As we created in the last example with type aliases, object types can be created using TypeScript's **interface** syntax. An interface is created with the `interface` keyword, followed by its name, followed by the bits that make up the `interface` in curly brackets:

```
interface Product {

  ...

}
```

Go to the TypeScript Playground that contains the code from the type alias exploration, and follow along to explore interfaces:

1. Start by replacing the `Product` type alias with a `Product` interface as follows:

    ```
    interface Product {
      name: string;
      unitPrice?: number;
    }
    ```

    The `table` variable assignment has a type error because the `purchase` property doesn't exist yet – we'll add this in *step 4*. However, the `chair` variable assignment compiles without error.

2. An interface can extend another interface using the `extends` keyword. Replace the `DiscountedProduct` type alias with the following interface:

    ```
    interface DiscountedProduct extends Product {
      discount: number;
    }
    ```

    Notice that the `chairOnSale` variable assignment compiles without error.

3. An interface can also be used to represent a function. Add the following interface to represent a function, replacing the type alias version:

    ```
    interface Purchase {(quantity: number): void}
    ```

    The interface syntax for creating functions isn't as intuitive as using a type alias.

4. Add the `Purchase` interface to the `Product` interface as follows:

    ```
    interface Product {
      name: string;
    ```

```
  unitPrice?: number;
  purchase: Purchase;
}
```

The type error on the `table` variable declarations is resolved now, but type errors are raised on the `chair` and `chairOnSale` variable declarations.

5. Click the **Run** option to run the code that purchases four tables. **"Purchased 4 tables"** is output to the console.

In the preceding steps, we carried out the same tasks using an interface as we did using a type alias. So, the obvious question is, *when should I use a type alias instead of an interface and vice versa?* The capabilities of type aliases and interfaces for creating object types are very similar – so the simple answer is that it is down to preference for object types. Type aliases can create types that interfaces can't, though, such as union types, which we shall cover later in this chapter.

> **Note**
>
> See the following link for more information on the differences between type aliases and interfaces: `https://www.typescriptlang.org/docs/handbook/2/everyday-types.html#differences-between-type-aliases-and-interfaces`.
>
> The rest of this book uses type aliases rather than interfaces to define types.

Next, we will learn how to use TypeScript with classes.

Creating classes

A **class** is a standard JavaScript feature that acts as a template for creating an object. Properties and methods defined in the class are automatically included in objects created from the class.

Open the TypeScript Playground, remove any existing code, and carry out the following steps to explore classes in TypeScript:

1. Add the following code to create a class to represent a product with properties for the name and unit price:

```
class Product {
  name;
  unitPrice;
}
```

If you hover over the `name` and `unitPrice` properties, you'll see that they have the `any` type. As we know, that means no type checking will occur on them.

2. Add the following type annotations to the properties:

```
class Product {
    name: string;
    unitPrice: number;
}
```

Unfortunately, TypeScript raises the following error:

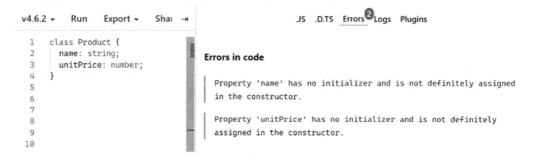

Figure 2.22 – Type errors on the class properties

The error is because when an instance of the class is created, those property values would be undefined, which isn't within the string or number types.

3. A solution would be to make the properties optional so that they can accept undefined as a value. Try this solution by adding a ? symbol at the start of the type annotations:

```
class Product {
    name?: string;
    unitPrice?: number;
}
```

4. If we don't want the values to initially be undefined, we can assign initial values like so:

```
class Product {
    name = "";
    unitPrice = 0;
}
```

If you hover over the properties now, you will see that name has been inferred to be a string type, and unitPrice has been inferred to be a number type.

5. Another method of adding types to class properties is in a constructor. Remove the values assigned to the properties and add a constructor to the class as follows:

```
class Product {
  name;
  unitPrice;
  constructor(name: string, unitPrice: number) {
    this.name = name;
    this.unitPrice = unitPrice;
  }
}
```

If you hover over the properties, you'll see that the correct types have been inferred.

6. In fact, the properties don't need to be defined if the constructor parameters are marked as public.

```
class Product {
  constructor(public name: string, public unitPrice:
    number) {
    this.name = name;
    this.unitPrice = unitPrice;
  }
}
```

TypeScript will automatically create properties for constructor parameters that are marked as public.

7. Type annotations can be added to method parameters and return values, just like we have previously done for functions:

```
class Product {
  constructor(public name: string, public unitPrice:
    number) {
    this.name = name;
    this.unitPrice = unitPrice;
  }
  getDiscountedPrice(discount: number): number {
    return this.unitPrice - discount;
  }
}
```

8. Now create an instance of the class and output its discounted price to the console:

    ```
    const table = new Product("Table", 45);
    console.log(table.getDiscountedPrice(5));
    ```

    If you run the code, **40** is output to the console.

In summary, class properties can be given a type in a constructor or by assigning a default value. Class methods can be strongly-typed just like regular JavaScript functions.

> **Note**
>
> For more information on classes, see the following link: `https://developer.mozilla.org/en-US/docs/Web/JavaScript/Reference/Classes`.

Next, we will learn how to create a type to represent a range of values.

Creating enumerations

Enumerations allow us to declare a meaningful set of friendly names that a variable can be set to. We use the enum keyword, followed by the name we want to give to it, and then its possible values in curly braces.

Let's explore an example in the TypeScript Playground:

1. Start by creating the enumeration for Level containing Low, Medium, and High values:

    ```
    enum Level {
      Low,
      Medium,
      High
    }
    ```

2. Now, create a level variable and assign it to the values Low and then High from the Level enumeration. Also, output the level values to the console:

    ```
    let level = Level.Low;
    console.log(level);
    level = Level.High
    console.log(level);
    ```

    Notice that you get IntelliSense as you reference the enumeration.

3. Click the **Run** option to execute the code and observe the enumeration values:

```
v4.6.2 ▾    Run    Export ▾    Share        ⇥     JS  .D.TS  Errors  Logs  Plugins

 1   enum Level {
 2      Low,                                     [LOG]: 0
 3      Medium,
 4      High                                     [LOG]: 2
 5   }
 6
 7   let level = Level.Low;
 8   console.log(level);
 9   level = Level.High
10   console.log(level);
```

Figure 2.23 – Output of enumeration values

By default, enumerations are zero-based numbers (this means that the first enumeration value is 0, the next is 1, the next is 2, and so on). In the preceding example, Level.Low is 0, Level. Medium is 1, and Level.High is 2.

4. Instead of the default values, custom values can be explicitly defined against each enumeration item after the equals (=) symbol. Explicitly set the values to be between 1 and 3:

```
enum Level {
   Low = 1,
   Medium = 2,
   High = 3
}
```

You can rerun the code to verify this works.

5. Now, let's do something interesting. Assign level to a number greater than 3:

```
level = 10;
```

Notice that a type error *doesn't* occur. This is a little surprising – number-based enumerations aren't as type-safe as we would like.

6. Instead of using number enumeration values, let's try strings. Replace all of the current code with the following:

```
enum Level {
   Low = "L",
   Medium = "M",
   High = "H"
}
```

```
let level = Level.Low;
console.log(level);
level = Level.High
console.log(level);
```

If this code is run, we see **L** and **H** output to the console as expected.

7. Add another line that assigns `level` to the following strings:

```
level = "VH";
level = "M"
```

We immediately see type errors raised on these assignments:

Figure 2.24 – Confirmation that string enumerations are type-safe

In summary, enumerations are a way of representing a range of values with user-friendly names. They are zero-based numbers by default and not as type-safe as we would like. However, we can make enumerations string-based, which is more type-safe.

Next, we will learn about union types in TypeScript.

Creating union types

A **union type** is the mathematical union of multiple other types to create a new type. Like enumerations, union types can represent a range of values. As mentioned earlier, type aliases can be used to create union types.

An example of a union type is as follows:

```
type Level = "H" | "M" | "L";
```

This `Level` type is similar to the enumeration version of the `Level` type we created earlier. The difference is that the union type only contains values (`"H"`, `"M"`, `"L"`) rather than a name (`"High"`, `"Medium"`, `"Large"`) and a value.

Clear any existing code in the TypeScript Playground, and let's have a play with union types:

1. Start by creating a type to represent `"red"`, `"green"`, or `"blue"`:

    ```
    type RGB = "red" | "green" | "blue";
    ```

    Note that this type is a union of strings, but a union type can consist of any types – even mixed types!

2. Create a variable with the RGB type and assign a valid value:

    ```
    let color: RGB = "red";
    ```

3. Now try assigning a value outside the type:

    ```
    color = "yellow";
    ```

    A type error occurs, as expected:

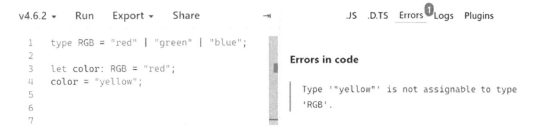

Figure 2.25 – Type error on the union type

Union types consisting of strings are great when a type can only hold a specific set of strings, as in the preceding example.

Here's a recap of what we have learned about creating types:

*   Objects and functions can be represented using type aliases or interfaces. They have very similar capabilities, but the type alias syntax is a little more intuitive for representing functions.

*   The ? symbol can specify that an object property or function parameter is optional.

*   Type annotations can be added to class properties and constructor and method parameters to make them type-safe.

- Like string-based union types, string-based enumerations are great for a specific set of strings. A string union type is the simplest approach if the strings are meaningful. If the strings aren't meaningful, then a string enumeration can be used to make them readable.

Now that we have covered types, next, we will learn about the TypeScript compiler.

Using the TypeScript compiler

In this section, we will learn how to use the TypeScript compiler to type check code and transpile it into JavaScript. First, we will use Visual Studio Code and create a simple TypeScript project containing code we have written in a previous section. We will then use the terminal within Visual Studio Code to interact with the TypeScript compiler.

Open Visual Studio Code in a blank folder of your choice, and carry out the following steps:

1. In the **EXPLORER** panel in Visual Studio Code, create a file called package.json containing the following content:

```
{
    "name": "tsc-play",
    "dependencies": {
        "typescript": "^4.6.4"
    },
    "scripts": {
        "build": "tsc src/product.ts"
    }
}
```

The file defines a project name of tsc-play and sets TypeScript as the only dependency. The file also defines an npm script called build that will invoke the TypeScript compiler (tsc), passing it to the product.ts file in the src folder. Don't worry that product.ts doesn't exist – we will create it in *step 3*.

2. Now open the Visual Studio Code terminal by selecting **New Terminal** from the **Terminal** menu, then enter the following command:

```
npm install
```

This will install all the libraries listed in the dependencies section of package.json. So, this will install TypeScript.

3. Create a folder called src and then create a file called product.ts within it.

4. Open `product.ts` and add the following content:

```typescript
class Product {
  constructor(public name: string, public unitPrice:
    number) {
    this.name = name;
    this.unitPrice = unitPrice;
  }
  getDiscountedPrice(discount: number): number {
    return this.unitPrice - discount;
  }
}

const table = new Product("Table", 45);
console.log(table.getDiscountedPrice(5));
```

This code will be familiar from the section on using classes. The code can be copied from https://github.com/PacktPublishing/Learn-React-with-TypeScript-2nd-Edition/blob/main/Chapter2/Section4-Using-the-compiler/src/product.ts.

5. Enter the following command in the terminal:

```
npm run build
```

This will run the npm `build` script we defined in the first step.

After the command finishes, notice that a `product.js` file appears next to `product.ts` in the `src` folder.

6. Open the transpiled `product.js` file and read the content. It will look as follows:

```javascript
var Product = /** @class */ (function () {
  function Product(name, unitPrice) {
    this.name = name;
    this.unitPrice = unitPrice;
    this.name = name;
    this.unitPrice = unitPrice;
  }
  Product.prototype.getDiscountedPrice = function
    (discount) {
    return this.unitPrice - discount;
```

```
  };
  return Product;
})();
var table = new Product("Table", 45);
console.log(table.getDiscountedPrice(5));
```

Notice that the type annotations have been removed because they aren't valid JavaScript. Notice also that it has been transpiled to JavaScript, capable of running in very old browsers.

The default configuration that the TypeScript compiler uses isn't ideal. For example, we probably want the transpiled JavaScript in a completely separate folder, and are likely to want to target newer browsers.

7.   The TypeScript compiler can be configured using a file called `tsconfig.json`. Add a `tsconfig.json` file at the root of the project, containing the following code:

```
{
  "compilerOptions": {
    "outDir": "build",
    "target": "esnext",
    "module": "esnext",
    "lib": ["DOM", "esnext"],
    "strict": true,
    "jsx": "react",
    "moduleResolution": "node",
    "noEmitOnError": true
  },
  "include": ["src/**/*"],
  "exclude": ["node_modules", "build"]
}
```

This code can be copied from `https://github.com/PacktPublishing/Learn-React-with-TypeScript-2nd-Edition/blob/main/Chapter2/Section4-Using-the-compiler/tsconfig.json`.

Here's an explanation of each setting in the `compilerOptions` field:

- `outDir`: This is the folder that the transpiled JavaScript is placed in.

- `target`: This is the version of JavaScript we want to transpile to. The `esnext` target means the next version.

- `Module`: This is the type of module used within the code. The `esnext` module means standard JavaScript modules.

- Lib: Gives the standard library types included in the type checking process. DOM gives the browser DOM API types, and esnext are types for APIs in the next version of JavaScript.

- Strict: When set to true, means the strictest level of type checking.

- Jsx: When set to React, allows the compiler to transpile React's JSX.

- moduleResolution: This is how dependencies are found. We want TypeScript to look in the node_modules folder, so we have chosen node.

- noEmitOnError: When set to true, means the transpilation won't happen if a type error is found.

The include field specifies the TypeScript files to compile, and the exclude field specifies the files to exclude.

> **Note**
>
> For more information on the TypeScript compiler options, see the following link: https://www.typescriptlang.org/tsconfig.

8. The TypeScript compiler configuration now specifies all files in the src folder to be compiled. So, remove the file path on the build script in package.json:

```
{
  ...,
  "scripts": {
    "build": "tsc"
  }
}
```

9. Delete the previous transpiled product.js in the src folder.

10. Rerun the build command in the terminal:

```
npm run build
```

This time the transpiled file is placed in a build folder. You will also notice that the transpiled JavaScript now uses classes that are supported in modern browsers.

11. The final thing we are going to try is a type error. Open product.ts and update the constructor to reference an incorrect property name:

```
class Product {
  constructor(public name: string, public unitPrice:
    number) {
    this.name = name;
```

```
        this.price = unitPrice;
    }

    . . .

}
```

12. Delete the `build` folder to remove the previously transpiled JavaScript file.

13. Rerun the `build` command in the terminal:

```
npm run build
```

The type error is reported in the terminal. Notice that the JavaScript file is not transpiled.

In summary, TypeScript has a compiler, called `tsc`, that we can use to carry out type checking and transpilation as part of a continuous integration process. The compiler is very flexible and can be configured using a file called `tsconfig.json`. It is worth noting that Babel is often used to transpile TypeScript (as well as React), leaving TypeScript to focus on type checking.

Next, we will recap what we have learned in this chapter.

Summary

TypeScript complements JavaScript with a rich type system, and in this chapter, we experienced catching errors early using TypeScript's type checking.

We also learned that JavaScript types, such as `number` and `string`, can be used in TypeScript, as well as types that only exist in TypeScript, such as `Date` and `unknown`.

We explored union types and learned that these are great for representing a specific set of strings. We now understand that string enumerations are an alternative to string union types if the string values aren't very meaningful.

New types can be created using type aliases. We learned that type aliases could be based on objects, functions, or even union types. We now know that the ? symbol in a type annotation makes an object property or function parameter optional.

We also learned a fair bit about the TypeScript compiler and how it can work well in different use cases because it is very configurable. This will be important when we start to use TypeScript with React in the next chapter. There, we will learn different ways of setting up React and TypeScript projects before learning to strongly-type React props and state.

Questions

Answer the following questions to check what you have learned about TypeScript:

1. What would the inferred type be for the `flag` variable in the following code?

   ```
   let flag = false;
   ```

2. What is the return type in the following function?

   ```
   function log(message: string) {
     return console.log(message);
   }
   ```

3. What is the type annotation for an array of dates?

4. Will a type error occur in the following code?

   ```
   type Point = {x: number; y: number; z?: number};
   const point: Point = { x: 24, y: 65 };
   ```

5. Use a type alias to create a number that can only hold integer values between and including 1 and 3.

6. What TypeScript compiler option can be used to prevent the transpilation process when a type error is found?

7. The following code raises a type error because `lastSale` can't accept `null` values:

   ```
   type Product = {
     name: string;
     lastSale: Date;
   }
   const table: Product = {name: "Table", lastSale: null}
   ```

   How can the `Product` type be changed to allow `lastSale` to accept `null` values?

Answers

1. The `flag` variable would be inferred to be a `boolean` type.

2. The return type in the function is `void`.

3. An array of dates can be represented as `Date[]` or `Array<Date>`.

4. A type error will not be raised on the `point` variable. It doesn't need to include the z property because it is optional.

5. A type for numbers 1-3 can be created as follows:

```
type OneToThree = 1 | 2 | 3;
```

6. The noEmitOnError compiler option (set to true) can be used to prevent the transpilation process when a type error is found.

7. A union type can be used for the lastSale property to allow it to accept null values:

```
type Product = {
  name: string;
  lastSale: Date | null;
}
const table: Product = {name: "Table", lastSale: null}
```

3

Setting Up React and TypeScript

In this chapter, we will learn how to use both React and TypeScript together. We will start by going through the steps for creating a React and TypeScript project using a tool called webpack. Then we will create another project, but this time using a tool called Create React App to show you how to speed up the process of creating a React and TypeScript project.

This chapter will then cover how to use TypeScript to make React props and states type-safe, extending the alert component built in the first chapter. Lastly, we will learn how to debug your app with React's DevTools.

In this chapter, we'll cover the following topics:

- Creating a project with webpack
- Creating a project with Create React App
- Creating a React and TypeScript component

Technical requirements

We will use the following technologies in this chapter:

- **Node.js** and **npm**: React and TypeScript are dependent on these. You can install them from https://nodejs.org/en/download/.
- **Visual Studio Code**: We'll use this editor to write code and execute terminal commands. You can install it from https://code.visualstudio.com/.

All the code snippets in this chapter can be found online at https://github.com/PacktPublishing/Learn-React-with-TypeScript-2nd-Edition/tree/main/Chapter3.

Creating a project with webpack

Setting up a React and TypeScript project is tricky because both JSX and TypeScript code needs to be transpiled into JavaScript. In this section, we will cover how to set up a React and TypeScript project step by step, with the help of a tool called webpack.

Introducing webpack

Webpack is a tool that bundles JavaScript source code files together. It can also bundle CSS and images. It can run other tools such as Babel to transpile React and the TypeScript type checker as it scans the files. It is a mature and incredibly popular tool used in the React community that powers many React projects.

Webpack is incredibly flexible but, unfortunately, it requires a lot of configuration. We will witness this as we create our project with webpack.

It is important to understand that webpack isn't a project creation tool. For example, it won't install React or TypeScript – we have to do that separately. Instead, webpack brings tools such as React and TypeScript together once installed and configured. So, we won't use webpack until later in this section.

Creating the folder structure

We will start by creating a simple folder structure for the project. The structure will separate the project's configuration files from the source code. Carry out the following steps to do this:

1. Open Visual Studio Code in the folder where you want the project to be.
2. In the **Explorer** panel, create a folder called `src`. A folder can be created by right-clicking in the **Explorer** panel and choosing **New Folder**. Note that `src` is short for source code.

So, the `src` folder will hold all the source code for the app. The project configuration files will be placed at the root of the project.

Next, we will define the critical information about the project.

Creating package.json

The `package.json` file defines our project name, description, npm scripts, dependent npm modules, and much more.

Create a `package.json` file at the root of the project with the following content:

```
{
    "name": "my-app",
    "description": "My React and TypeScript app",
```

```
    "version": "0.0.1"
  }
```

This file contains minimal information at the moment. However, it will eventually contain other details, such as React and TypeScript as the app's dependencies.

> **Note**
>
> More information can be found on `package.json` at the following link: `https://docs.npmjs.com/cli/v8/configuring-npm/package-json`.

Next, we will add the web page that will host the React app.

Adding a web page

An HTML page is going to host the app. In the `src` folder, create a file called `index.html` with the following content:

```html
<!DOCTYPE html>
<html>
  <head>
    <meta charset="utf-8" />
    <title>My app</title>
  </head>
  <body>
    <div id="root"></div>
  </body>
</html>
```

This code snippet can be copied and pasted from `https://github.com/PacktPublishing/Learn-React-with-TypeScript-2nd-Edition/blob/main/Chapter3/Section1-Creating-a-project-with-Webpack/src/index.html`.

The React app will be injected into the `div` element with an `id` attribute value of `"root"`. We will cover the injection of the React app in a later section, *Adding React*.

Adding TypeScript

Next, we will install TypeScript into the project. To do this, carry out the following steps:

1. Start by opening the Visual Studio Code terminal by opening the **Terminal** menu and clicking **New Terminal**.

2. We know from the last chapter that using `npm install` without specifying any options will install the dependencies listed inside `package.json`. The `install` command has options for the specific packages to be installed that aren't in `package.json` yet. Execute the following command in the terminal to install `typescript`:

```
npm install --save-dev typescript
```

We have also included a `--save-dev` option to specify that `typescript` should be installed as a **development-only** dependency. This is because TypeScript is only required during development and not at runtime.

3. After the command has finished, open `package.json`. You will see that `typescript` is now listed as a development dependency in the `devDependencies` section:

```
{
    "name": "my-app",
    "description": "My React and TypeScript app",
    "version": "0.0.1",
    "devDependencies": {
        "typescript": "^4.6.4"
    }
}
```

Note that the version (`4.6.4`) of `typescript` in the preceding code snippet will probably be different in your example. This is because `npm install` installs the latest version of the dependency unless a version is specified in the command.

4. Next, we will create a TypeScript configuration file. Note that we aren't going to configure TypeScript to do any transpilation – we will use Babel for that, which is covered later. So, the TypeScript configuration will be focused on type checking.

To do this, create a file called `tsconfig.json` in the `root` folder and enter the following content into it:

```
{
    "compilerOptions": {
        "noEmit": true,
        "lib": [
            "dom",
            "dom.iterable",
            "esnext"
        ],
        "moduleResolution": "node",
```

```
    "allowSyntheticDefaultImports": true,
    "esModuleInterop": true,
    "jsx": "react",
    "forceConsistentCasingInFileNames": true,
    "strict": true
  },
  "include": ["src"],
  "exclude": ["node_modules", "dist"]
}
```

This code snippet can be copied and pasted from https://github.com/PacktPublishing/Learn-React-with-TypeScript-2nd-Edition/blob/main/Chapter3/Section1-Creating-a-project-with-Webpack/tsconfig.json.

Here is an explanation of each setting that has been configured that wasn't explained in the last chapter:

- Setting noEmit to true suppresses the TypeScript compiler from doing any transpilation.

- Setting allowSyntheticDefaultImports and esModuleInterop to true allows React to be imported as a default import, like the following:

```
import React from 'react'
```

  - Without these settings set to true, React would have to be imported like this:

```
import * as React from 'react'
```

- Setting forceConsistentCasingInFileNames to true enables the type-checking process to check the casing of referenced filenames in import statements are consistent.

> **Note**
>
> For more information on the TypeScript compiler options, see the following link: https://www.typescriptlang.org/docs/handbook/compiler-options.html.

Adding React

Next, we will install React and its TypeScript types into the project. We will then add a React root component. To do this, carry out the following steps:

1. Execute the following command in the terminal to install React:

```
npm install react react-dom
```

Reacts comes in two libraries:

- The core library is called react, which is used in all variants of React.

- The specific React variant, which is the variant used to build web apps, is called react-dom. An example of a different variant would be the React Native variant used to build mobile apps.

2. React doesn't include TypeScript types – instead, they are in a separate npm package. Let's install these now:

```
npm install --save-dev @types/react @types/react-dom
```

3. The root component will be in a file called index.tsx in the src folder. Create this file with the following content:

```tsx
import React, { StrictMode } from 'react';
import { createRoot } from 'react-dom/client';

const root = createRoot(
  document.getElementById('root') as HTMLElement
);

function App() {
  return <h1>My React and TypeScript App!</h1>;
}

root.render(
  <StrictMode>
    <App />
  </StrictMode>
);
```

This code snippet can be copied and pasted from https://github.com/ PacktPublishing/Learn-React-with-TypeScript-2nd-Edition/blob/ main/Chapter3/Section1-Creating-a-project-with-Webpack/src/ index.tsx.

The structure of this file is similar to the index.js file in the alert component project from the first chapter. It injects the React app into a DOM element with an id of 'root'. The app is straightforward – it displays a heading called **My React and TypeScript App!**.

Notice that the file extension for index is .tsx rather than .js. This allows Babel and TypeScript to detect TypeScript files containing JSX in the transpilation and type-checking processes. A .ts extension can be used for TypeScript code that doesn't contain any JSX.

Also, notice as HTMLElement in the call to createRoot:

```
const root = createRoot(
  document.getElementById('root') as HTMLElement
);
```

This is called a **type assertion**, which tells TypeScript what the type should be. Without the type assertion, TypeScript will infer the type as HTMLElement | null because document.getElementById may not find an element and return null. However, we are confident that the element will be found because we specified it in the index.html file, so it is safe to narrow the type to HTMLElement using a type assertion.

React is now installed in the project, and the project also contains a simple React app.

Adding Babel

As mentioned earlier, Babel will transpile both React and TypeScript code into JavaScript in this project. Carry out the following steps to install and configure Babel:

1. Start by installing the core Babel library using the following command in Visual Studio Code's terminal:

    ```
    npm install --save-dev @babel/core
    ```

    Babel is installed as a development dependency because it is only needed during development to transpile code and not when the app runs.

    A shortened version of this command is as follows:

    ```
    npm i -D @babel/core
    ```

    i is short for install, and -D is short for --save-dev.

2. Next, install a Babel plugin called @babel/preset-env that allows the latest JavaScript features to be used:

    ```
    npm i -D @babel/preset-env
    ```

3. Now, install a Babel plugin called @babel/preset-react that enables React code to be transformed into JavaScript:

    ```
    npm i -D @babel/preset-react
    ```

4. Similarly, install a Babel plugin called @babel/preset-typescript that enables TypeScript code to be transformed into JavaScript:

    ```
    npm i -D @babel/preset-typescript
    ```

5. The last two plugins to install allow the use of the async and await features in JavaScript:

    ```
    npm i -D @babel/plugin-transform-runtime @babel/runtime
    ```

6. Babel can be configured in a file called .babelrc.json. Create this file at the root of the project with the following content:

    ```json
    {
      "presets": [
        "@babel/preset-env",
        "@babel/preset-react",
        "@babel/preset-typescript"
      ],
      "plugins": [
        [
          "@babel/plugin-transform-runtime",
          {
            "regenerator": true
          }
        ]
      ]
    }
    ```

    This code snippet can be found at https://github.com/PacktPublishing/Learn-React-with-TypeScript-2nd-Edition/blob/main/Chapter3/Section1-Creating-a-project-with-Webpack/.babelrc.json.

    The preceding configuration tells Babel to use the installed plugins. Babel is now installed and configured.

> **Note**
>
> For more information about Babel, see the following link: https://babeljs.io/.

Next, we will glue everything together with webpack.

Adding webpack

Webpack is a popular tool that primarily bundles JavaScript source code files together. It can run other tools, such as Babel, as it scans the files. So, we will use webpack to scan all the source files and transpile them into JavaScript. The output from the webpack process will be a single JavaScript bundle that is referenced in `index.html`.

Installing webpack

Carry out the following steps to install webpack and its associated libraries:

1. Start by installing webpack using the following command in the terminal in Visual Studio Code:

   ```
   npm i -D webpack webpack-cli
   ```

   This installs the core webpack library as well as its command-line interface.

   Webpack has TypeScript types in the `webpack` package, so we don't need to install them separately.

2. Next, run the following command to install webpack's development server:

   ```
   npm i -D webpack-dev-server
   ```

   Webpack's development server is used during developments to host the web app and automatically updates as changes are made to the code.

3. A webpack plugin is required to allow Babel to transpile the React and TypeScript code into JavaScript. This plugin is called `babel-loader`. Install this using the following command:

   ```
   npm i -D babel-loader
   ```

4. Webpack can create the `index.html` file that hosts the React app. We want webpack to use the `index.html` file in the `src` folder as a template and add the React app's bundle to it. A plugin called `html-webpack-plugin` is capable of doing this. Install this plugin using the following command:

   ```
   npm i -D html-webpack-plugin
   ```

Webpack and its associated libraries are now installed.

Configuring webpack

Next, we will configure webpack to do everything we need. Separate configurations for development and production can be created because the requirements are slightly different. However, we will focus on a configuration for development in this chapter. Carry out the following steps to configure webpack:

1. First, install a library called `ts-node`, which allows the configuration to be defined in a TypeScript file:

   ```
   npm i -D ts-node
   ```

2. Now, we can add the development configuration file. Create a file called `webpack.dev.config.ts` in the project root. The code to go in this file is lengthy and can be copied and pasted from the following link: `https://github.com/PacktPublishing/Learn-React-with-TypeScript-2nd-Edition/blob/main/Chapter3/Section1-Creating-a-project-with-Webpack/webpack.dev.config.ts`. In the following steps, we will explain the different parts of this file.

3. The configure file starts with various import statements and a type for the configuration object:

```typescript
import path from 'path';
import HtmlWebpackPlugin from 'html-webpack-plugin';
import {
  Configuration as WebpackConfig,
  HotModuleReplacementPlugin,
} from 'webpack';
import {
  Configuration as WebpackDevServerConfig
} from 'webpack-dev-server';

type Configuration = WebpackConfig & {
  devServer?: WebpackDevServerConfig;
}
```

Let's review the most important points:

- The `path` node library will tell webpack where to place the bundle.

- `HtmlWebpackPlugin` will be used to create `index.html`.

- The webpack configuration TypeScript types come from both the `webpack` and `webpack-dev-server` packages. So, we combine them using an intersect type, creating a type called `Configuration`.

4. The configuration object is then defined as follows:

```typescript
const config: Configuration = {
  mode: 'development',
  output: {
    publicPath: '/',
  },
  entry: './src/index.tsx',

  ...
```

```
};

export default config;
```

Let's review the most important points here:

- The `mode` property tells webpack the configuration is for development, meaning that the React development tools are included in the bundle

- The `output.publicPath` property is the root path in the app, which is important for deep linking in the dev server to work correctly

- The `entry` property tells webpack where the React app's entry point is, which is `index.tsx` in our project

- Webpack expects the configuration object to be a default export, so we export the `config` object as a default export

5. Further configuration is highlighted by the following code:

```
const config: Configuration = {
  ...,
  module: {
    rules: [
      {
        test: /\.(ts|js)x?$/i,
        exclude: /node_modules/,
        use: {
          loader: 'babel-loader',
          options: {
            presets: ['@babel/preset-env', '@babel/
              preset-react', '@babel/preset-typescript'],
          },
        },
      },
    ],
  },
  resolve: {
    extensions: ['.tsx', '.ts', '.js'],
  }
};
```

The `module` property informs webpack how different modules should be processed. We need to tell webpack to use `babel-loader` for files with `.js`, `.ts`, and `.tsx` extensions.

The `resolve.extensions` property tells webpack to look for TypeScript files and JavaScript files during module resolution.

6. Next, a couple of plugins are defined:

```
const config: Configuration = {
  ...,
  plugins: [
    new HtmlWebpackPlugin({
      template: 'src/index.html',
    }),
    new HotModuleReplacementPlugin(),
  ]
};
```

As mentioned earlier, `HtmlWebpackPlugin` creates the HTML file. It has been configured to use `index.html` in the `src` folder as a template.

`HotModuleReplacementPlugin` allows modules to be updated while an application is running, without a full reload.

7. Lastly, the following properties complete the configuration:

```
const config: Configuration = {
  ...,
  devtool: 'inline-source-map',
  devServer: {
    static: path.join(__dirname, 'dist'),
    historyApiFallback: true,
    port: 4000,
    open: true,
    hot: true,
  }
};
```

The `devtool` property tells webpack to use full inline source maps, which allow the original source code to be debugged before transpilation.

The devServer property configures the webpack development server. It configures the web server root to be the dist folder and to serve files on port 4000. Now, historyApiFallback is required for deep links to work, and we have also specified to open the browser after the server has been started.

The development configuration is now complete. But before we try to run the app in development mode, we need to create an npm script to run webpack.

8. First, open package.json and add a scripts section with a start script:

```
{
  ...,
  "scripts": {
    "start": "webpack serve --config webpack.dev.config.
      ts"
  }
}
```

9. Now, we can run the app in development mode by running the following command in the terminal:

```
npm run start
```

The npm run command executes a script in the scripts section of package.json. The start script is commonly used to run a program in development mode. It is so common that npm recognizes this without the run part. So, the command can be shortened to the following:

```
npm start
```

After a few seconds, the app opens in the default browser:

My React and TypeScript App!

Figure 3.1 – The app running in a browser in development mode

10. Leave the app running and open the index.tsx file. Change the content of the h1 element to something slightly different:

```
function App() {
  return <h1>My Super React and TypeScript App!</h1>;
}
```

When the file is saved, notice that the running app automatically refreshes:

My Super React and TypeScript App!

Figure 3.2 – The app is automatically refreshed

That completes the setup of the React and TypeScript project using webpack. Here's a recap of the key points of the setup:

- An HTML file is required to host the React app

- Webpack transpiles the app's React and TypeScript code into JavaScript with the help of Babel and then references it in the HTML file

- Webpack has a development server that automatically refreshes the app as we write code

> **Note**
> More information about webpack is available at the following link: `https://webpack.js.org/`.

That was an incredible amount of work to set up a React and TypeScript app, and it only does a fraction of what we will need to build a real app. For example, CSS can't be used, and the setup doesn't support unit testing. Luckily, there is a much easier way to create React and TypeScript projects, which we will learn in the next section. What you have learned in this section is really important though, because the tool we are about to use also uses webpack under the hood.

Creating a project with Create React App

Create React App is a popular tool for creating React projects. It is based on webpack, so the knowledge from the last section will give you an understanding of how Create React App works. In this section, we will use Create React App to create a React and TypeScript project.

Using Create React App

Unlike the setup in the last section, Create React App generates a React and TypeScript project with all the common tools we will likely require, including CSS and unit testing support.

To use Create React App, open Visual Studio Code in a blank folder of your choice and run the following command:

```
npx create-react-app myapp --template typescript
```

npx allows npm packages to temporarily be installed and run. It is a common method of running project scaffolding tools such as Create React App.

create-react-app is the package for the Create React App tool that creates the project. We have passed it the app name, myapp. We have also specified that the typescript template should be used to create the project.

It takes a minute or so for the project to be created, but this is much quicker than creating it manually with webpack!

When the command has finished creating the project, reopen the project in Visual Studio Code in the myapp folder. Note that your directory might be slightly different if you called the app something different. It is important to be in the app name folder; otherwise, the dependencies may be installed in the wrong location.

Next, we will understand what linting is and add an extension for it into Visual Studio Code.

Adding linting to Visual Studio Code

Linting is the process of checking code for potential problems. It is common practice to use linting tools to catch problems early in the development process as code is written. **ESLint** is a popular tool that can lint React and TypeScript code. Fortunately, Create React App has already installed and configured ESLint in our project.

Editors such as Visual Studio Code can be integrated with ESLint to highlight potential problems. Carry out the following steps to install an ESLint extension into Visual Studio Code:

1. Open up the **Extensions** area in Visual Studio Code. The **Extensions** option is in the **Preferences** menu in the **File** menu on Windows *or* in the **Preferences** menu in the **Code** menu on a Mac.

2. A list of extensions will appear on the left-hand side and the search box above the extensions list can be used to find a particular extension. Enter eslint into the extensions list search box.

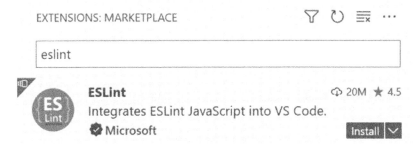

Figure 3.3 – The Visual Studio Code ESLint extension

An extension by Microsoft called ESLint should appear at the top of the list.

3.   Click the **Install** button to install the extension.

4.   Now, we need to make sure the ESLint extension is configured to check React and TypeScript. So, open the **Settings** area in Visual Studio Code. The **Settings** option is in the **Preferences** menu in the **File** menu on Windows or in the **Preferences** menu in the **Code** menu on a Mac.

5.   In the settings search box, enter `eslint: probe` and select the **Workspace** tab:

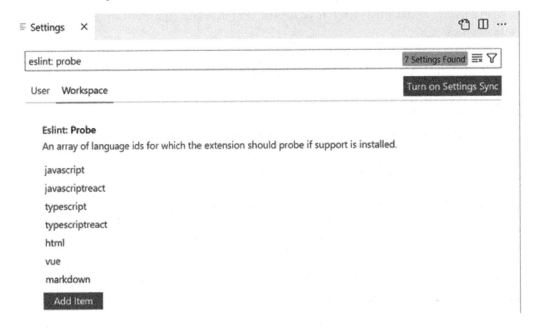

Figure 3.4 – Visual Studio Code ESLint Probe settings

This setting defines the languages to use when ESLint checks code.

6.   Make sure that **typescript** and **typescriptreact** are on the list. If not, add them using the **Add Item** button.

The ESLint extension for Visual Studio Code is now installed and configured in the project.

> **Note**
>
> For more information about ESLint, see the following link: `https://eslint.org/`.

Next, we will add automatic code formatting to the project.

Adding code formatting

The next tool we will set up automatically formats code. Automatic code formatting ensures code is consistently formatted, which helps its readability. Having consistently formatted code also helps developers see the important changes in a code review – rather than differences in formatting.

Prettier is a popular tool capable of formatting React and TypeScript code. Unfortunately, Create React App doesn't install and configure it for us. Carry out the following steps to install and configure Prettier in the project:

1. Install Prettier using the following command in the terminal in Visual Studio Code:

   ```
   npm i -D prettier
   ```

   Prettier is installed as a development dependency because it is only used during development time and not at runtime.

2. Prettier has overlapping style rules with ESLint, so install the following two libraries to allow Prettier to take responsibility for the styling rules from ESLint:

   ```
   npm i -D eslint-config-prettier eslint-plugin-prettier
   ```

   `eslint-config-prettier` disables conflicting ESLint rules, and `eslint-plugin-prettier` is an ESLint rule that formats code using Prettier.

3. The ESLint configuration needs to be updated to allow Prettier to manage the styling rules. Create React App allows ESLint configuration overrides in an `eslintConfig` section in `package.json`. Add the Prettier rules to the `eslintConfig` section in `package.json` as follows:

   ```
   {
     ...,
     "eslintConfig": {
       "extends": [
         "react-app",
         "react-app/jest",
         "plugin:prettier/recommended"
       ]
     },
     ...
   }
   ```

4. Prettier can be configured in a file called `.prettierrc.json`. Create this file with the following content in the root folder:

```json
{
    "printWidth": 100,
    "singleQuote": true,
    "semi": true,
    "tabWidth": 2,
    "trailingComma": "all",
    "endOfLine": "auto"
}
```

We have specified the following:

- Lines wrap at 100 characters
- String qualifiers are single quotes
- Semicolons are placed at the end of statements
- The indentation level is two spaces
- A trailing comma is added to multi-line arrays and objects
- Existing line endings are maintained

> **Note**
>
> More information on the configuration options can be found at the following link: `https://prettier.io/docs/en/options.html`.

Prettier is now installed and configured in the project.

Visual Studio Code can integrate with Prettier to automatically format code when source files are saved. So, let's install a Prettier extension into Visual Studio Code:

1. Open the **Extensions** area in Visual Studio Code and enter `prettier` into the extensions list search box. An extension called **Prettier – Code formatter** should appear at the top of the list:

Figure 3.5 – The Visual Studio Code Prettier extension

2. Click the **Install** button to install the extension.

3. Next, open the **Settings** area in Visual Studio Code. Select the **Workspace** tab and make sure the **Format On Save** option is ticked:

Figure 3.6 – Visual Studio Code "Format On Save" setting

This setting tells Visual Studio Code to automatically format code in files that are saved.

4. There is one more setting to set. This is the default formatter that Visual Studio Code should use to format code. Click the **Workspace** tab and make sure **Default Formatter** is set to **Prettier - Code formatter**:

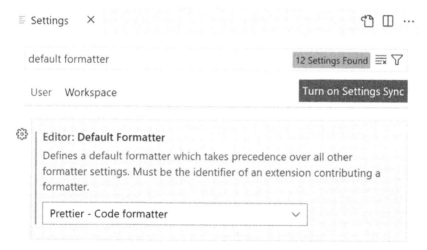

Figure 3.7 – Setting Default Formatter to Prettier - Code formatter

The Prettier extension for Visual Studio Code is now installed and configured in the project. Next, we will run the app in development mode.

Starting the app in development mode

Carry out the following steps to start the app in development mode:

1. Create React App has already created an npm script called `start`, which runs the app in development mode. Run this script in the terminal as follows:

    ```
    npm start
    ```

    After a few seconds, the app will appear in the default browser:

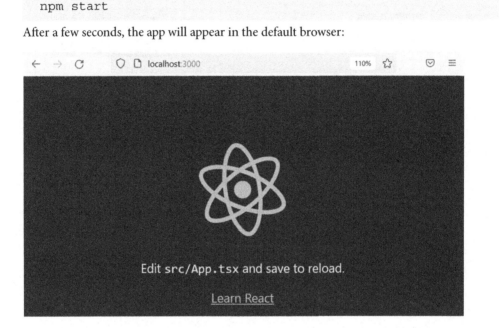

Figure 3.8 – The React app running in development mode

If your app reports Prettier formatting issues, open the file in question and save it. This will correctly format the file and resolve the errors.

2. Open `App.tsx` and change the **Learn React** link to **Learn React and TypeScript**:

    ```
    <a
      className="App-link"
      href="https://reactjs.org"
      target="_blank"
      rel="noopener noreferrer"
    >
      Learn React and TypeScript
    </a>;
    ```

After the file is saved, the running app is automatically refreshed with the updated link text:

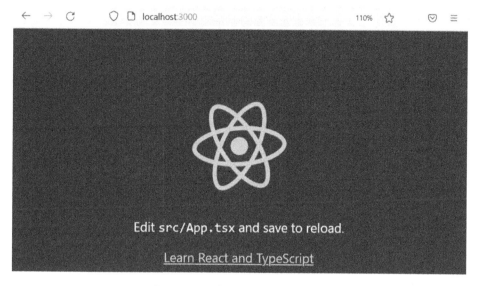

Figure 3.9 – The updated React app

3. Experiment with the code in App.tsx. Add a used variable and pass an invalid prop in a JSX element:

```
function App() {
  const unused = 'something';
  return (
    <div className="App" invalidProp="something">
      ...
    </div>
  );
}
```

As expected, the problems are caught and reported in Visual Studio Code. The issues are also reported in the browser.

```
 5    function App() {
 6      const unused = 'something';
 7      return (
 8        <div className="App" invalidProp="something">
 9          <Alert heading="Success" closable>
10            Everything is really good!
11          </Alert>
12        </div>
13      );
14    }
```

PROBLEMS 2   OUTPUT ···   Filter (e.g. text, **/*.ts, !**/node_modules/**)

∨ TS App.tsx src 2

⊗ Type '{ children: Element; className: string; invalidProp: string; }' is not assignable to type 'Det... ts(2322) [Ln 8, Col 26] ∧
  Property 'invalidProp' does not exist on type 'DetailedHTMLProps<HTMLAttributes<HTMLDivElement>, HTMLDivElement>'.

⚠ 'unused' is assigned a value but never used. eslint(@typescript-eslint/no-unused-vars) [Ln 6, Col 9]

Figure 3.10 – Problems caught by Visual Studio Code

4. Remove the invalid code and stop the app from running before continuing. The shortcut key for stopping the app is *Ctrl + C*.

We have now seen how Create React App provides a productive development experience. Next, we will produce a production build.

Producing a production build

Carry out the following steps to produce a build of the app that can be deployed into production:

1. Create React App has already created an npm script called `build` that produces all the artifacts for deployment to production. Run this script in the terminal as follows:

    ```
    npm run build
    ```

    After a few seconds, the deployment artifacts are placed in a `build` folder.

2. Open the `build` folder – it contains many files. The root file is `index.html`, which references the other JavaScript, CSS, and image files. All the files are optimized for production with whitespace removed and the JavaScript minified.

This completes the production build and the React and TypeScript project set up with Create React App. Here's a recap of the key points of the setup:

- The npx tool can execute the Create React App library, specifying the `typescript` template to create a React and TypeScript project.

- Create React App sets up many useful project features, such as linting, CSS support, and SVG support.

- Create React App also sets up npm scripts to run the app in development mode and produce a production build.

- One feature that Create React App doesn't set up is automatic code formatting. However, Prettier can be installed and configured manually to provide this capability.

Keep this project safe because we will continue to use it in the next section.

Next, we will learn how to create a React component that uses TypeScript for type checking.

Creating a React and TypeScript component

In *Chapter 1, Introducing React*, we built an alert component using React. In this section, we will use TypeScript to make the component strongly typed and experience the benefits. We start by adding a type to the alert component's props and then experiment with defining a type for its state. After completing the alert component, we will inspect the component using React's DevTools.

Adding a props type

We will continue using the React and TypeScript project created in the last section with Create React App. Take the following steps to add a strongly typed version of the alert component:

1. Open the project in Visual Studio Code if it isn't already open. Make sure you open the project in the app name folder so that `package.json` is at the root.

2. Create a new file in the `src` folder called `Alert.tsx`. Paste in the JavaScript version of the alert component, which can be found on GitHub at `https://github.com/PacktPublishing/Learn-React-with-TypeScript-2nd-Edition/blob/main/Chapter1/Section7-Using-events/Alert.js`.

   Notice that type errors are reported on some of the props because they can only be inferred as having the any type.

3. Add the following type just above the component. This will be the type for the component props:

```
type Props = {
  type?: string;
  heading: string;
  children: React.ReactNode;
  closable?: boolean;
  onClose?: () => void;
};
```

The `heading` and `children` props are required but the rest of the props are optional.

The `children` prop is given a special type called `React.ReactNode`. This allows it to accept JSX elements as well as strings.

The name of the type can be anything, but it is common practice to call it `Props`.

Remember from the *Creating interfaces* section in *Chapter 2, Introducing TypeScript*, that the interface syntax can be used to create types as an alternative to type aliases. An interface version of the `Props` type is as follows:

```
interface Props {
  type?: string;
  heading: string;
  children: React.ReactNode;
  closable?: boolean;
  onClose?: () => void;
}
```

As mentioned in the last chapter, it is largely personal preference whether you choose type aliases or interfaces for the type of component props.

4. Now, assign the `Props` type to the alert component after the destructed parameters:

```
export function Alert({
  type = "information",
  heading,
  children,
  closable,
  onClose,
}: Props) {
  ...
}
```

The alert props are now strongly typed.

5. Open `App.tsx` and replace the header element with the alert component. Don't forget to import the alert component before using it in the JSX. Don't pass any props into `Alert` to test the type checking:

```
import React from 'react';
import './App.css';
import { Alert } from './Alert';
```

```
function App() {
  return (
    <div className="App">
      <Alert />
    </div>
  );
}
```

```
export default App;
```

As expected, a type error is raised on `Alert`:

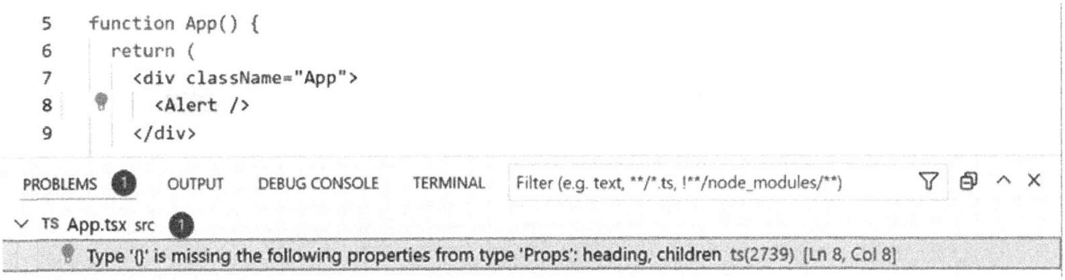

```
5    function App() {
6      return (
7        <div className="App">
8    💡    <Alert />
9        </div>
```

PROBLEMS ❶   OUTPUT   DEBUG CONSOLE   TERMINAL   Filter (e.g. text, **/*.ts, !**/node_modules/**)   ▽ ⧉ ∧ ✕

∨ TS App.tsx src ❶

💡 Type '{}' is missing the following properties from type 'Props': heading, children ts(2739) [Ln 8, Col 8]

Figure 3.11 – Type error on the Alert component

6. Pass in a `header` prop to `Alert`, and give it some content:

    ```
    <Alert heading="Success">Everything is really good!</
    Alert>
    ```

    The type errors will disappear.

7. Start the app in development mode if not already running (`npm start`). After that, the app component appears on the page as expected.

Next, we will learn how to explicitly give the React component state a type.

Adding a state type

Follow these steps to experiment with the `visible` state type in the alert component:

1. Open `Alert.tsx` and hover over the `visible` state variable to determine its inferred type. It has been inferred to be `boolean` because it has been initialized with the `true` value. The `boolean` type is precisely what we want.

2. As an experiment, remove the initial value of `true` passed into `useState`. Then, hover over the `visible` state variable again. It has been inferred to be `undefined` because no default value has been passed into `useState`. This obviously isn't the type we want.

3. Sometimes, the `useState` type isn't inferred to be the type we want, like in the previous step. In these cases, the type of the state can be explicitly defined using a **generic argument** on `useState`. Explicitly give the `visible` state a `boolean` type by adding the following generic argument:

```
const [visible, setVisible] = useState<boolean>();
```

> **Note**
>
> A generic argument is like a regular function argument but defines a type for the function. A generic argument is specified using angled brackets after the function name.

4. Restore the `useState` statement to what it originally was, with it initialized as `true` and no explicit type:

```
const [visible, setVisible] = useState(true);
```

5. Stop the app from running by pressing *Ctrl + C*.

In summary, always check the inferred state type from `useState` and use its generic argument to explicitly define the type if the inferred type is not what is required.

Next, we will learn how to use the React browser development tools.

Using React DevTools

React DevTools is a browser extension available for Chrome and Firefox. The tools allow React apps to be inspected and debugged. The links to the extensions are as follows:

- Chrome: `https://chrome.google.com/webstore/detail/react-developer-tools/fmkadmapgofadopljbjfkapdkoienihi/`

- Firefox: `https://addons.mozilla.org/en-GB/firefox/addon/react-devtools/`

To install the extension, click the **Add to Chrome** or **Add to Firefox** button. You will need to reopen the browser for the tools to be available.

Carry out the following steps to explore the tools:

1. In Visual Studio Code, start the app in development mode by running `npm start` in a terminal. After a few seconds, the app will appear in the browser.

2. Open the browser's development tools by pressing *F12*. React DevTools adds two panels called **Components** and **Profiler**.

3. First, we will explore the **Components** panel, so select this panel:

Figure 3.12 – The React DevTools Components panel

The React component tree appears on the left-hand side. Selecting a React component reveals the current props and state values on the right-hand side.

4. Notice that the state isn't named – it has a generic name, **State**. Click the wand icon at the right of the **hooks** section.

The name of the state now appears in brackets:

Figure 3.13 – State variable name after wand is clicked

5. In Visual Studio Code, open `App.tsx` and pass the `closable` prop to `Alert`:

```
<Alert heading="Success" closable>
  Everything is really good!
</Alert>
```

The app refreshes and the close button appears.

6. Click the close button and notice that the `visible` state changes to `false` in DevTools.

    The **Components** panel is useful when debugging a large component tree to quickly understand the values of the props and state.

7. Refresh the browser so that the alert appears again. While still in the **Components** panel in React DevTools, open the settings by clicking the cog icon. Tick the **Highlight updates when components render.** option in the **General** section, if not already ticked.

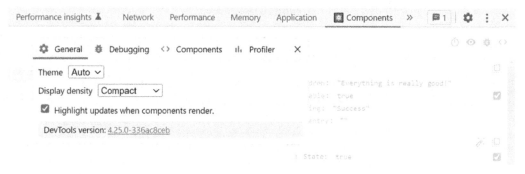

Figure 3.14 – Re-render highlight option

This option will highlight when a component is re-rendered.

8. Before we try the re-render highlight, open `Alert.tsx` and update it to render **Gone!** when the `visible` state is `false`:

    ```
    if (!visible) {
      return <div>Gone!</div>;
    }
    ```

    Before this change, the re-render highlight would have no element to highlight.

9. Now, click the close button on the alert in the browser. The re-rendered alert component will be highlighted with a green border:

Gone!

Figure 3.15 – Re-render highlight

This completes our exploration of the **Components** panel. Press *F5* to refresh the browser so that the alert component reappears before continuing.

10. Now, we will explore the **Profiler** panel, so select this panel. This tool allows interactions to be profiled, which is useful for tracking performance problems.

11. Click the **Start profiling** option, which is the blue circle icon.

12. Click the close button in the alert.

13. Click the **Stop profiling** option, which is the red circle icon. A timeline appears of all the component re-renders:

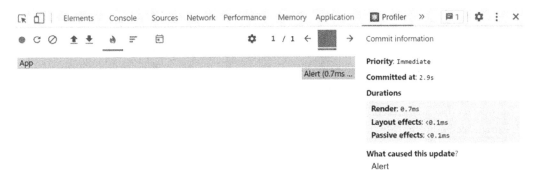

Figure 3.16 – React DevTools components

This shows that Alert was re-rendered when the close button was clicked, taking 0.7 milliseconds.

This tool is helpful in quickly spotting the slow components for a particular user interaction.

14. This completes our exploration of React DevTools. Undo the change we made to the Alert component so that it renders null again when invisible:

```
if (!visible) {
    return null;
}
```

That completes this section. Here's a recap:

- A type can be added to component props to make them type-safe

- A state can be inferred from its initial value but can be explicitly defined using a generic argument on useState

- React DevTools can be installed in a browser to inspect the component tree in a running app and help track down performance problems

That brings us to the end of the chapter.

Summary

We started the chapter by creating a React and TypeScript project with the help of webpack and Babel. Lots of steps were involved and we only set up a fraction of what we would need for a real project. For example, we have not set up the ability to produce an optimized bundle for production.

We moved on to use Create React App for creating a React and TypeScript project. We saw how this approach is a much faster and more thorough way of creating a project. Then, we used ESLint for linting and Prettier for automatic code formatting. As a result of that exercise, we now understand how TypeScript, ESLint, and Prettier can be used together to create a high-quality React and TypeScript project environment.

In the final section, we learned how to create React components with strongly typed props and states. We experienced how this helps to catch problems quickly. We also played with React's DevTools, which allows a React component tree to be inspected and the performance profiled.

In the next chapter, we will learn about React's common hooks.

Questions

The following questions will check what you have learned in this chapter:

1. What type will the `name` prop have in the following component, which has no type annotation?

    ```
    export function Name({ name }) {
      return <span>{name}</span>;
    }
    ```

2. What type will the `firstName` state have in the following `useState` statement?

    ```
    const [firstName, setFirstName] = useState("");
    ```

3. A `ContactDetails` component has the following type for its props:

    ```
    type Props = {
      firstName?: string;
      email: string;
    };
    export function ContactDetails({ firstName, email }:
    Props) {

      ...

    }
    ```

The preceding component is referenced in another component's JSX as follows:

```
<ContactDetails email="fred@somewhere.com" />
```

Will a type error be raised?

4. A `status` state variable can hold the `"Good"` and `"Bad"` values and is initially `"Good"`. It is defined in the following code:

```
const [status, setStatus] = useState("Good");
```

What is the type given to `status`? How can its type be narrowed to only `"Good"` or `"Bad"`?

5. A `FruitList` component takes in an array of fruit names and displays them in a list. It is referenced in another component's JSX as follows:

```
<FruitList fruits={["Banana", "Apple", "Strawberry"]} />;
```

What type would you define for the `FruitList` component?

6. An `email` state variable can hold `null` or an email address and is initially `null`. How would you define this state using the `useState` hook?

7. The following component allows the user to agree:

```
export function Agree({ onAgree }: Props) {
  return (
    <button onClick={() => onAgree()}>
      Click to agree
    </button>
  );
}
```

What would you define as the type definition for `Props`?

Answers

Here are the answers to the questions in the preceding section.

1. The `name` prop will have the `any` type.

2. The `firstName` state will be given the `string` type because `string` will be inferred from the initial value `""`.

3. There will be no type error even though `firstName` is not passed because it is defined as optional.

4. The inferred type of `status` is `string`. An explicit type can be defined for the state using a generic type argument as follows:

```
const [status, setStatus] = useState<'Good' |
'Bad'>('Good');
```

5. The type for the `FruitList` component could be as follows:

```
type Props = {
   fruits: string[];
}
```

Alternatively, it could be defined using an interface as follows:

```
interface Props {
   fruits: string[];
}
```

6. The `email` state could be defined as follows:

```
const [email, setEmail] = useState<string | null>(null);
```

An explicit type needs to be defined; otherwise, an initial value of `null` would give `email` a type of `null`.

7. The type for `Props` could be as follows:

```
type Props = {
   onAgree: () => void;
};
```

Alternatively, it could be defined using an interface as follows:

```
interface Props {
   onAgree: () => void;
}
```

4

Using React Hooks

In this chapter, we will learn about React's common Hooks and how to use them with TypeScript. We will implement the knowledge of all these Hooks in a React component that allows a user to adjust a score for a person. We will start by exploring the effect Hook and begin to understand use cases where it is useful. We will then delve into two state Hooks, `useState` and `useReducer`, understanding when it is best to use each one. After that, we will cover the ref Hook and how it differs from the state Hook, and then the memo and callback Hooks, looking at how they can help performance.

So, we'll cover the following topics:

- Using the effect Hook
- Using state Hooks
- Using the ref Hook
- Using the memo Hook
- Using the callback Hook

Technical requirements

We will use the following technologies in this chapter:

- **Browser**: A modern browser such as Google Chrome
- **Node.js** and **npm**: You can install them from `https://nodejs.org/en/download/`
- **Visual Studio Code**: You can install it from `https://code.visualstudio.com/`

All the code snippets in this chapter can be found online at `https://github.com/PacktPublishing/Learn-React-with-TypeScript-2nd-Edition/tree/main/Chapter4`.

Using the effect Hook

In this section, we will learn about the effect Hook and where it is useful. We will then create a new React project and a component that makes use of the effect Hook.

Understanding the effect Hook parameters

The effect Hook is used for component side effects. A component side effect is something executed outside the scope of the component such as a web service request. The effect Hook is defined using the `useEffect` function from React. `useEffect` contains two parameters:

- A function that executes the effect; at a minimum, this function runs each time the component is rendered

- An optional array of dependencies that cause the effect function to rerun when changed

Here's an example of the `useEffect` Hook in a component:

```
function SomeComponent() {
  function someEffect() {
    console.log("Some effect");
  }
  useEffect(someEffect);
  return ...
}
```

The preceding effect Hook is passed an effect function called `someEffect`. No effect dependencies have been passed, so the effect function is executed each time the component renders.

Often, an anonymous arrow function is used for the effect function. Here's the same example but with an anonymous effect function instead:

```
function SomeComponent() {
  useEffect(() => {
    console.log("Some effect");
  });
  return ...
}
```

As you can see, this version of the code is a little shorter and arguably easier to read.

Here's another example of an effect:

```
function SomeOtherComponent({ search }) {
  useEffect(() => {
    console.log("An effect dependent on a search prop",
      search);
  }, [search]);
  Return ...;
}
```

This time the effect has a dependency on a `search` prop. So, the `search` prop is defined in an array in the effect Hook's second parameter. The effect function will run every time the value of `search` changes.

The rules of Hooks

There are some rules that all Hooks, including `useEffect`, must obey:

- A Hook can only be called at the top level of a function component. So, a Hook can't be called in a loop or in a nested function such as an event handler.

- A Hook can't be called conditionally.

- A Hook can only be used in function components and not class components.

The following example is a violation of the rules:

```
export function AnotherComponent() {
  function handleClick() {
    useEffect(() => {
      console.log("Some effect");
    });
  }
  return <button onClick={handleClick}>Cause effect</button>;
}
```

This is a violation because `useEffect` is called in a handler function rather than at the top level. A corrected version is as follows:

```
export function AnotherComponent() {
  const [clicked, setClicked] = useState(false);
  useEffect(() => {
```

```
    if (clicked) {
      console.log("Some effect");
    }
  }, [clicked]);
  function handleClick() {
    setClicked(true);
  }
  return <button onClick={handleClick}>Cause effect</button>;
}
```

useEffect has been lifted to the top level and now depends on the clicked state that is set in the handler function.

The following is another example that violates the rules of Hooks:

```
function YetAnotherComponent({ someProp }) {
  if (!someProp) {
    return null;
  }
  useEffect(() => {
    console.log("Some effect");
  });
  return ...
}
```

The violation is because useEffect is called conditionally. If someProp is falsy, null is returned from the component and useEffect is never called. So, the condition is that useEffect is only called when someProp is truthy.

A corrected version is as follows:

```
function YetAnotherComponent({someProp}) {
  useEffect(() => {
    if (someProp) {
      console.log("Some effect");
    }
  });
  if (!someProp) {
    return null
```

```
    }
    return ...
}
```

useEffect has been lifted above the condition. The condition has also been put inside the effect function so that its logic is only executed when someProp is truthy.

Effect cleanup

An effect can return a function that performs cleanup logic when the component is unmounted. Cleanup logic ensures nothing is left that could cause a memory leak. Let's consider the following example:

```
function ExampleComponent({onClickAnywhere}) {
  useEffect(() => {
    function handleClick() {
      onClickAnywhere();
    }
    document.addEventListener("click", handleClick);
  });
  return ...
}
```

The preceding effect function attaches an event handler to the document element. The event handler is never detatched though, so multiple event handlers will become attached to the document element as the effect is rerun. This problem is resolved by returning a cleanup function that detaches the event handler as follows:

```
function ExampleComponent({ onClickAnywhere }) {
  useEffect(() => {
    function handleClick() {
      onClickAnywhere();
    }
    document.addEventListener("click", listener);
    return function cleanup() {
      document.removeEventListener("click", listener);
    };
  });
  return ...;
}
```

Often, an anonymous arrow function is used for the cleanup function:

```
function ExampleComponent({ onClickAnywhere }) {
  useEffect(() => {
    function handleClick() {
      onClickAnywhere();
    }
    document.addEventListener("click", listener);
    return () => {
      document.removeEventListener("click", listener);
    };
  });
  return ...;
```

An anonymous arrow function is a little shorter than the named function in the previous example.

Next, we will explore a common use case for the effect Hook.

Creating the project

Let's start by creating a new project in Visual Studio Code using Create React App. We learned how to do this in *Chapter 3, Setting Up React and TypeScript* – the steps are as follows:

1. Open Visual Studio Code in a blank folder of your choice and run the following command:

    ```
    npx create-react-app app --template typescript
    ```

    Create React App will take a minute or so to create the project. The app is called app in the proceeding command, but feel free to change this.

2. Reopen Visual Studio Code in the app folder that has just been created (or whatever you called the app).

3. Install Prettier and its libraries to allow it to work with ESLint. Run the following command in the terminal to do this:

    ```
    npm i -D prettier eslint-config-prettier eslint-plugin-
    prettier
    ```

4. Enable Visual Studio Code to automatically format code as files are saved. To do this, create a .vscode folder in the project root and create a settings.json file containing the following:

    ```
    {
        "editor.formatOnSave": true,
    ```

```
    "editor.defaultFormatter": "esbenp.prettier-vscode"
}
```

5. Update the ESLint configuration to allow Prettier to manage the styling rules. To do this, add the following highlighted line to the `eslintConfig` section in `package.json`:

```
{
  ...,
  "eslintConfig": {
    "extends": [
      "react-app",
      "react-app/jest",
      "plugin:prettier/recommended"
    ]
  },
  ...
}
```

6. Add the following Prettier configuration in a file called `.prettierrc.json`:

```
{
  "printWidth": 100,
  "singleQuote": true,
  "semi": true,
  "tabWidth": 2,
  "trailingComma": "all",
  "endOfLine": "auto"
}
```

7. Remove the following files from the `src` folder, because these aren't needed in this project:

- `App.test.tsx`

- `Logo.svg`

8. Open `index.tsx` and save the file without making any changes. This will remove any formatting issues.

9. Open `App.tsx` and replace the content with the following:

```
import React from 'react';
import './App.css';
```

```
function App() {
  return <div className="App"></div>;
}
export default App;
```

10. Start the app running in development mode by running npm start in the terminal. The app contains a blank page at the moment. Keep the app running as we explore the different Hooks in a React component.

That's the project created. Next, we will use the effect Hook.

Fetching data using the effect Hook

A common use of the effect Hook is fetching data. Carry out the following steps to implement an effect that fetches a person's name:

1. Create a function that will simulate a data request. To do this, create a file called getPerson. ts in the src folder and then add the following content to this file:

```
type Person = {
  name: string,
};
export function getPerson(): Promise<Person> {
  return new Promise((resolve) =>
    setTimeout(() => resolve({ name: "Bob" }), 1000)
  );
}
```

The function asynchronously returns an object, { name: "Bob" }, after a second has elapsed.

Notice the type annotation for the return type, Promise<Person>. The Promise type represents a JavaScript Promise, which is something that will eventually be completed. The Promise type has a generic argument for the item type that is resolved in the promise, which is Person in this example. For more information on JavaScript promises, see the following link: https://developer.mozilla.org/en-US/docs/Web/JavaScript/Reference/Global_Objects/Promise.

2. Next, we will create a React component that will eventually display a person and a score. Create a file called PersonScore.tsx in the src folder and then add the following contents to the file:

```
import { useEffect } from 'react';
import { getPerson } from './getPerson';
```

```
export function PersonScore() {
  return null;
}
```

The useEffect Hook has been imported from React and the getPerson function we have just created has also been imported. At the moment, the component simply returns null.

3. Add the following effect above the return statement:

```
export function PersonScore() {
  useEffect(() => {
    getPerson().then((person) => console.log(person));
  }, []);
  return null;
}
```

The effect calls the getPerson function and outputs the returned person to the console. The effect is only executed after the component is initially rendered because an empty array has been specified as the effect dependencies in its second argument.

4. Open App.tsx and render the PersonScore component inside the div element:

```
import React from 'react';
import './App.css';
import { PersonScore } from './PersonScore';

function App() {
  return (
    <div className="App">
      <PersonScore />
    </div>
  );
}
export default App;
```

5. Go to the running app in the browser and go to the **Console** panel in the browser's DevTools. Notice that the person object appears in the console, which verifies that the effect that fetches the person data ran properly:

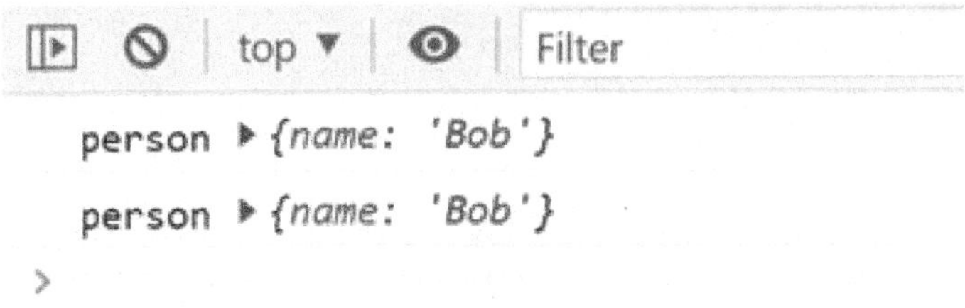

Figure 4.1 – The effect output

You may also notice that the effect function has been executed twice rather than once. This behavior is intentional and only happens in development mode with React Strict Mode. This will eventually allow a future React feature to preserve the state when sections of the UI are removed. See this blog post from the React team for more information on this behavior: `https://reactjs.org/blog/2022/03/29/react-v18.html#new-strict-mode-behaviors`.

6. Next, we will refactor how the effect function is called to expose an interesting problem. Open `PersonScore.tsx` and change the `useEffect` call to use the `async/await` syntax:

```
useEffect(async () => {
  const person = await getPerson();
  console.log(person);
}, []);
```

> **Note**
>
> The `async/await` syntax is an alternative way to write asynchronous code. Many developers prefer it because it reads like synchronous code. For more information on `async/await`, see the following link: `https://developer.mozilla.org/en-US/docs/Learn/JavaScript/Asynchronous/Promises#async_and_await`.

The preceding code is arguably more readable, but React raises an error. Look in the browser's console and you'll see the following error:

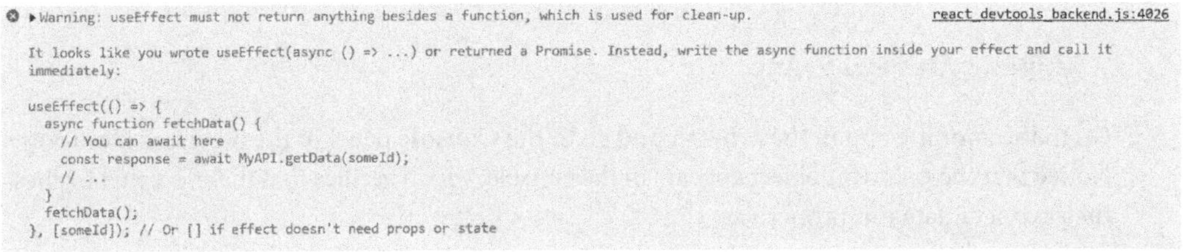

Figure 4.2 – Effect async error

The error is very informative – the useEffect Hook doesn't allow a function marked with async to be passed into it.

7. Next, update the code and use the approach suggested in the error message:

```
useEffect(() => {
  async function getThePerson() {
    const person = await getPerson();
    console.log(person);
  }
  getThePerson();
}, []);
```

A nested asynchronous function has been defined and immediately called in the effect function; this works nicely.

8. This implementation of the effect is arguably less readable than the initial version. So, switch back to that version before continuing to the next section. The code is available to copy from the following link: https://github.com/PacktPublishing/Learn-React-with-TypeScript-2nd-Edition/blob/main/Chapter4/Section1-Using-the-effect-hook/src/PersonScore.tsx.

That completes our exploration of the effect Hook – here's a recap:

*   The effect Hook is used to execute component side effects when a component is rendered or when certain props or states change.

*   A common use case for the effect Hook is fetching data. Another use case is where DOM events need to be manually registered.

*   Any required effect cleanup can be done in a function returned by the effect function.

Next, we will learn about the two state Hooks in React. Keep the app running as we move to the next section.

Using state Hooks

We have already learned about the useState Hook in previous chapters, but here we will look at it again and compare it against another state Hook we haven't covered yet, useReducer. We will expand the PersonScore component we created in the last section to explore these state Hooks.

Using useState

As a reminder, the useState Hook allows state to be defined in a variable. The syntax for useState is as follows:

```
const [state, setState] = useState(initialState);
```

We will enhance the PersonScore component we created in the last section to store the person's name in state. We will also have state for a score that is incremented, decremented, and reset using some buttons in the component. We will also add the loading state to the component, which will show a loading indicator when true.

Carry out the following steps:

1. Open PersonScore.tsx and add useState to the React import statement:

    ```
    import { useEffect, useState } from 'react';
    ```

2. Add the following state definitions for name, score, and loading at the top of the component function, above the useEffect call:

    ```
    export function PersonScore() {
      const [name, setName] = useState<string | undefined>();
      const [score, setScore] = useState(0);
      const [loading, setLoading] = useState(true);

      useEffect( ... );

      return null;
    }
    ```

    The score state is initialized to 0 and loading is initialized to true.

3. Change the effect function to set the loading and name state values after the person data has been fetched. This should replace the existing console.log statement:

    ```
    useEffect(() => {
      getPerson().then((person) => {
        setLoading(false);
        setName(person.name);
      });
    }, []);
    ```

    After the person has been fetched, loading is set to false, and name is set to the person's name.

4. Next, add the following `if` statement in between the `useEffect` call and the return statement:

```
useEffect( ... );
if (loading) {
  return <div>Loading ...</div>;
}
return ...
```

This displays a loading indicator when the `loading` state is `true`.

5. Change the component's return statement from outputting nothing to outputting the following:

```
if (loading) {
  return <div>Loading ...</div>;
}
return (
  <div>
    <h3>
      {name}, {score}
    </h3>
    <button>Add</button>
    <button>Subtract</button>
    <button>Reset</button>
  </div>
);
```

The person's name and score are displayed in a header with **Add**, **Subtract**, and **Reset** buttons underneath (don't worry that the output is unstyled – we will learn how to style components in the next chapter):

Bob, 0

Figure 4.3 – The PersonScore component after data has been fetched

6. Update the **Add** button so that it increments the score when clicked:

```
<button onClick={() => setScore(score + 1)}>Add</button>
```

The button click event calls the score state setter to increment the state.

There is an alternative method of updating the state values based on their previous value. The alternative method uses a parameter in the state setter that gives the previous state value, so our example could look as follows:

```
setScore(previousScore => previousScore + 1)
```

This is arguably a little harder to read, so we'll stick to our initial method.

7. Add score state setters to the other buttons as follows:

```
<button onClick={() => setScore(score - 1)}>Subtract</
button>
<button onClick={() => setScore(0)}>Reset</button>
```

8. In the running app, click the different buttons. They should change the score as you would expect.

Bob, 3

Figure 4.4 – The PersonScore component after the button is clicked

9. Before we finish this exercise, let's take some time to understand when the state values are actually set. Update the effect function to output the state values after they are set:

```
useEffect(() => {
  getPerson().then((person) => {
    setLoading(false);
    setName(person.name);
    console.log("State values", loading, name);
  });
}, []);
```

Perhaps we would expect `false` and `"Bob"` as the output to the console? However, `true` and `undefined` are the output to the console. This is because updating state values is not immediate – instead, they are batched and updated before the next render. So, it isn't until the next render that `loading` will be `false`, and `name` will be `"Bob"`.

We no longer need the `console.log` statement we added in this step, so remove it before continuing.

Next, we will learn about an alternative React Hook for using state.

Understanding useReducer

useReducer is an alternative method of managing state. It uses a **reducer** function for state changes, which takes in the current state value and returns the new state value.

Here is an example of a useReducer call:

```
const [state, dispatch] = useReducer(reducer, initialState);
```

So, useReducer takes in a reducer function and the initial state value as parameters. It then returns a tuple containing the current state value and a function to **dispatch** state changes.

The dispatch function takes in an argument that describes the change. This object is called an **action**. An example dispatch call is as follows:

```
dispatch({ type: 'add', amount: 2 });
```

There is no defined structure for an action, but it is common practice for it to contain a property, such as type, to specify the type of change. Other properties in the action can vary depending on the type of change. Here's another example of a dispatch call:

```
dispatch({ type: 'loaded' });
```

This time, the action only needs the type to change the necessary state.

Turning our attention to the reducer function, it has parameters for the current state value and the action. Here's an example code snippet of a reducer:

```
function reducer(state: State, action: Action): State {
  switch (action.type) {
    case 'add':
      return { ...state, total: state.total + action.amount };
    case ...

      ...

    default:
      return state;
  }
}
```

The reducer function usually contains a switch statement based on the action type. Each switch branch makes the required changes to the state and returns the updated state. A new state object is created during the state change – the current state is never mutated. A mutating state would result in the component not re-rendering.

> **Note**
>
> In the preceding code snippet, inside the `"add"` branch the **spread syntax** is used on the `state` variable (`...state`). The spread syntax copies all the properties from the object after the three dots. In the preceding code snippet, all the properties are copied from the `state` variable into the new state object returned. The `total` property value will then be overwritten by `state.total + action.amount` because this is defined after the spread operation in the new object creation. For more information on the spread syntax, see the following link: `https://developer.mozilla.org/en-US/docs/Web/JavaScript/Reference/Operators/Spread_syntax`.

The types for `useReducer` can be explicitly defined in its generic parameter as follows:

```
const [state, dispatch] = useReducer<Reducer<State, Action>>(
  reducer,
  initialState
);
```

`Reducer` is a standard React type that has generic parameters for the type of state and the type of action.

So, `useReducer` is more complex than `useState` because state changes go through a reducer function that we must implement. This benefits complex state objects with related properties or when a state change depends on the previous state value.

Next, we will implement state using `useReducer`.

Using useReducer

We will refactor the `PersonScore` component we have been working on to use `useReducer` instead of `useState`. To do this, carry out the following steps. The code snippets used are available to copy from `https://github.com/PacktPublishing/Learn-React-with-TypeScript-2nd-Edition/blob/main/Chapter4/Section2-Using-state-hooks/2-Using-useReducer/src/PersonScore.tsx`:

1. Open `PersonScore.tsx` and import `useReducer` instead of `useState` from React:

    ```
    import { useEffect, useReducer } from 'react';
    ```

2. We will have the state in a single object, so define a type for the state beneath the import statements:

    ```
    type State = {
      name: string | undefined;
      score: number;
    ```

```
        loading: boolean;
    };
```

3. Next, let's also define types for all the action objects:

```
type Action =
    | {
        type: 'initialize';
        name: string;
      }
    | {
        type: 'increment';
      }
    | {
        type: 'decrement';
      }
    | {
        type: 'reset';
      };
```

These action objects represent all the ways in which state can change. The action object types are combined using a union type, allowing an action to be any of these.

4. Now, define the following reducer function underneath the type definitions:

```
function reducer(state: State, action: Action): State {
  switch (action.type) {
    case 'initialize':
      return { name: action.name, score: 0, loading:
false };
    case 'increment':
      return { ...state, score: state.score + 1 };
    case 'decrement':
      return { ...state, score: state.score - 1 };
    case 'reset':
      return { ...state, score: 0 };
    default:
      return state;
  }
}
```

The reducer function contains a `switch` statement that makes appropriate state changes for each type of action.

Notice the nice IntelliSense when referencing the `state` and `action` parameters:

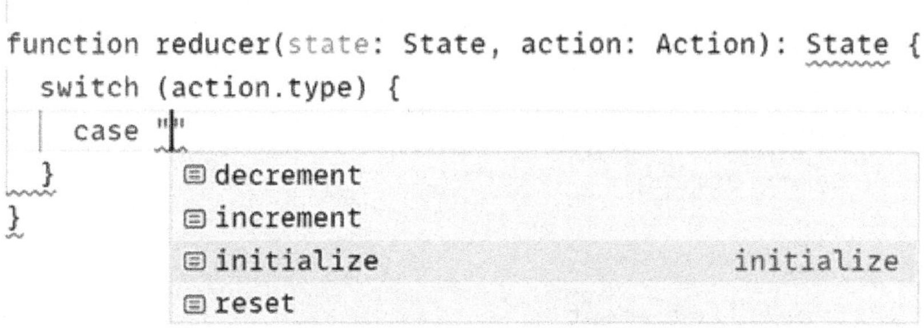

```
function reducer(state: State, action: Action): State {
  switch (action.type) {
    case ""
  }
}
```

▣ decrement	
▣ increment	
▣ initialize	initialize
▣ reset	

Figure 4.5 – IntelliSense inside the reducer function

5. Inside the `PersonScore` component, replace the `useState` calls with the following `useReducer` call:

```
const [{ name, score, loading }, dispatch] = useReducer(
  reducer,
  {
    name: undefined,
    score: 0,
    loading: true,
  }
);
```

The state has been initialized with an `undefined` name, a score of 0, and `loading` set to `true`.

The current state value has been destructured into `name`, `score`, and `loading` variables. If you hover over these destructured state variables, you will see that their types have been inferred correctly.

6. We now need to amend the places in the component that update the state. Start with the effect function and dispatch an initialize action after the person has been returned:

```
useEffect(() => {
  getPerson().then(({ name }) =>
    dispatch({ type: 'initialize', name })
  );
}, []);
```

7.   Lastly, dispatch the relevant actions in the button click handlers:

```
<button onClick={() => dispatch({ type: 'increment' })}>
  Add
</button>
<button onClick={() => dispatch({ type: 'decrement' })}>
  Subtract
</button>
<button onClick={() => dispatch({ type: 'reset' })}>
  Reset
</button>
```

8.   If you try clicking the buttons in the running app, they will correctly update.

That completes our exploration of the useReducer Hook. It is more useful for complex state management situations than useState, for example, when the state is a complex object with related properties and state changes depend on previous state values. The useState Hook is more appropriate when the state is based on primitive values independent of any other state.

We will continue to expand the PersonScore component in the following sections. Next, we will learn how to move the focus to the **Add** button using the ref Hook.

Using the ref Hook

In this section, we will learn about the ref Hook and where it is useful. We will then walk through a common use case of the ref Hook by enhancing the PersonScore component we have been working on.

Understanding the ref Hook

The ref Hook is called useRef and it returns a variable whose value is persisted for the lifetime of a component. This means that the variable doesn't lose its value when a component re-renders.

The value returned from the ref Hook is often referred to as a **ref**. The ref can be changed without causing a re-render.

Here's the syntax for useRef:

```
const ref = useRef(initialValue);
```

An initial value can optionally be passed into useRef. The type of the ref can be explicitly defined in a generic argument for useRef:

```
const ref = useRef<Ref>(initialValue);
```

The generic argument is useful when no initial value is passed or is null. This is because TypeScript won't be able to infer the type correctly.

The value of the ref is accessed via its current property:

```
console.log("Current ref value", ref.current);
```

The value of the ref can be updated via its current property as well:

```
ref.current = newValue;
```

A common use of the useRef Hook is to access HTML elements imperatively. HTML elements have a ref attribute in JSX that can be assigned to a ref. The following is an example of this:

```
function MyComponent() {
  const inputRef = useRef<HTMLInputElement>(null);
  function doSomething() {
    console.log(
      "All the properties and methods of the input",
      inputRef.current
    );
  }
  return <input ref={inputRef} type="text" />;
}
```

The ref used here is called inputRef and is initially null. So, it is explicitly given a type of HTMLInputElement, which is a standard type for input elements. The ref is then assigned to the ref attribute on an input element in JSX. All the input's properties and methods are then accessible via the ref's current property.

Next, we will use the useRef Hook in the PersonScore component.

Using the ref Hook

We will enhance the PersonScore component we have been working on to use useRef to move the focus to the **Add** button. To do this, carry out the following steps. All the code snippets used are available at https://github.com/PacktPublishing/Learn-React-with-

`TypeScript-2nd-Edition/blob/main/Chapter4/Section3-Using-the-ref-`
`hook/src/PersonScore.tsx`:

1. Open `PersonScore.tsx` and import `useRef` from React:

   ```
   import { useEffect, useReducer, useRef } from 'react';
   ```

2. Create a ref for the **Add** button just below the `useReducer` statement:

   ```
   const [ ... ] = useReducer( ... );

   const addButtonRef = useRef<HTMLButtonElement>(null);

   useEffect( ... )
   ```

   The ref is named `addButtonRef` and is initially `null`. It is given the standard `HTMLButtonElement` type.

> **Note**
>
> All the standard HTML elements have corresponding TypeScript types for React. Right-click on the `HTMLButtonElement` type and choose **Go to Definition** to discover all these types. The React TypeScript types will open containing all the HTML element types.

3. Assign the ref to the `ref` attribute on the **Add** button JSX element:

   ```
   <button
     ref={addButtonRef}
     onClick={() => dispatch({ type: 'increment' })}
   >
     Add
   </button>
   ```

4. Now that we have a reference to the **Add** button, we can invoke it's `focus` method to move the focus to it when the person's information has been fetched. Let's add another effect to do this below the existing effect that fetches the person:

   ```
   useEffect(() => {
     getPerson().then(({ name }) =>
       dispatch({ type: 'initialize', name })
     );
   }, []);
   ```

```
useEffect(() => {
  if (!loading) {
    addButtonRef.current?.focus();
  }
}, [loading]);

if (loading) {
  return <div>Loading ...</div>;
}
```

The effect is executed when the `loading` state is `true`, which will be after the person has been fetched.

Notice the `?` symbol after the `current` property on the ref. This is the **optional chaining** operator, and it allows the `focus` method to be invoked without having to check that `current` is not `null`. Visit the following link for more information about optional chaining: `https://developer.mozilla.org/en-US/docs/Web/JavaScript/Reference/Operators/Optional_chaining`.

We could have moved the focus to the **Add** button in the existing effect as follows:

```
useEffect(() => {
  getPerson().then(({ name }) => {
    dispatch({ type: 'initialize', name });
    addButtonRef.current?.focus();
  });
}, []);
```

However, this is mixing the concerns of fetching data, setting state, and setting focus to a button. Mixing concerns like this can make components hard to understand and change.

5. If you refresh the browser containing the running app, you will see a focus indicator on the **Add** button:

Bob, 0

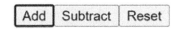

Figure 4.6 – The focused Add button

If you press the *Enter* key, you will see that the **Add** button is clicked and the score incremented. This proves that the **Add** button is focused.

That completes the enhancement and our exploration of the ref Hook.

To recap, the `useRef` Hook creates a mutatable value and doesn't cause a re-render when changed. It is commonly used to access HTML elements in React imperatively.

Next, we will learn about the memo Hook.

Using the memo Hook

In this section, we will learn about the memo Hook and where it is useful. We will then walk through an example in the `PersonScore` component we have been working on.

Understanding the memo Hook

The memo Hook creates a memoized value and is beneficial for values that have computationally expensive calculations. The Hook is called `useMemo` and the syntax is as follows:

```
const memoizedValue = useMemo(() => expensiveCalculation(),
[]);
```

A function that returns the value to memoize is passed into `useMemo` as the first argument. The function in this first argument should perform the expensive calculation.

The second argument passed to `useMemo` is an array of dependencies. So, if the `expensiveCalculation` function has dependencies a and b, the call will be as follows:

```
const memoizedValue = useMemo(
  () => expensiveCalculation(a, b),
  [a, b]
);
```

When any dependencies change, the function in the first argument is executed again to return a new value to memoize. In the previous example, a new version of `memoizedValue` is created every time a or b changes.

The type of the memoized value is inferred but can be explicitly defined in a generic parameter on `useMemo`. The following is an example of explicitly defining that the memoized value should have a `number` type:

```
const memoizedValue = useMemo<number>(
  () => expensiveCalculation(),
  []
);
```

Next, we will experiment with `useMemo`.

Using the memo Hook

We will use the `PersonScore` component we have been working on to play with the `useMemo` Hook. To do so, carry out the following steps. The code snippets used are available at `https://github.com/PacktPublishing/Learn-React-with-TypeScript-2nd-Edition/tree/main/Chapter4/Section4-Using-the-memo-hook`:

1. Open `PersonScore.tsx` and import `useMemo` from React:

    ```
    import {
      useEffect,
      useReducer,
      useRef,
      useMemo
    } from 'react';
    ```

2. Add the following expensive function below the import statements:

    ```
    function sillyExpensiveFunction() {
      console.log("Executing silly function");
      let sum = 0;
      for (let i = 0; i < 10000; i++) {
        sum += i;
      }
      return sum;
    }
    ```

    The function adds all the numbers between `0` and `10000` and will take a while to execute.

3. Add a call to the function in the `PersonScore` component beneath the effects:

    ```
    useEffect( ... );

    const expensiveCalculation = sillyExpensiveFunction();

    if (loading) {
      return <div>Loading ...</div>;
    }
    ```

4. Add the result of the function call to the JSX underneath `name` and `score`:

```
<h3>
  {name}, {score}
</h3>
<p>{expensiveCalculation}</p>
<button ... >
  Add
</button>
```

5. Refresh the browser containing the app and click the buttons. If you look in the console, you will see that the expensive function is executed every time the component is re-rendered after a button click.

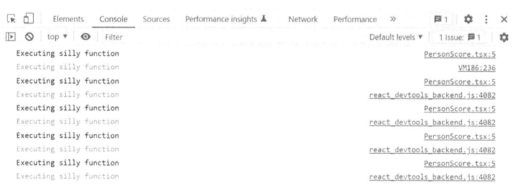

Figure 4.7 – The expensive function executed multiple times

Remember that a double render occurs in development mode and React's Strict Mode. So, once a button is clicked, you will see **Executing silly function** in the console twice.

An expensive function executing each time a component is re-rendered can lead to performance problems.

6. Rework the call to `sillyExpensiveFunction` as follows:

```
const expensiveCalculation = useMemo(
  () => sillyExpensiveFunction(),
  []
);
```

The useMemo Hook is used to memoize the value from the function call.

7. Refresh the browser containing the running app and click the buttons. If you look in the console, you will see that the expensive function isn't executed when the buttons are clicked because the memoized value is used instead.

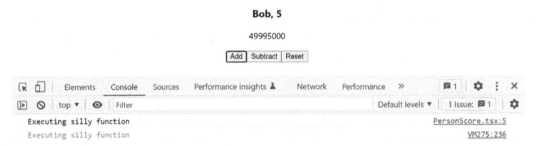

Figure 4.8 – The expensive function call memoized

That completes our exploration of the useMemo Hook. The takeaway from this section is that the useMemo Hook helps improve the performance of function calls by memoizing their results and using the memoized value when the function is re-executed.

Next, we will look at another Hook that can help performance.

Using the callback Hook

In this section, we will learn about the callback Hook and where it is useful. We will then use the Hook in the PersonScore component we have been working on.

Understanding the callback Hook

The callback Hook memoizes a function so that it isn't recreated on each render. The Hook is called useCallback and the syntax is as follows:

```
const memoizedCallback = useCallback(() => someFunction(), []);
```

A function that executes the function to memoize is passed into useCallback as the first argument. The second argument passed to useCallback is an array of dependencies. So, if the someFunction function has dependencies a and b, the call will be as follows:

```
const memoizedCallback = useCallback(
    () => someFunction(a, b),
    [a, b]
);
```

When any dependencies change, the function in the first argument is executed again to return a new function to memoize. In the previous example, a new version of memoizedCallback is created every time a or b changes.

The type of the memoized function is inferred but can be explicitly defined in a generic parameter on useCallback. Here is an example of explicitly defining that the memoized function has no parameters and returns void:

```
const memoizedValue = useCallback<() => void>(
  () => someFunction (),
  []
);
```

A common use case for useCallback is to prevent unnecessary re-renders of child components. Before trying useCallback, we will take the time to understand when a component is re-rendered.

Understanding when a component is re-rendered

We already understand that a component re-renders when its state changes. Consider the following component:

```
export function SomeComponent () {
  const [someState, setSomeState] = useState ('something');
  return (
    <div>
      <ChildComponent />
      <AnotherChildComponent something={someState} />
      <button
        onClick={() => setSomeState ('Something else')}
      ></button>
    </div>
  );
}
```

When someState changes, SomeComponent will re-render – for example, when the button is clicked. In addition, ChildComponent and AnotherChildComponent will re-render when someState changes. This is because a component is re-rendered when its parent is re-rendered.

It may seem like this re-rendering behavior will cause performance problems – particularly when a component is rendered near the top of a large component tree. However, it rarely does cause performance issues. This is because the DOM will only be updated after a re-render if the virtual DOM changes, and updating the DOM is the slow part of the process. In the preceding example, the DOM for `ChildComponent` won't be updated when `SomeComponent` is re-rendered if the definition of `ChildComponent` is as follows:

```
export function ChildComponent() {
  return <span>A child component</span>;
}
```

The DOM for `ChildComponent` won't be updated during a re-render because the virtual DOM will be unchanged.

While this re-rendering behavior generally doesn't cause performance problems, it can cause performance issues if a computationally expensive component is frequently re-rendered or a component with a slow side effect is frequently re-rendered. For example, we would want to avoid unnecessary re-renders in components with a side effect that fetches data.

There is a function called `memo` in React that can be used to prevent unnecessary re-renders. The `memo` function can be applied as follows to `ChildComponent` to prevent unnecessary re-renders:

```
export const ChildComponent = memo(() => {
  return <span>A child component</span>;
});
```

The `memo` function wraps the component and memoizes the result for a given set of props. The memoized function is then used during a re-render if the props are the same. Note that the preceding code snippet uses arrow function syntax so that the component can be a named export.

In summary, React's `memo` function can prevent the unnecessary re-rendering of slow components.

Next, we will use the `memo` function and the `useCallback` Hook to prevent unnecessary re-renders.

Using the callback Hook

We will now refactor the `PersonScore` component by extracting the **Reset** button into a separate component called `Reset`. This will lead to unnecessary re-rendering of the `Reset` component, which we will resolve using React's `memo` function and the `useCallback` Hook.

To do so, carry out the following steps. The code snippets used are available at `https://github.com/PacktPublishing/Learn-React-with-TypeScript-2nd-Edition/tree/main/Chapter4/Section5-Using-the-callback-hook`:

1. Start by creating a new file in the `src` folder for the reset button called `Reset.tsx` with the following content:

    ```
    type Props = {
      onClick: () => void,
    ```

```
};
export function Reset({ onClick }: Props) {
  console.log("render Reset");
  return <button onClick={onClick}>Reset</button>;
}
```

The component takes in a click handler and displays the reset button. The component also outputs **render Reset** to the console so that we can clearly see when the component is re-rendered.

2. Open `PersonScore.tsx` and import the `Reset` component:

    ```
    import { Reset } from './Reset';
    ```

3. Replace the existing reset button with the new `Reset` component as follows:

    ```
    <div>
      ...
      <button onClick={() => dispatch({ type: 'decrement'
    })}>
        Subtract
      </button>
      <Reset onClick={() => dispatch({ type: 'reset' })} />
    </div>;
    ```

4. Go to the app running in the browser and open React's DevTools. Make sure the **Highlight updates when components render.** option is ticked in the **Components** panel's settings:

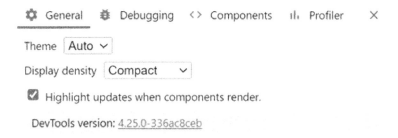

Figure 4.9 – The re-render highlight option

5. In the browser, the **Reset** button will work as it did before. Click this button as well as the **Add** and **Subtract** buttons. If you look at the console you'll notice that `Reset` is unnecessarily re-rendered. You will also see the re-render highlight around the **Reset** button.

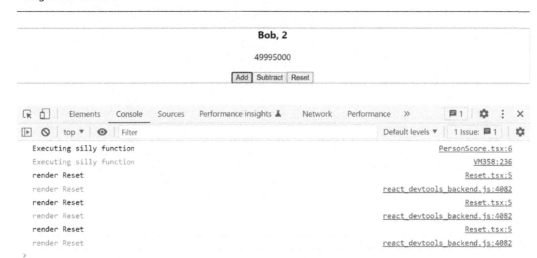

Figure 4.10 – The unnecessary re-renders of the Reset component

6.   Use the browser's DevTools to inspect the DOM. To do this, right-click on the **Reset** button and choose **Inspect**. Click the buttons and observe the DOM elements. The DevTools in Chrome highlight elements when they are updated. You will see that only the h3 element content was updated – none of the other elements are highlighted due to an update occurring.

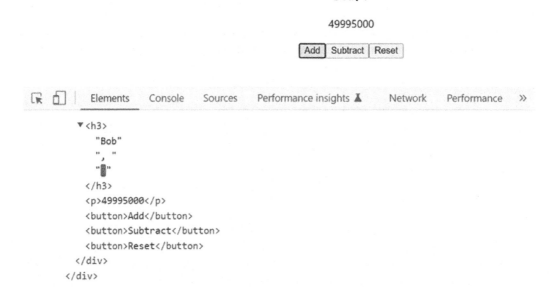

Figure 4.11 – The h3 element was updated after a re-render

Even though Reset is unnecessarily re-rendered, it doesn't result in a DOM update. In addition, Reset isn't computationally expensive and doesn't contain any side effects. So, the unnecessary render isn't really a performance problem. However, we will use this example to learn how to use React's memo function, and the useCallback Hook can prevent the unnecessary render.

7. We will now add React's memo function to try to prevent unnecessary re-renders. Open React.tsx and add a React import statement to import memo at the top of the file:

```
import { memo } from 'react';
```

8. Now, wrap memo around the Reset component as follows:

```
export const Reset = memo(({ onClick }: Props) => {
  console.log("render Reset");
  return <button onClick={onClick}>Reset</button>;
});
```

9. In addition, add the following line beneath the Reset component definition so that it has a meaningful name in React's DevTools:

```
Reset.displayName = 'Reset';
```

10. In the browser, click the **Add**, **Subtract**, and **Reset** buttons. Then, look at the console and notice that Reset is *still* unnecessarily re-rendered.

11. We will use React's DevTools to start to understand why Reset is still unnecessarily re-rendered when its result is memoized. Open the **Profiler** panel and click the cog icon to open the settings. Go to the **Profiler** settings section and make sure **Record why each component rendered while profiling.** is ticked:

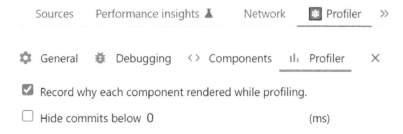

Figure 4.12 – Ensuring the Record why each component rendered while profiling. option is ticked

12. Click the blue circle icon to start profiling and then click the **Add** button in our app. Click the red circle icon to stop profiling.

13. In the flamegraph that appears, click the **Reset** bar. This gives useful information about the Reset component re-render:

Figure 4.13 – Information about the Reset re-render

So, the unnecessary Reset render is happening because the onClick prop changes. The onClick handler contains the same code, but a new instance of the function is created on every render. This means onClick will have a different reference on each render. The changing onClick prop reference means that the memorized result from Reset isn't used and a re-render occurs instead.

14. We can use the useCallback Hook to memoize the onClick handler and prevent the re-render. Open PersonScore.tsx and start by refactoring the handler into a named function:

```
function handleReset() {
  dispatch({ type: 'reset' });
}

if (loading) {
  return <div>Loading ...</div>;
}

return (
  <div>

    ...

    <Reset onClick={handleReset} />
  </div>
);
```

15. Now, add useCallback to the React import statement:

```
import {
  useEffect,
  useReducer,
```

```
    useRef,
    useMemo,
    useCallback
} from 'react';
```

16. Lastly, wrap `useCallback` around the click handler we just created:

```
const handleReset = useCallback(
  () => dispatch({ type: 'reset' }),
  []
);
```

17. Now, if you click the **Add**, **Subtract**, and **Reset** buttons, you will notice that `Reset` is no longer unnecessarily re-rendered.

    That completes our exploration of the `useCallback` Hook.

Here's a quick recap of everything we learned in this section:

- A component is re-rendered when its parent is re-rendered.

- React's `memo` function can be used to prevent unnecessary re-renders to child components.

- `useCallback` can be used to memoize functions. This can be used to create a stable reference for function props passed to child components to prevent unnecessary re-renders.

- React's `memo` function and `useCallback` should be used wisely – make sure they help performance before using them because they increase the complexity of the code.

Next, we will summarize the chapter.

Summary

In this chapter, we learned that all React Hooks must be called at the top level of a function component and can't be called conditionally.

The `useEffect` Hook can be used to execute component side effects when it is rendered. We learned how to use `useEffect` to fetch data, which is a common use case.

`useReducer` is an alternative to `useState` for using state, and we experienced using both approaches in our `PersonScore` example component. `useState` is excellent for primitive state values. `useReducer` is great for complex object state values, particularly when state changes depend on previous state values.

The `useRef` Hook creates a mutable value and doesn't cause a re-render when changed. We used `useRef` to set focus to an HTML element after it was rendered, which is a common use case.

The useMemo and useCallback Hooks can be used to memoize values and functions, respectively, and can be used for performance optimization. The examples we used for these Hooks were a little contrived and using useCallback didn't improve performance, so remember to check that the use of these Hooks does improve performance.

So far in this book, the components we have created are unstyled. In the next chapter, we will learn several approaches for styling React components.

Questions

Answer the following questions to check what you have learned about React Hooks:

1. The following component renders some text for 5 seconds. This is problematic though – what is the problem?

```
export function TextVanish({ text }: Props) {
  if (!text) {
    return null;
  }
  const [textToRender, setTextToRender] = useState(text);
  useEffect(() => {
    setTimeout(() => setTextToRender(""), 5000);
  }, []);
  return <span>{textToRender}</span>;
}
```

2. The following code is a snippet from a React component that fetches some data and stores it in state. There are several problems with this code though – can you spot any of the problems?

```
const [data, setData] = useState([]);
useEffect(async () => {
  const data = await getData();
  setData(data);
});
```

3. How many times will the following component re-render in production mode when the button is clicked? Also, what will the button content be after one click?

```
export function Counter() {
  const [count, setCount] = useState(0);
  return (
    <button
```

```
      onClick={() => {
        setCount(count + 1);
        setCount(count + 1);
        setCount(count + 1);
      }}
    >
      {count}
    </button>
  );
}
```

4. How many times will the following component re-render in production mode when the button is clicked? Also, what will the button content be after one click?

```
export function CounterRef() {
  const count = useRef(0);
  return (
    <button
      onClick={() => {
        count.current = count.current + 1;
      }}
    >
      {count.current}
    </button>
  );
}
```

5. Consider the following reducer function:

```
type State = { steps: number };
type Action =
  | { type: 'forward'; steps: number }
  | { type: 'backwards'; steps: number };

function reducer(state: State, action: Action): State {
  switch (action.type) {
    case 'forward':
      return { ...state, steps: state.steps + action.
steps };
```

```
    case 'backwards':
      return { ...state, steps: state.steps - action.
        steps };
    default:
      return state;
  }
}
```

What will the type of the `action` parameter be narrowed down to in the `"backwards"` switch branch?

6. Consider the following `Counter` component:

```
export function Counter() {
  const [count, setCount] = useState(0);
  const memoCount = useMemo(() => count, []);
  return (
    <div>
      <button onClick={() => setCount(count + 1)}>
        {memoCount}
      </button>
    </div>
  );
}
```

What will the button content be after it is clicked once?

7. Consider the following `Counter` component:

```
export function Counter() {
  const [count, setCount] = useState(0);
  const handleClick = useCallback(() => {
    setCount(count + 1);
  }, []);
  return (
    <div>
      <button onClick={handleClick}>{count}</button>
    </div>
  );
}
```

What will the button content be after it is clicked twice?

Answers

1. The problem with the component is that both `useState` and `useEffect` are called conditionally (when the `text` prop is defined), and React doesn't allow its Hooks to be called conditionally. Placing the Hooks before the `if` statement resolves the problem:

```
export function TextVanish({ text }: Props) {
  const [textToRender, setTextToRender] = useState(text);
  useEffect(() => {
    setTimeout(() => setTextToRender(""), 5000);
  }, []);
  if (!text) {
    return null;
  }
  return <span>{textToRender}</span>;
}
```

2. The main problem with the code is that the effect function can't be marked as asynchronous with the `async` keyword. A solution is to revert to the older promise syntax:

```
const [data, setData] = useState([]);
useEffect(() => {
  getData().then((theData) => setData(theData));
});
```

The other major problem is that no dependencies are defined in the call to `useEffect`. This means the effect function will be executed on every render. The effect function sets some state, which causes a re-render. So, the component will keep re-rendering, and the effect function will keep executing indefinitely. An empty array passed into the second argument of `useEffect` will resolve the problem:

```
useEffect(() => {
  getData().then((theData) => setData(theData));
}, []);
```

Another problem is that the `data` state will have the `any []` type, which isn't ideal. In this case, it is probably better to explicitly define the type of the state as follows:

```
const [data, setData] = useState<Data[]>([]);
```

The last problem is that the data state could be set after the component has been unmounted, which can lead to memory leaks. A solution is to set a flag when the component is unmounted and not set the state when the flag is set:

```
useEffect(() => {
  let cancel = false;
  getData().then((theData) => {
    if (!cancel) {
      setData(theData);
    }
  });
  return () => {
    cancel = true;
  };
}, []);
```

3.   The button will only render once in production mode because state changes are batched.

The state isn't changed until the next render, so clicking the button once will result in count being set to 1, which means the button content will be 1.

4.   The button will not re-render when the button is clicked because changes to a ref don't cause a re-render.

The counter ref will be incremented when the button is clicked. However, because a re-render doesn't occur, the button content will still be 0.

5.   TypeScript will narrow the type of the action parameter to { type: 'backwards'; steps: number } in the 'backwards' switch branch.

6.   The button's content will always be 0 because the initial count of 0 is memoized and never updated.

7.   The button content will be 1 after one click and will stay as 1 after subsequent clicks. So, after two clicks, it will be 1.

The key here is that the handleClick function is only created when the component is initially rendered because useCallback memoizes it. So, the count state will always be 0 within the memoized function. This means the count state will always be updated to 1, which will appear in the button content.

Part 2:
App Fundamentals

This part covers the fundamental topics for building apps that are outside the core of React. These topics are styling, clientside routing, and forms. Each topic involves different approaches that you can take, along with the benefits of each one. We will also cover several popular third-party libraries that are commonly used for these parts of an application.

This part includes the following chapters:

- *Chapter 5, Approaches to Styling React Frontends*
- *Chapter 6, Routing with React Router*
- *Chapter 7, Working with Forms*

Approaches to Styling React Frontends

In this chapter, we will style the alert component we worked on in previous chapters using four different approaches. First, we will use plain CSS and understand the downsides of this approach. Then, we will move on to use **CSS modules**, which will resolve plain CSS's main problem. We will then use a **CSS-in-JS** library called Emotion and a library called Tailwind CSS and will understand the benefits of each of these libraries.

We will also learn how to use SVGs in React apps and use them in the alert component for the information and warning icons.

We'll cover the following topics:

- Using plain CSS
- Using CSS modules
- Using CSS-in-JS
- Using Tailwind CSS
- Using SVGs

Technical requirements

We will use the following technologies in this chapter:

- **Browser**: A modern browser such as Google Chrome
- **Node.js** and **npm**: You can install them from `https://nodejs.org/en/download/`
- **Visual Studio Code**: You can install it from `https://code.visualstudio.com/`

All the code snippets used in this chapter can be found online at `https://github.com/PacktPublishing/Learn-React-with-TypeScript-2nd-Edition/tree/main/Chapter5`.

Using plain CSS

We will start this section by setting up a React and TypeScript project with the alert component from *Chapter 3, Setting Up React and TypeScript*. Next, we will add the alert component from *Chapter 3* and style it using plain CSS. Finally, we will look at one of the challenges with plain CSS and discover how we could mitigate it.

Creating the project

The project we will be using is the one we completed at the end of *Chapter 3*. This can be found at the following location: `https://github.com/PacktPublishing/Learn-React-with-TypeScript-2nd-Edition/tree/main/Chapter3/Section2-Creating-a-project-with-Create-React-App/myapp`. To copy this locally, carry out the following steps:

1. Open Visual Studio Code in a folder of your choice.

2. Run the following command in the terminal to clone the GitHub repository for the book:

   ```
   git clone https://github.com/PacktPublishing/Learn-React-
   with-TypeScript-2nd-Edition.git
   ```

3. Reopen Visual Studio Code in the `Learn-React-with-TypeScript-2nd-Edition\Chapter3\Section2-Creating-a-project-with-Create-React-App\myapp` subfolder. This contains the project in the form it was in at the end of *Chapter 3*.

4. Run the following command to install all the dependencies:

   ```
   npm i
   ```

The project is now set up. Next, we will take some time to understand how to use plain CSS in React components.

Understanding how to reference CSS

Create React App has already enabled the use of plain CSS in the project. In fact, if you look in `App.tsx`, it already uses plain CSS:

```
...
import './App.css';
...
```

```
function App() {
  return (
    <div className="App">
      ...
    </div>
  );
}
...
```

CSS styles from the App.css file are imported, and the App CSS class is referenced on the outer div element.

React uses a className attribute rather than class because class is a reserved word in JavaScript. The className attribute is converted to a class attribute during transpilation.

The CSS import statement is a webpack feature. As webpack processes all the files, it will include all the imported CSS in the bundle.

Carry out the following steps to explore the CSS bundle that the project produces:

1. Start by opening and looking at App.css. As we have seen already, App.css is used within App.tsx. However, it contains CSS classes that are no longer used, such as App-header and App-logo. These classes were referenced in the App component before we removed them when we added the alert component. Leave the redundant CSS classes in place.

2. Open the index.tsx file and you'll notice that index.css is imported. However, no CSS classes are referenced within this file. If you open index.css, you will notice that it only contains CSS rules that target element names and no CSS classes.

3. Run the following command in the terminal to produce a production build:

    ```
    npm run build
    ```

    After a few seconds, the build artifacts will appear in a build folder at the project's root.

4. Open index.html in the build folder and notice all the whitespace has been removed because it is optimized for production. Next, find the link element that references the CSS file and note down the path – it will be something similar to /static/css/main.073c9b0a.css.

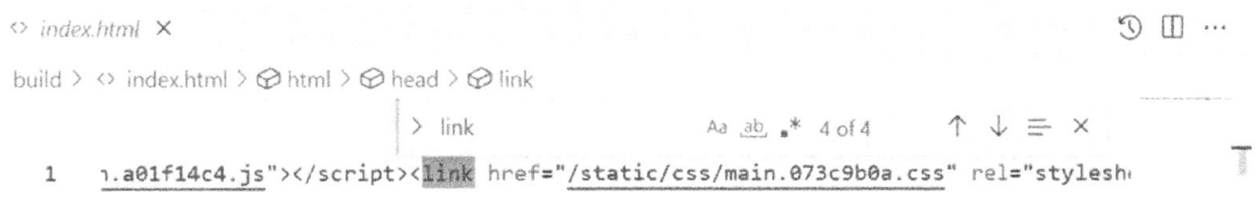

Figure 5.1 – The link element in index.html

5.   Open up the referenced CSS file. All the whitespace has been removed because it is optimized for production. Notice that it contains all the CSS from index.css and App.css, including the redundant App-header and App-logo CSS classes.

```
# main.073c9b0a.css  ✕
build > static > css > # main.073c9b0a.css > ⅍ body
  1    )s linear infinite}}.App-header{align-items:center;background-color:█#282c34;
  2
```

Figure 5.2 – The bundled CSS file, including redundant App-header CSS class

The key point here is that webpack doesn't remove any redundant CSS – it will include all the content from all the CSS files that have been imported.

Next, we will style the alert component with plain CSS.

Using plain CSS in the alert component

Now that we understand how to use plain CSS within React, let's style the alert component. Carry out the following steps:

1.   Add a CSS file called Alert.css in the src folder. This is available in GitHub at https://github.com/PacktPublishing/Learn-React-with-TypeScript-2nd-Edition/blob/main/Chapter5/Section1-Using-plain-CSS/app/src/Alert.css to copy.

2.   We will add the CSS classes step by step and understand the styles in each class. Start by adding a container class into Alert.css:

```
.container {
  display: inline-flex;
  flex-direction: column;
  text-align: left;
  padding: 10px 15px;
  border-radius: 4px;
  border: 1px solid transparent;
}
```

This will be used on the outer div element. The style uses an inline flexbox, with the items flowing vertically and left-aligned. We've also added a nice rounded border and a bit of padding between the border and child elements.

3. Add the following additional classes that can be used within `container`:

```
.container.warning {
  color: #e7650f;
  background-color: #f3e8da;
}
.container.information {
  color: #118da0;
  background-color: #dcf1f3;
}
```

We will use these classes for the different types of alerts to color them appropriately.

4. Add the following class for the header container element:

```
.header {
  display: flex;
  align-items: center;
  margin-bottom: 5px;
}
```

This will be applied to the element that contains the icon, heading, and close button. It uses a flexbox that flows horizontally with child elements vertically centered. It also adds a small gap at the bottom before the alert message.

5. Now add the following class for the icon to give it a width of 30 px:

```
.header-icon {
  width: 30px;
}
```

6. Next, add the following class to apply to the heading to make it bold:

```
.header-text {
  font-weight: bold;
}
```

7. Add the following class to apply to the close button:

```
.close-button {
  border: none;
  background: transparent;
  margin-left: auto;
```

```
  cursor: pointer;
}
```

This removes the border and background. It also aligns the button to the right of the header and gives it a pointer mouse cursor.

8. Add the following class for the content element:

```
.content {
  margin-left: 30px;
  color: #000;
}
```

This adds a left margin so the message horizontally aligns with the heading and sets the text color to black.

That completes all the CSS class definitions.

9. Open `Alert.tsx` and add an import statement for the CSS file we just created:

```
import './Alert.css';
```

10. Now we are going to reference the CSS classes we just created in the elements of the alert component. Add the following highlighted CSS class name references in the alert JSX to do this:

```
<div className={`container ${type}`}>
  <div className="header">
    <span

      . . .

      className="header-icon"

    >
      {type === "warning" ? "⚠" : "i"}
    </span>
    <span className="header-text">{heading}</span>
  </div>
  {closable && (
    <button

      . . .

      className="close-button"

    >

      . . .

    </button>
```

```
    ) }
    <div className="content">{children}</div>
  </div>
```

The elements in the alert component are now being styled by the CSS classes in the imported CSS file.

11. Move the close button so that it is located inside the header container, under the header element:

```
<div className={`container ${type}`}>
  <div className="header">
    . . .
    <span className="header-text">{heading}</span>
    {closable && (
      <button
        aria-label="Close"
        onClick={handleCloseClick}
        className="close-button"
      >
        <span role="img" aria-label="Close">
          ✕
        </span>
      </button>
    )}
  </div>
  <div className="content">{children}</div>
</div>;
```

12. Start the app in development mode by running npm start in the terminal.

    After a few seconds an improved alert component will appear in the browser:

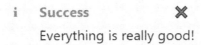

Figure 5.3 – A styled alert component with plain CSS

That completes the alert component's styling, but let's continue so that we can observe a downside of plain CSS.

Experiencing CSS clashes

We will now see an example of CSS with different components clashing. Keep the app running in development mode and then follow these steps:

1. Open App.tsx and change the referenced CSS class from App to container on the div element:

    ```
    <div className="container">
      <Alert ...>

        ...

      </Alert>
    </div>
    ```

2. Open App.css and rename the App CSS class to container and also add 20px of padding to it:

    ```
    .container {
      text-align: center;
      padding: 20px;
    }
    ```

3. Now, look at the running app and notice that the alert is no longer centered horizontally on the page. Inspect the elements using the browser DevTools. If you inspect the div element from the App component, you will see that styles from the container CSS class in the alert component have been applied to it as well as the container CSS class we just added. So, the text-align CSS property is left rather than center.

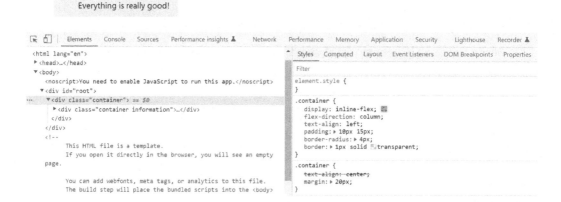

Figure 5.4 – Clashing CSS classes

4. Stop the running app before continuing by pressing *Ctrl + C*.

The key point here is that plain CSS classes are scoped to the whole app and not just the file it is imported into. This means that CSS classes can clash if they have the same name, as we have just experienced

A solution to CSS clashes is to carefully name them using **BEM**. For example `container` in the App component could be called `App__container`, and `container` in the `Alert` component could be called `Alert__container`. However, this requires discipline from all members of a development team.

> **Note**
>
> **BEM** stands for **Block, Element, Modifier** and is a popular naming convention for CSS class names. More information can be found at the following link: `https://css-tricks.com/bem-101/`.

Here's a quick recap of this section:

*   Create React App configures webpack to process CSS so that CSS files can be imported into React component files
*   All the styles in an imported CSS file are applied to the app – there is no scoping or removing redundant styles

Next, we will learn about a styling approach that doesn't suffer from CSS clashes across components.

Using CSS modules

In this section, we will learn about an approach to styling React apps called **CSS modules**. We will start by understanding CSS modules and then we will use them within the alert component that we have been working on.

Understanding CSS modules

CSS modules is an open source library available on GitHub at `https://github.com/css-modules/css-modules`, which can be added to the webpack process to facilitate the automatic scoping of CSS class names.

A CSS module is a CSS file, just like in the previous section; however, the filename has an extension of `.module.css` rather than `.css`. This special extension allows webpack to differentiate a CSS module file from a plain CSS file so that it can be processed differently.

A CSS module file is imported into a React component file as follows:

```
import styles from './styles.module.css';
```

This is similar to the syntax of importing plain CSS, but a variable is defined to hold CSS class name mapping information. In the preceding code snippet, the CSS class name information is imported into a variable called `styles`, but the variable name can be anything we choose.

The CSS class name mapping information variable is an object containing property names corresponding to the CSS class names. Each class name property contains a value of a scoped class name to be used on a React component. Here is an example of the mapping object that has been imported into a component called `MyComponent`:

```
{
  container: "MyComponent_container__M7tzC",
  error: "MyComponent_error__vj8Oj"
}
```

The scope CSS class name starts with the component filename, then the original CSS class name, followed by a random string. This naming construct prevents class names from clashing.

Styles within a CSS module are referenced in a component's `className` attribute as follows:

```
<span className={styles.error}>A bad error</span>
```

The CSS class name on the element would then resolve to the scoped class name. In the preceding code snippets, `styles.error` would resolve to `MyComponent_error__ vj8Oj`. So, the styles in the running app will be the scoped style names and not the original class names.

Projects created using Create React App already have CSS modules installed and configured with webpack. This means we don't have to install CSS modules in order to start using them in our project.

Next, we will use CSS modules in the alert component we have worked on.

Using CSS modules in the alert component

Now that we understand CSS modules, let's use them in the alert component. Carry out the following steps:

1. Start by renaming `Alert.css` to `Alert.module.css`; this file can now be used as a CSS module.

2. Open `Alert.module.css` and change the CSS class names to camel case rather than kebab case. This will allow us to reference the scoped CSS class names more easily in the component – for example, `styles.headerText` rather than `styles["header-text"]`. The changes are as follows:

```
...
.headerIcon {
  ...
```

```
}
.headerText {

  ...

}
.closeButton {

  ...

}
```

3. Now, open `Alert.tsx` and change the CSS import statement to import the CSS module as follows:

    ```
    import styles from './Alert.module.css';
    ```

4. In the JSX, change the class name references to use the scoped names from the CSS module:

    ```jsx
    <div className={`${styles.container} ${styles[type]}`}>
      <div className={styles.header}>
        <span

          ...

          className={styles.headerIcon}
        >
          {type === "warning" ? "⚠" : "i"}
        </span>
        {heading && (
          <span className={styles.headerText}>{heading}</
            span>
        )}
        {closable && (
          <button

            ...

            className={styles.closeButton}
          >

            ...

          </button>
        )}
      </div>
      <div className={styles.content}>{children}</div>
    </div>
    ```

5. Start the app by running `npm start` in the terminal.

    After a few seconds, the styled alert will appear. This time the alert will be horizontally centered, which is a sign that styles are no longer clashing.

6. Inspect the elements in the DOM using the browser's DevTools. You will see that the alert component is now using scoped CSS class names. This means the alert container styles no longer clash with the app container styles.

Figure 5.5 – The CSS module scoped class names

7. Stop the running app before continuing by pressing *Ctrl + C*.

8. To round off our understanding of CSS modules, let's see what happens to the CSS in a production build. However, before we do that, let's add a redundant CSS class at the bottom of `Alert.module.css`:

```
...
.content {
  margin-left: 30px;
  color: #000;
}
.redundant {
  color: red;
}
```

9. Now create a production build by executing `npm run build` in the terminal.

    After a few seconds, the build artifacts are created in the `build` folder.

10. Open the bundled CSS file and you will notice the following points:

- It contains all the CSS from `index.css`, `App.css`, and the CSS module we just created.

- The class names from the CSS module are scoped. This will ensure that the styles in production don't clash, as they did not in development mode.

- It contains the redundant CSS class name from the CSS module.

```
#  main.4e8b03b1.css  ✕

build > static > css > #  main.4e8b03b1.css > ...
  1    :__YqM9b{color: ■ #000;margin-left:30px}.Alert_redundant__qwosS{color: ■red}
  2
```

Figure 5.6 – The redundant CSS class included in CSS bundle

That completes the refactoring of the alert component to use CSS modules.

> **Note**
>
> For more information on CSS modules, visit the GitHub repository at `https://github.com/css-modules/css-modules`.

Here's a recap of what we have learned about CSS modules:

- CSS modules allow CSS class names to be automatically scoped to a React component. This prevents styles for different React components from clashing.

- CSS modules isn't a standard browser feature; instead, it is an open source library that can be added to the webpack process.

- CSS modules are pre-installed and pre-configured in projects created with Create React App.

- Similar to plain CSS, redundant CSS classes are not pruned from the production CSS bundle.

Next, we will learn about another approach to styling React apps.

Using CSS-in-JS

In this section, we start by understanding CSS-in-JS and its benefits. We will then refactor the alert component we have used to implement CSS-in-JS and observe how it differs from CSS modules.

Understanding CSS-in-JS

CSS-in-JS isn't a browser feature, and it isn't even a specific library – instead, it is a type of library. Popular examples of CSS-in-JS libraries are **styled-components** and **Emotion**. There isn't a significant difference between styled-components and Emotion – they are both popular and have similar APIs. We will use Emotion in this chapter.

Emotion generates styles that are scoped, similar to CSS modules. However, you write the CSS in JavaScript rather than in a CSS file – hence the name *CSS-in-JS*. In fact, you can write the CSS directly on JSX elements as follows:

```
<span
  css={css`
    font-weight: 700;
    font-size: 14;
  `}
>
  {text}
</span>
```

Each CSS-in-JS library's syntax is slightly different – the preceding example is a code snippet from Emotion styling.

Having styles directly on the component allows a developer to fully understand the component without having to visit another file. This obviously increases the file size, which can make the code harder to read. However, child components can be identified and extracted out of the file to mitigate large file sizes. Alternatively, styles can be extracted from component files into a JavaScript function that is imported.

A massive benefit of CSS-in-JS is that you can mix logic into the style, which is really useful for highly interactive apps. The following example contains a conditional `font-weight` dependent on an `important` prop and a conditional `font-size` dependent on a `mobile` prop:

```
<span
  css={css`
    font-weight: ${important ? 700 : 400};
    font-size: ${mobile ? 15 : 14};
  `}
>
  {text}
</span>
```

JavaScript string interpolation is used to define the conditional statement.

The equivalent plain CSS would be similar to the following example, with separate CSS classes created for the different conditions:

```
<span
  className={`${important ? "text-important" : ""} ${
    mobile ? "text-important" : ""
  }`}
>
  {text}
</span>
```

If a style on an element is highly conditional, then CSS-in-JS is arguably easier to read and certainly easier to write.

Next, we will use Emotion in the alert component we have worked on.

Using Emotion in the alert component

Now that we understand CSS-in-JS, let's use Emotion in the alert component. To do so, carry out the following steps. All the code snippets used can be found at `https://github.com/PacktPublishing/Learn-React-with-TypeScript-2nd-Edition/blob/main/Chapter5/Section3-Using-CSS-in-JS/app/src/Alert.tsx`:

1. Create React App doesn't install and set up Emotion, so we first need to install Emotion. Run the following command in the terminal:

    ```
    npm i @emotion/react
    ```

    This will take a few seconds to install.

2. Open `Alert.tsx` and remove the CSS module import.

3. Add an import for the `css` prop from Emotion with a special comment at the top of the file:

    ```
    /** @jsxImportSource @emotion/react */
    import { css } from '@emotion/react';
    import { useState } from 'react';
    ```

    This special comment changes JSX elements to be transpiled using Emotion's `jsx` function instead of React's `createElement` function. Emotion's `jsx` function adds styles to elements containing Emotion's `css` prop.

4. In the JSX, we need to replace all the `className` props with the equivalent Emotion `css` attributes. The styles are largely the same as defined in the CSS file we created earlier, so the explanations won't be repeated.

    We will style one element at a time, starting with the outer `div` element:

    ```
    <div
      css={css`
        display: inline-flex;
        flex-direction: column;
        text-align: left;
        padding: 10px 15px;
        border-radius: 4px;
        border: 1px solid transparent;
        color: ${type === "warning" ? "#e7650f" : "#118da0"};
        background-color: ${type === "warning"
          ? "#f3e8da"
          : "#dcf1f3"};
      `}
    >
      ...
    </div>
    ```

    There are a few important points to explain in this code snippet:

    - The `css` attribute isn't usually valid on JSX elements. The special comment at the top of the file (`/** @jsxImportSource @emotion/react */`) allows this.

    - The `css` attribute is set to a **tagged template literal**. This is a special string that gets processed by the function specified before it, which is a function called `css` in this case. For more information on tagged template literals, see `https://developer.mozilla.org/en-US/docs/Web/JavaScript/Reference/Template_literals`.

    - The tagged template literal converts the style to a CSS class at runtime. We will verify this in *step 14*.

    - String interpolation is used to implement the conditional styles for the colors. Remember that we had to define three CSS classes using plain CSS or CSS modules. This CSS-in-JS version is arguably more readable and certainly more concise.

5. Next, style the header container:

    ```
    <div
      css={css`
    ```

```
    display: flex;
    align-items: center;
    margin-bottom: 5px;
  `}
>
  <span role="img" ... > ... </span>
  <span ...>{heading}</span>
  {closable && ...}
</div>
```

6. Next, style the icon as follows:

```
<span
  role="img"
  aria-label={type === "warning" ? "Warning" :
    "Information"}
  css={css`
    width: 30px;
  `}
>
  {type === "warning" ? "⚠" : "i"}
</span>
```

7. Then, style the heading as follows:

```
<span
  css={css`
    font-weight: bold;
  `}
>
  {heading}
</span>
```

8. Now, style the close button as follows:

```
{closable && (
  <button
    ...
    css={css`
```

```
            border: none;
            background: transparent;
            margin-left: auto;
            cursor: pointer;
          `}
        >
          ...
        </button>
    )}
```

9. Finally, style the message container as follows:

```
<div
    css={css`
        margin-left: 30px;
        color: #000;
    `}
>
    {children}
</div>
```

10. Run the app by running `npm start` in the terminal. The alert component will appear like it was before.

11. Inspect the elements in the DOM using the browser's DevTools. The alert component uses scoped CSS class names, similar to CSS modules:

Figure 5.7 – Emotion's scoped class names

12. Stop the running app before continuing by pressing *Ctrl + C*.

13. To round off our understanding of Emotion, let's see what happens to the CSS in a production build. First, create a production build by executing `npm run build` in the terminal.

    After a few seconds, the build artifacts are created in the `build` folder.

14. Open the bundled CSS file from the `build/static/css` folder. Notice that the Emotion styles are not there. This is because Emotion generates the styles at runtime via JavaScript rather than at build time. If you think about it, the styles can't be generated at build time because they may depend on JavaScript variables whose values are only known at runtime.

This completes the refactoring of the alert component to use CSS-in-JS.

> **Note**
>
> For more information on emotion, visit their website at `https://emotion.sh/docs/introduction`.

Here's a recap of what we learned about Emotion and CSS-in-JS:

- Styles for a CSS-in-JS library are defined in JavaScript rather than a CSS file.

- Emotion's styles can be defined directly on a JSX element using a `css` attribute.

- A huge benefit is that conditional logic can be added directly to the styles, which helps us style interactive components more quickly.

- Emotion styles are applied at runtime rather than at build time because they depend on JavaScript variables. While this allows conditional styling logic to be elegantly defined, it does mean a small performance penalty because the styles are created and applied at runtime.

Next, we will learn about another different approach to styling React frontends.

Using Tailwind CSS

In this section, we will start by understanding Tailwind CSS and its benefits. We will then refactor the alert component we have been using to use Tailwind and observe how it differs from other approaches we have tried.

Understanding Tailwind CSS

Tailwind is a set of prebuilt CSS classes that can be used to style an app. It is referred to as a **utility-first CSS framework** because the prebuilt classes can be thought of as flexible utilities.

An example CSS class is bg-white, which styles the background of an element white – *bg* is short for *background*. Another example is bg-orange-500, which sets the background color to a 500 shade of orange. Tailwind contains a nice color palette that can be customized.

The utility classes can be used together to style an element. The following example styles a button element in JSX:

```
<button className="border-none rounded-md bg-emerald-700 text-
white cursor-pointer">
  . . .
</button>
```

Here's an explanation of the classes used in the preceding example:

- border-none removes the border of an element.
- rounded-md rounds the corners of an element border. The *md* stands for *medium*. Alternatively, lg (large) could have been used or even full, for more rounded borders.
- bg-emerald-700 sets the element background color to a 700 shade of emerald.
- text-white sets the element text color to white.
- cursor-pointer sets the element cursor to a pointer.

The utility classes are low-level and focused on styling a very specific thing. This makes the classes flexible, allowing them to be highly reusable.

Tailwind can specify that a class should be applied when the element is in a hover state by prefixing it with hover:. The following example sets the button background to a darker shade of emerald when hovered:

```
<button className="md border-none rounded-md bg-emerald-700
text-white cursor-pointer hover:bg-emerald-800">
  . . .
</button>
```

So, a key point of Tailwind is that we don't write new CSS classes for each element we want to style – instead, we use a large range of well-thought-through existing classes. A benefit of this approach is that it helps an app look nice and consistent.

> **Note**
>
> For more information on Tailwind, refer to their website at the following link: `https://tailwindcss.com/`. The Tailwind website is a crucial resource for searching and understanding all the different utility classes that are available.

Next, we will install and configure Tailwind in the project containing the alert component we have been working on.

Installing and configuring Tailwind CSS

Now that we understand Tailwind, let's install and configure it in the alert component project. To do this, carry out the following steps:

1. In the Visual Studio project, start by installing Tailwind by running the following command in a terminal:

    ```
    npm i -D tailwindcss
    ```

    The Tailwind library is installed as a development dependency because it's not required at runtime.

2. Tailwind integrates into Create React App projects using a library called **PostCSS**. PostCSS is a tool that transforms CSS using JavaScript and Tailwind runs as a plugin in it. Install PostCSS by running the following command in the terminal:

    ```
    npm i -D postcss
    ```

3. Tailwind also recommends another PostCSS called **Autoprefixer**, which adds vendor prefixes to CSS. Install this by running the following command in the terminal:

    ```
    npm i -D autoprefixer
    ```

4. Next, run the following command in a terminal to generate configuration files for Tailwind and PostCSS:

    ```
    npx tailwindcss init -p
    ```

    After a few seconds, the two configuration files are created. The Tailwind configuration file is called `tailwind.config.js`, and the PostCSS configuration file is called `postcss.config.js`.

5. Open `tailwind.config.js` and specify the path to the React components as follows:

    ```
    module.exports = {
      content: [
        './src/**/*.{js,jsx,ts,tsx}'
    ```

```
        ],
        theme: {
          extend: {},
        },
        plugins: [],
    }
```

6. Now, open `index.css` in the `src` folder and add the following three lines at the top of the file:

```
@tailwind base;
@tailwind components;
@tailwind utilities;
```

These are called **directives** and will generate the CSS required by Tailwind during the build process.

Tailwind is now installed and ready to use.

Next, we will use Tailwind to style the alert component we have been working on.

Using Tailwind CSS

Now, let's use Tailwind to style the alert component. We will remove emotion's `css` JSX attribute and replace it with Tailwind utility class names in the JSX `className` attribute. To do this, carry out the following steps:

1. Open `Alert.tsx` and start by removing the special emotion comment and the `css` import statement from the top of the file.

2. Replace the `css` attribute with a `className` attribute on the outermost `div` element as follows:

```
<div
  className={`inline-flex flex-col text-left px-4 py-3
    rounded-md border-1 border-transparent`}
>

  ...
</div>
```

Here is an explanation of the utility classes that were just used:

-   `inline-flex` and `flex-col` create an inline flexbox that flows vertically
-   `text-left` aligns items to the left
-   `px-4` adds 4 spacing units of left and right padding
-   `py-3` adds 3 spacing units of top and bottom padding

- We have encountered `rounded-md` before – this rounds the corners of the `div` element

- `border-1` and `border-transparent` add a transparent 1 px border

> **Note**
>
> Spacing units are defined in Tailwind and are a proportional scale. One spacing unit is equal to `0.25rem`, which translates roughly to 4px.

3. Still on the outermost `div` element, add the following conditional styles using string interpolation:

```
<div
    className={`inline-flex flex-col text-left px-4 py-3
rounded-md border-1 border-transparent ${
        type === 'warning' ? 'text-amber-900' : 'text-
            teal-900'
    } ${type === 'warning' ? 'bg-amber-50' : 'bg-teal-
        50'}`}
>
    ...
</div>
```

The text color is set to a 900 amber shade for warning alerts and a 900 teal shade for information alerts. The background color is set to a 50 amber shade for warning alerts and a 50 teal shade for information alerts.

4. Next, replace the `css` attribute with a `className` attribute on the header container as follows:

```
<div className="flex items-center mb-1">
    <span role="img" ... > ... </span>
    <span ... >{heading}</span>
    {closable && ...}
</div>
```

Here is an explanation of the utility classes that were just used:

- `flex` and `items-center` create a horizontal flowing flexbox where the items are centered vertically

- `mb-1` adds a 1 spacing unit margin at the bottom of the element

5. Replace the `css` attribute with a `className` attribute on the icon as follows:

```
<span role="img" ... className="w-7">
    {type === 'warning' ? '⚠' : 'i'}
```

```
</span>
```

w-7 sets the element to a width of 7 spacing units.

6. Replace the css attribute with a className attribute on the heading as follows:

```
<span className="font-bold">{heading}</span>
```

font-bold sets the font weight to be bold on the element.

7. Replace the css attribute with a className attribute on the close button as follows:

```
{closable && (
  <button

    . . .

    className="border-none bg-transparent ml-auto cursor-
      pointer"

  >

    . . .

  </button>
)}
```

Here, border-none removes the element border, and bg-transparent makes the element background transparent. ml-auto sets the left margin to automatic, which right aligns the element. cursor-pointer sets the mouse cursor to a pointer.

8. Finally, replace the css attribute with a className attribute on the message container as follows:

```
<div className="ml-7 text-black">
  {children}
</div>
```

ml-7 sets the left margin on the element to 7 spacing units and text-black sets the text color to black.

9. Run the app by running npm start in the terminal. After a few seconds, the app will appear in the browser.

Notice that the alert component looks a bit nicer because of Tailwind's default color palette and consistent spacing.

10. Inspect the elements in the DOM using the browser's DevTools. Notice the Tailwind utility classes being used and notice the spacing units use CSS rem units.

A key point to notice is that no CSS class name scoping occurs. There is no need for any scoping because the classes are general and reusable and not specific to any element.

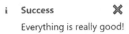

Figure 5.8 – A styled alert using Tailwind

11. Stop the running app before continuing by pressing *Ctrl + C*.

12. To round off our understanding of Tailwind, let's see what happens to the CSS in a production build. First, create a production build by executing `npm run build` in the terminal.

    After a few seconds, the build artifacts are created in the `build` folder.

13. Open the bundled CSS file from the `build/static/css` folder. Notice the base Tailwind styles at the start of the file. You will also see that all the Tailwind classes that we used are in this file.

```
# main.67504d25.css 5 ✕

build > static > css > # main.67504d25.css > ⁑ .rounded-md
1                                           > rounded-md    Aa ab .* 1 of 1        ↑ ↓ ≡ ✕
2
3    ion:column}.items-center{align-items:center}.rounded-md{border-radius:.375rem}.border-none{border-sty
4
```

Figure 5.9 – Tailwind CSS classes in a bundled CSS file

> **Note**
>
> An important point is that Tailwind doesn't add all its CSS classes – that would produce a massive CSS file! Instead, it only adds the CSS classes used in the app.

That completes the process of refactoring the alert component to use Tailwind.

Here's a recap of what we learned about Tailwind:

- Tailwind is a well-thought-through collection of reusable CSS classes that can be applied to React elements
- Tailwind has a nice default color palette and a 4 px spacing scale, both of which can be customized
- Tailwind is a plugin for PostCSS and executed at build time
- Tailwind does not incur a runtime performance penalty like Emotion, because the styles aren't created and applied at runtime
- Only classes used on React elements are included in the CSS build bundle

Next, we will make the icons in the alert component look a bit nicer.

Using SVGs

In this section, we will learn how to use SVG files in React and how to use them for the icons in the alert component.

Understanding how to use SVGs in React

SVG stands for **Scalable Vector Graphics** and it is made up of points, lines, curves, and shapes based on mathematical formulas rather than specific pixels. This allows them to scale when resized without distortion. The quality of icons is important to get right – if they are distorted, they make the whole app feel unprofessional. Using SVGs for icons is common in modern web development.

Create React App configures webpack to use SVG files when a project is created. In fact, `logo.svg` is referenced in the template App component as follows:

```
import logo from './logo.svg';
...
function App() {
  return (
    <div className="App">
      <header className="App-header">
        <img src={logo} className="App-logo" alt="logo" />
          ...
      </header>
    </div>
  );
}
export default App;
```

In the preceding example, `logo` is imported as a path to the SVG file, which is then used on the `src` attribute on the `img` element to display the SVG.

An alternate way of referencing SVGs is to reference them as a component as follows:

```
import { ReactComponent as Logo } from './logo.svg';

function SomeComponent() {
  return (
    <div>
      <Logo />
    </div>
  );
}
```

SVG React components are available in a named import called `ReactComponent`. In the preceding example, the SVG component is aliased with the name `Logo`, which is then used in the JSX.

Next, we will learn how to use SVGs in the alert component.

Adding SVGs to the alert component

Carry out the following steps to replace the emoji icons in the alert component with SVGs:

1. First, create three files called `cross.svg`, `info.svg`, and `warning.svg` in the `src` folder. Then, copy and paste the content of these from the GitHub repository at `https://github.com/PacktPublishing/Learn-React-with-TypeScript-2nd-Edition/tree/main/Chapter5/Section5-Using-SVGs/app/src`.

2. Open `Alert.tsx` and add the following import statements to import the SVGs as React components:

    ```
    import { ReactComponent as CrossIcon } from './cross.svg';
    import { ReactComponent as InfoIcon } from './info.svg';
    import { ReactComponent as WarningIcon } from './warning.svg';
    ```

    We have given the SVG components appropriately named aliases.

3. Update the `span` element containing the emoji icons to use SVG icon components as follows:

    ```
    <span
      role="img"
    ```

```
aria-label={type === 'warning' ? 'Warning' :
  'Information'}
className="inline-block w-7"
>
  {type === 'warning ' ? (
    <WarningIcon className="fill-amber-900 w-5 h-5" />
  ) : (
    <InfoIcon className="fill-teal-900 w-5 h-5" />
  )}
</span>;
```

We have used Tailwind to size and color the icons appropriately.

4.   Next, update the emoji close icon to the SVG close icon as follows:

```
<button
  aria-label="Close"
  onClick={handleCloseClick}
  className="border-none bg-transparent ml-auto cursor-
    pointer"
>
  <CrossIcon />
</button>
```

5.   Run the app by running npm start in the terminal. After a few seconds, the app will appear in a browser containing the improved alert component:

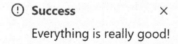

Figure 5.10 – An alert with an SVG icon

That completes the alert component – it is looking much better now.

Here's a quick recap of what we learned about using SVGs in React apps:

- Webpack needs to be configured to bundle SVG files and Create React App does this configuration for us

- The default import for an SVG file is the path to the SVG, which can then be used in an img element

- A named import called `ReactComponent` can be used to reference the SVG as a React component in JSX

Next, we will summarize what we have learned in this chapter.

Summary

In this chapter, we learned about four methods of styling.

First, we learned that plain CSS could be used to style React apps, but all the styles in the imported CSS file are bundled regardless of whether a style is used. Also, the styles are not scoped to a specific component – we observed the `container` CSS class names clashing with the `App` and `Alert` components.

Next, we learned about CSS modules, which allows us to write plain CSS files imported in a way that scopes styles to the component. We learned that CSS modules is an open source library pre-installed and pre-configured in projects created with Create React App. We saw how this resolved the CSS clashing problem but didn't remove redundant styles.

Then, we discussed CSS-in-JS libraries, which allow styles to be defined directly on the React component. We used emotion's `css` prop to style the alert component without an external CSS file. The nice thing about this approach is that conditional-style logic can be implemented more quickly. We learned that emotion's styles are scoped like CSS modules, but the scoping happens at runtime rather than at build time. We also understood that the small performance cost of this approach is because of the styles being created at runtime.

The fourth styling approach we looked at was using Tailwind CSS. We learned that Tailwind provides a set of reusable CSS classes that can be applied to React elements, including a nice default color palette and a 4 px spacing scale, both of which can be customized. We learned that only the used Tailwind classes are included in the production build.

Finally, we learned that Create React App configures webpack to enable the use of SVG files. SVGs can be referenced as a path in an `img` element or as a React component using a `ReactComponent` named `import`.

In the next chapter, we will look at implementing multiple pages in React apps with a popular library called React Router.

Questions

Answer the following questions to check what you have learned about React styling:

1. Why could the following use of plain CSS be problematic?

   ```
   <div className="wrapper"></div>
   ```

2. We have a component styled using CSS modules as follows:

    ```
    import styles from './styles1.module.css';

    function ComponentOne() {
      return <div className={styles.wrapper}></div>;
    }
    ```

    We have another component styled using CSS modules as follows:

    ```
    import styles from './styles2.module.css';

    function ComponentTwo() {
      return <div className={styles.wrapper}></div>;
    }
    ```

    Will the styles of these div elements clash, given that they are using the wrapper class name?

3. We have a component styled using CSS modules as follows:

    ```
    import styles from './styles3.module.css';

    function ComponentThree() {
      return <div className={styles.wrapper}>
    </div>
    }
    ```

    The styles in styles3.module.css are as follows:

    ```
    .wrap {
      display: flex;
      align-items: center;
      background: #e7650f;
    }
    ```

    The styles aren't being applied when the app is run. What is the problem?

4. We are defining a reusable button component with a kind prop that can be "square" or "rounded". The rounded button should have a 04 px border radius, and the square button should have no border radius. How could we define this conditional style using Emotion's css prop?

5. We are styling a button element using Tailwind. It is currently styled as follows:

    ```
    <button className="bg-blue-500 text-white font-bold py-2
    px-4 rounded">
    ```

```
    Button
  </button>
```

How can we enhance the style by making the button background a 700 shade of blue when the user hovers over it?

6. A logo SVG is referenced as follows:

```
import Logo from './logo.svg';

function LogoComponent() {
  return <Logo />;
}
```

However, the logo isn't rendered. What is the problem?

7. We are styling a button element using Tailwind that has a `color` prop to determine its color and is styled as follows:

```
<button className={`bg-${color}-500 text-white font-bold
py-2 px-4 rounded`}>
    Button
  </button>
```

However, the button color doesn't work. What is the problem?

Answers

1. The wrapper CSS class could clash with other classes. To reduce this risk, the class name can be manually scoped to the component:

```
<div className="card-wrapper"></div>
```

2. The CSS won't clash because CSS modules will scope the class names to each component.

3. The wrong class name is referenced in the component – it should be `wrap` rather than `wrapper`:

```
import styles from './styles3.module.css';

function ComponentThree() {
  return <div className={styles.wrap}>
</div>
}
```

4. The `css` prop on the button could be as follows:

```
<button
  css={css`
    border-radius: ${kind === "rounded" ? "4px" : "0px"};
  `}
>
  ...
</button>
```

5. The style can be adjusted as follows to include the hover style:

```
<button className="bg-blue-500 hover:bg-blue-700 text-white font-bold py-2 px-4 rounded">
  ...
</button
```

6. Logo will hold the path to the SVG rather than a component. The import statement can be adjusted as follows to import a logo component:

```
import { ReactComponent as Logo } from './logo.svg';

function LogoComponent() {
  return <Logo />;
}
```

7. The `bg-${color}-500` class name is problematic because this can only be resolved at runtime because of the `color` variable. The used Tailwind classes are determined at build time and added to the bundle, meaning the relevant background color classes won't be bundled. This means that the background color style won't be applied to the button.

6

Routing with React Router

In this chapter, we will build a simple app implementing the following pages:

- A home page that welcomes the user
- A products list page that lists all the products
- A product page that provides details about a particular product
- An admin page for privileged users

This will all be managed using a library called **React Router**.

Through this, we will learn how to implement static links from the products list to the product page and implement route parameters on the product page for the product ID. We will also learn about form navigation and query parameters when it comes to the search feature of our app.

Finally, the chapter will end with how to lazily load code for a page to improve performance.

So, in this chapter, we will cover the following topics:

- Introducing React Router
- Declaring routes
- Creating navigation
- Using nested routes
- Using route parameters
- Creating an error page
- Using index routes
- Using search parameters
- Navigating programmatically

- Using form navigation
- Implementing lazy loading

Technical requirements

We will use the following technologies in this chapter:

- **Browser**: A modern browser such as Google Chrome
- **Node.js** and **npm**: You can install them from `https://nodejs.org/en/download/`
- **Visual Studio Code**: You can install it from `https://code.visualstudio.com/`

All the code snippets in this chapter can be found online at `https://github.com/PacktPublishing/Learn-React-with-TypeScript-2nd-Edition/tree/main/Chapter6`.

Introducing React Router

In this section, we start by creating a new React project for the app before understanding what React Router is and how to install it.

Creating the project

We will develop the app locally using Visual Studio Code, which requires a new Create React App-based project setup. We have covered this several times, so we will not cover the steps in this chapter – instead, see *Chapter 3, Setting Up React and TypeScript*. Create the project for the app with a name of your choice.

We will style the app with Tailwind CSS. We covered how to install and configure Tailwind in Create React App in *Chapter 5, Approaches to Styling Frontends*, so after you have created the React and TypeScript project for the app, install and configure Tailwind.

Understanding React Router

As the name suggests, React Router is a routing library for React apps. A router is responsible for selecting what to show in the app for a requested path. For example, React Router is responsible for determining what components to render when a path of `/products/6` is requested. For any app containing multiple pages, a router is essential, and React Router has been a popular router library for React for many years.

Installing React Router

React Router is in a package called `react-router-dom`. Install this in the project using the following command in the terminal:

```
npm i react-router-dom
```

TypeScript types are included in `react-router-dom`, so there is no need for a separate installation.

Next, we will create a page in the app and declare a route that shows it.

Declaring routes

We will start this section by creating a page component that lists the app's products. We will then learn how to create a router and declare routes using React Router's `createBrowserRouter` function.

Creating the products list page

The products list page component will contain the list of the React tools in the app. Carry out the following steps to create this:

1. We will start by creating the data source for the page. First, create a folder called `data` in the `src` folder and then a file called `products.ts` within `data`.

2. Add the following content into `products.ts` (you can copy and paste it from the GitHub repository at `https://github.com/PacktPublishing/Learn-React-with-TypeScript-2nd-Edition/blob/main/Chapter6/src/data/products.ts`):

```
export type Product = {
  id: number,
  name: string,
  description: string,
  price: number,
};

export const products: Product[] = [
  {
    description:
      'A collection of navigational components that
        compose declaratively with your app',
    id: 1,
    name: 'React Router',
    price: 8,
```

```
    },
    {
      description: 'A library that helps manage state
        across your app',
      id: 2,
      name: 'React Redux',
      price: 12,
    },
    {
      description: 'A library that helps you implement
        robust forms',
      id: 3,
      name: 'React Hook Form',
      price: 9,
    },
    {
      description: 'A library that helps you interact with
        a REST API',
      id: 4,
      name: 'React Apollo',
      price: 10,
    },
    {
      description: 'A library that provides utility CSS
        classes',
      id: 5,
      name: 'Tailwind CSS',
      price: 7,
    },
  ];
```

This is a list of all the React tools in the app held in a JavaScript array.

> **Note**
>
> Usually, this kind of data is on a server somewhere, but this adds complexity beyond the scope of this chapter. We cover how to interact with server data in detail in *Chapter 9, Interacting with RESTful APIs*, including how to do this efficiently with React Router.

3. We will create the products list page component now. First, create a folder for all the page components in the src folder called pages. Next, create a file called ProductsPage.tsx in the pages folder for the products list page component.

4. Add the following import statement into ProductsPage.tsx to import the products we just created:

```
import { products } from '../data/products';
```

5. Next, start to create the ProductsPage component by outputting a heading for the page:

```
export function ProductsPage() {
  return (
    <div className="text-center p-5">
      <h2 className="text-xl font--bold text-slate-600">
        Here are some great tools for React
      </h2>
    </div>
  );
}
```

This uses Tailwind classes to make the heading large, bold, gray, and horizontally centered.

6. Next, add the list of the products in the JSX:

```
<div className="text-center p-5 text-xl">
  <h2 className="text-base text-slate-600">
    Here are some great tools for React
  </h2>
  <ul className="list-none m-0 p-0">
    {products.map((product) => (
      <li key={product.id} className="p-1 text-base text-
        slate-800">
        {product.name}
      </li>
    ))}
  </ul>
</div>
```

The Tailwind classes remove the bullet points, margin, and padding from the unordered list element, and make the list items gray.

Notice that we use the products array `map` function to iterate over each product and return a `li` element. Using `Array.map` is common practice for JSX looping logic.

Notice the `key` prop on the list item elements. React requires this on elements in a loop to update the corresponding DOM elements efficiently. The value of the `key` prop must be unique and stable within the array, so we have used the product ID.

That completes the product page for now. This page won't show in the app yet because it isn't part of its component tree – we need to declare it as a page using React Router, which we'll do next.

Understanding React Router's router

A router in React Router is a component that tracks the browser's URL and performs navigation. Several routers are available in React Router, and the one recommended for web applications is called a **browser router**. As its name suggests, the `createBrowserRouter` function creates a browser router.

`createBrowserRouter` requires an argument containing all the **routes** in the application. A route contains a path and what component to render when the app's browser address matches that path. The following code snippet creates a router with two routes:

```
const router = createBrowserRouter([
  {
    path: 'some-page',
    element: <SomePage />,
  },
  {
    path: 'another-page',
    element: <AnotherPage />,
  }
]);
```

When the path is `/some-page`, the `SomePage` component will be rendered. When the path is `/another-page`, the `AnotherPage` component will be rendered.

The router returned by `createBrowserRouter` is passed to a `RouterProvider` component and placed high up in the React component tree, as shown here:

```
const root = ReactDOM.createRoot(
  document.getElementById('root') as HTMLElement
);
root.render(
  <React.StrictMode>
```

```
    <RouterProvider router={router} />
  </React.StrictMode>
);
```

Now that we are starting to understand React Router's router, we will use it in our project.

Declaring the products route

We will declare the products list page in the app using `createBrowserRouter` and `RouterProvider`. Carry out the following steps:

1. We will create our own component to hold all the route definitions. Create a file called `Routes.tsx` in the `src` folder containing the following `import` statements:

```
import {
  createBrowserRouter,
  RouterProvider,
} from 'react-router-dom';
import { ProductsPage } from './pages/ProductsPage';
```

   We have imported `createBrowserRouter` and `RouterProvider` from React Router. We have also imported `ProductsPage`, which we'll render in a `products` route next.

2. Add the following component underneath the `import` statements to define the router with a `products` route:

```
const router = createBrowserRouter([
  {
    path: 'products',
    element: <ProductsPage />,
  },
]);
```

   So, the `ProductsPage` component will be rendered when the path is `/products`.

3. Still in `Routes.tsx`, create a component called `Routes` under the router as follows:

```
export function Routes() {
  return <RouterProvider router={router} />;
}
```

   This component wraps `RouterProvider` with the router passed into it.

4. Open the index.tsx file and add an import statement for the Routes component we just created beneath the other import statements:

```
import { Routes } from './Routes';
```

5. Render Routes instead of App as the top-level component as follows:

```
root.render(
  <React.StrictMode>
    <Routes />
  </React.StrictMode>
);
```

This causes the products route we defined to be part of the component tree. This means the products list page will be rendered in the app when the path is /products.

6. Remove the import statement for the App component, as this is not needed at the moment.

7. Run the app using npm start.

An error screen appears explaining that the current route isn't found:

Unhandled Thrown Error!

404 Not Found

😀 Hey developer 🪨

You can provide a way better UX than this when your app throws errors by providing your own `errorElement` props on `<Route>`

Figure 6.1 – React Router's standard error page

The error page is from React Router. As the error message suggests, we can provide our own error screen, which we will do later in this chapter.

8. Change the browser URL to http://localhost:3000/products.

You will see the products list page component rendered as follows:

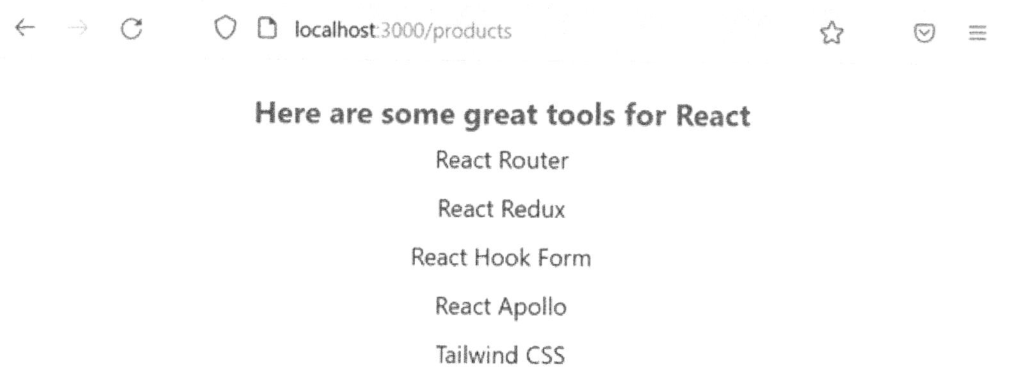

← → C   ○ 🗋 localhost:3000/products   ☆   ▽ ≡

Here are some great tools for React

React Router

React Redux

React Hook Form

React Apollo

Tailwind CSS

Figure 6.2 – Products list page

This confirms that the `products` route is working nicely. Keep the app running as we recap and move to the next section.

Here's a recap of what we have learned in this section:

- In a web app, routes in React Router are defined using `createBrowserRouter`
- Each route has a path and a component to render when the browser's URL matches that path
- The router returned from `createBrowserRouter` is passed into a `RouterProvider` component, which should be placed high up in the component tree

For more information on `createBrowserRouter`, see the following link in the React Router documentation: `https://reactrouter.com/en/main/routers/create-browser-router`. For more information on `RouterProvider`, see the following link in the React Router documentation: `https://reactrouter.com/en/main/routers/router-provider`.

Next, we will learn about React Router components that can perform navigation.

Creating navigation

React Router comes with components called `Link` and `NavLink`, which provide navigation. In this section, we will create a navigation bar at the top of the app containing the `Link` component from React Router. We will then swap `Link` for the `NavLink` component and understand the difference between the two components.

Using the Link component

Carry out the following steps to create an app header containing React Router's `Link` component:

1. Start by creating a file for the app header called `Header.tsx` in the `src` folder containing the following `import` statements:

   ```
   import { Link } from 'react-router-dom';
   import logo from './logo.svg';
   ```

   We have imported the `Link` component from React Router.

   We have also imported the React logo because we will include this in the app header with the navigation options.

2. Create the `Header` component as follows:

   ```
   export function Header() {
     return (
       <header className="text-center text-slate-50
         bg-slate-900 h-40 p-5">
         <img
           src={logo}
           alt="Logo"
           className="inline-block h-20"
         />
         <h1 className="text-2xl">React Tools</h1>
         <nav></nav>
       </header>
     );
   }
   ```

   The component contains a `header` element containing the React logo, the app title, and an empty `nav` element. We have used Tailwind classes to make the header gray with the logo and title horizontally centered.

3. Now, create a link inside the `nav` element:

   ```
   <nav>
     <Link
       to="products"
       className="text-white no-underline p-1"
     >
   ```

```
       Products
     </Link>
   </nav>
```

The `Link` component has a `to` prop that defines the path to navigate to. The text to display can be specified in the `Link` content.

4. Open `Routes.tsx` and add an import statement for the `Header` component we just created:

```
import { Header } from './Header';
```

5. In the `router` definition, add a root path that renders the `Header` component as follows:

```
const router = createBrowserRouter([
  {
    path: '/',
    element: <Header />,
  },
  {
    path: 'products',
    element: <ProductsPage />,
  },
]);
```

What we have just done isn't ideal because the `Header` component needs to show on all routes and not just the root route. However, it will allow us to explore React Router's `Link` component. We will tidy this up in the *Using nested routes* section.

6. In the running app, change the browser address to the root of the app. The new app header appears, containing the **Products** link:

Figure 6.3 – App header

7. Now, inspect the app header elements using the browser's DevTools:

Figure 6.4 – Header component inspection

We can see that the Link component is rendered as an HTML anchor element.

8. Select the **Network** tab in DevTools and clear any existing requests that are shown. Click on the **Products** link in the app header. The browser will navigate to the products list page.

    Notice that a network request wasn't made for the products list page. This is because React Router overrides the anchor element's default behavior with client-side navigation:

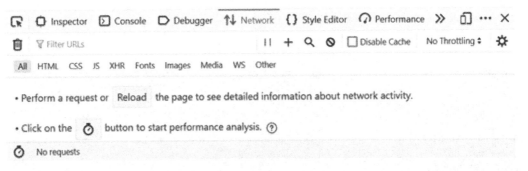

Figure 6.5 – Client-side navigation

Finally, notice that the app header disappears on the products list page, which is not what we want. We will resolve this in the *Using nested routes* section.

Keep the app running as we move to the next section.

The navigation is working well but it would be nice if the **Products** link had a different style when the products list page was active. We will make this improvement next.

Using the NavLink component

React Router's `NavLink` is like a `Link` element but allows it to be styled differently when active. This is really handy for a navigation bar.

Carry out the following steps to replace `Link` with `NavLink` in the app header:

1. Open `Header.tsx` and change the `Link` references to `NavLink`:

```
import { NavLink } from 'react-router-dom';
...
export function Header() {
  return (
    <header ...>

      ...

      <nav>
        <NavLink
          to="products"
          className="..."
        >
          Products
        </NavLink>
      </nav>
    </header>
  );
}
```

The app header will look and behave exactly the same at the moment.

2. The `className` prop on the `NavLink` component accepts a function that can be used to conditionally style it, depending on whether its page is active. Update the `className` attribute to the following:

```
<NavLink
  to="products"
```

```
className={({ isActive }) =>
  `text-white no-underline p-1 pb-0.5 border-solid
    border-b-2 ${
    isActive ? "border-white" : "border-transparent"
  }`
}
>
  Products
</NavLink>
```

The function takes in a parameter, isActive, for defining whether the link's page is active. We've added a bottom border to the link if it is active.

We can't see the impact of this change just yet, because the **Products** link doesn't appear on the products list page yet. We will resolve this in the next section.

That completes the app header and our exploration of the NavLink component.

To recap, NavLink is great for main app navigation when we want to highlight an active link, and Link is great for all the other links in our app.

For more information on the Link component, see the following link: https://reactrouter.com/en/main/components/link. For more information on the NavLink component, see the following link: https://reactrouter.com/en/main/components/nav-link.

Next, we will learn about nested routes.

Using nested routes

In this section, we will cover **nested routes** and the situations in which they are useful, before using a nested route in our app. The nested route will also resolve the disappearing app header problem we experienced in the previous sections.

Understanding nested routes

A nested route allows a segment of a route to render a component. For example, the following mock-up is commonly implemented using nested routes:

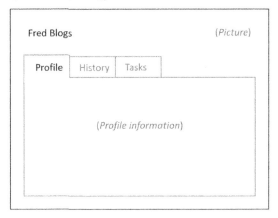

/customers/1234/profile

Figure 6.6 – Use case for nested routes

The mock-up displays information about a customer. The path determines the active tab – in the mockup, **Profile** is the active tab because that is the last segment in the path. If the user selects the **History** tab, the path would change to /customers/1234/history.

A Customer component could render the shell of this screen, including the customer's name, picture, and tab headings. The component that renders the tab contents could be decoupled from the Customer component and coupled to the path instead.

This feature is referred to as *nested routes* because Route components are nested inside each other. Here's what the routes for the mock-up could be:

```
const router = createBrowserRouter([
  {
    path: 'customer/:id',
    element: <Customer />,
    children: [
      {
        path: 'profile',
        element: <CustomerProfile />,
      },
      {
        path: 'history',
        element: <CustomerHistory />,
      },
      {
```

```
        path: 'tasks',
        element: <CustomerTasks />,
      },
    ],
  },
]);
```

This nested approach to defining routes makes them easy to read and understand, as you can see in the preceding code snippet.

A critical part of nested routes is where child components are rendered in their parent. In the preceding code snippet, where would the `CustomerProfile` component be rendered in the `Customer` component? The solution is React Router's `Outlet` component. Here's an example of `Outlet` in the `Customer` component from the mock-up:

```
export function Customer() {
  . . .
  return (
    <div>
      <Name ... />
      <Picture ... />
      <nav>
        <NavLink to="profile" ... >Profile</NavLink>
        <NavLink to="history" ... >History</NavLink>
        <NavLink to="tasks" ... >Tasks</NavLink>
      </nav>
      <Outlet />
    </div>
  );
}
```

So, in this example, the `CustomerProfile` component would be rendered after the navigation options in the `Customer` component. Notice that the `Customer` component is decoupled from the nested content. This means new tabs can be added to the customer page without changing the `Customer` component. This is another benefit of nested routes.

Next, we will use a nested route within our app.

Using nested routes in the app

In our app, we will use the App component for the app's shell, which renders the root path. We will then nest the products list page within this:

1. Open App.tsx and replace all the existing content with the following:

```
import { Outlet } from 'react-router-dom';
import { Header } from './Header';

export default function App() {
  return (
    <>
      <Header />
      <Outlet />
    </>
  );
}
```

The component renders the app header with nested content underneath it.

> **Note**
>
> The empty JSX elements, < > and < / >, are **React fragments**. React fragments are not added to the DOM and are used as a workaround to React components only being able to return a single element, so they are a way of returning multiple elements in a React component that keeps React happy.

2. Open Routes.tsx, import the App component we just modified, and remove the import component for Header:

```
import {
  createBrowserRouter,
  RouterProvider,
} from 'react-router-dom';
import { ProductsPage } from './pages/ProductsPage5';
import App from './App';
```

3. Update the router definition as follows:

```
const router = createBrowserRouter([
  {
```

```
    path: '/',
    element: <App />,
    children: [
      {
        path: 'products',
        element: <ProductsPage />,
      }
    ]
  }
]);
```

The products list page is now nested inside the App component.

4. If you return to the running app, you will see that the app header now appears on the products list page. You will also see the **Products** link underlined because it is an active link:

Figure 6.7 – App header on the products list page

To recap, nested routes allow components to be rendered for different path segments. An Outlet component is to render nested content within a parent component.

For more information on the Outlet component, see the following link: `https://reactrouter.com/en/main/components/outlet`.

Next, we will learn about route parameters.

Using route parameters

In this section, we will understand **route parameters** and how they are useful before using a route parameter in our app.

Understanding route parameters

A route parameter is a segment in the path that varies. The value of the variable segment is available to components so that they can render something conditionally.

In the following path, 1234 is the ID of a customer: /customers/1234/.

This can be defined as a route parameter in a route as follows:

```
{ path: '/customer/:id', element: <Customer /> }
```

A colon (:) followed by a name defines a route parameter. It is up to us to choose a parameter name that makes sense, so the :id segment in the path is the route parameter definition in the preceding route.

Multiple route parameters can be used in a path as follows:

```
{
  path: '/customer/:customerId/tasks/:taskId',
  element: <CustomerTask />,
}
```

Route parameter names obviously have to be unique within a path.

Route parameters are available to components using React Router's useParams hook. The following code snippet is an example of how the customerId and taskId route parameter values could be obtained:

```
const params = useParams<Params>();
console.log('Customer id', params.customerId);
console.log('Task id', params.taskId);
```

As we can see from the code snippet, `useParams` has a generic argument that defines the type for the parameters. The `type` definition for the preceding code snippet is as follows:

```
type Params = {
  customerId: string;
  taskId: string;
};
```

It is important to note that the route parameter values are always strings because they are extracted from paths, which are strings.

Now that we understand route parameters, we will use a route parameter in our app.

Using route parameters in the app

We will add a product page to our app to show the description and price of each product. The path to the page will have a route parameter for the product ID. Carry out the following steps to implement the product page:

1. We will start by creating the product page. In the `src/pages` folder, create a file called `ProductPage.tsx` with the following `import` statements:

    ```
    import { useParams } from 'react-router-dom';
    import { products } from '../data/products';
    ```

    We have imported the `useParams` hook from React Router, which will allow us to get the value of an `id` route parameter – the product's ID. We have also imported the `products` array.

2. Start creating the `ProductPage` component as follows:

    ```
    type Params = {
      id: string;
    };
    export function ProductPage() {
      const params = useParams<Params>();
      const id =
        params.id === undefined ? undefined :
          parseInt(params.id);
    }
    ```

    We use the `useParams` hook to obtain the `id` route parameter and turn it into an integer if it has a value.

3. Now, add a variable that is assigned to the product with the ID from the route parameter:

```
export function ProductPage() {
  const params = useParams<Params>();
  const id =
    params.id === undefined ? undefined :
      parseInt(params.id);
  const product = products.find(
    (product) => product.id === id
  );
}
```

4. Return the product information from the `product` variable in the JSX:

```
export function ProductPage() {
  ...
  return (
    <div className="text-center p-5 text-xl">
      {product === undefined ? (
        <h1 className="text-xl text-slate-900">
          Unknown product
        </h1>
      ) : (
        <>
          <h1 className="text-xl text-slate-900">
            {product.name}
          </h1>
          <p className="text-base text-slate-800">
            {product.description}
          </p>
          <p className="text-base text-slate-800">
            {new Intl.NumberFormat('en-US', {
              currency: 'USD',
              style: 'currency',
            }).format(product.price)}
          </p>
        </>
      )}
```

```
    </div>
  );
}
```

Unknown product is returned if the product can't be found. Its name, description, and price are returned if the product is found. We use JavaScript's Intl.NumberFormat function to nicely format the price.

That completes the product page.

5. The next task is to add the route for the product page. Open Routes.tsx and add an import statement for the product page:

```
import { ProductPage } from './pages/ProductPage';
```

6. Add the following highlighted route for the product page:

```
const router = createBrowserRouter([
  {
    path: '/',
    element: <App />,
    children: [
      {
        path: 'products',
        element: <ProductsPage />,
      },
      {
        path: 'products/:id',
        element: <ProductPage />,
      }
    ]
  }
]);
```

So, the /products/2 path should return a product page for React Redux.

7. In the running app, change the browser URL to http://localhost:3000/products/2. The React Redux product should show up:

Figure 6.8 – The product page

8. The last task in this section is to turn the products list on the products list page into links that open the relevant product page. Open ProductsPage.tsx and import the Link component from React Router:

```
import { Link } from 'react-router-dom';
```

9. Add a Link component around the product name in the JSX:

```
<ul className="list-none m-0 p-0">
  {products.map((product) => (
    <li key={product.id}>
      <Link
        to={`${product.id}`}
        className="p-1 text-base text-slate-800
          hover:underline"
      >
        {product.name}
      </Link>
    </li>
  ))}
</ul>
```

Link paths are relative to the component's path. Given that the component path is /products, we set the link path to the product ID, which should match the product route.

10. Return to the running app and go to the products list page. Hover over the products and you will now see that they are links:

localhost:3000/products/3

Figure 6.9 – Product list links

11. Click one of the products and the relevant product page will appear.

That completes this section on route parameters. Here's a quick recap:

- A route parameter is a varying segment in a path defined using a colon followed by the parameter name
- Route parameters can be accessed using React Router's useParams hook

For more information on the useParams hook, see the following link in the React Router documentation: https://reactrouter.com/en/main/hooks/use-params.

Remember React Router's error page we experienced in the *Declaring routes* section? Next, we will learn how to customize that error page.

Creating an error page

In this section, we will understand how error pages work in React Router before implementing one in our app.

Understanding error pages

Currently, a React Router built-in error page is shown when an error occurs. We can check this by entering an invalid path in the running app:

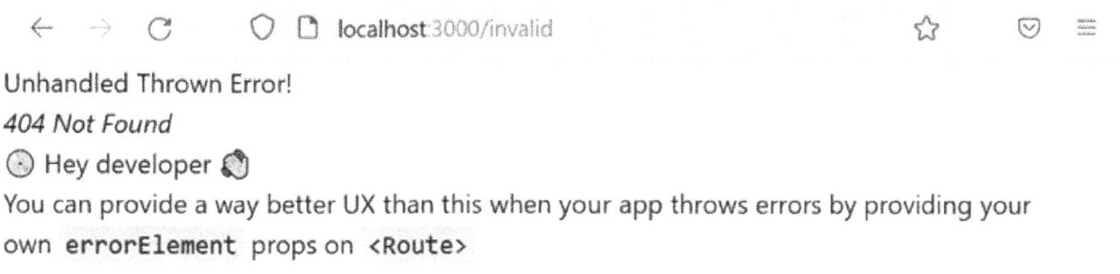

← → C   ○ □ localhost:3000/invalid   ☆   ♡   ≡

Unhandled Thrown Error!

404 Not Found

🙂 Hey developer 🗨

You can provide a way better UX than this when your app throws errors by providing your own **errorElement** props on **<Route>**

Figure 6.10 – Standard React Router error page

An error is raised because no matching routes are found in the router. The *404 Not Found* message on the error page confirms this.

This standard error page isn't ideal because the information is targeted at a developer rather than a real user. Also, the app header isn't shown, so users can't easily navigate to a page that does exist.

As the error message suggests, an `errorElement` prop can be used on a route to override the standard error page. The following is an example of a custom error page defined for a customer's route; if any error occurs on this route, the `CustomersErrorPage` component will be rendered:

```
const router = createBrowserRouter([
  ...,
  {
    path: 'customers',
    element: <CustomersPage />,
    errorElement: <CustomersErrorPage />
  },
  ...
]);
```

Now that we have started understanding error pages in React Router, we will implement one in our app.

Adding an error page

Carry out the steps below to create an error page in the app:

1. First, create a new page called `ErrorPage.tsx` in the `src/pages` folder with the following content:

```
import { Header } from '../Header';

export function ErrorPage() {
  return (
    <>
      <Header />
      <div className="text-center p--5 text-xl">
        <h1 className="text-xl text-slate-900">
          Sorry, an error has occurred
        </h1>
      </div>
    </>
  );
}
```

The component simply returns the app header with a *Sorry, an error has occurred* message underneath.

2. Open `Routes.tsx` and add an `import` statement for the error page:

```
import { ErrorPage } from './pages/ErrorPage';
```

3. Specify the error page on the root route as follows:

```
const router = createBrowserRouter([
  {
    path: '/',
    element: <App />,
    errorElement: <ErrorPage />,
    children: ...
  },
]);
```

Specifying the error page on the root route means that it will show if any routes have errors.

4. Switch back to the running app and change the browser URL to `http://localhost:3000/invalid`. The error page will be shown:

Figure 6.11 – Error page

5. This is a good start, but we can improve it by providing the user with more information, which we can get from React Router's `useRouteError` hook. Open `ErrorPage.tsx` again and add an `import` statement for `useRouteError`:

```
import { useRouteError } from 'react-router-dom';
```

6. Assign the error to an `error` variable before the component's `return` statement using `useRouteError`:

```
export function ErrorPage() {
  const error = useRouteError();
  return ...
}
```

7. The `error` variable is of the unknown type – you can verify this by hovering over it. We can use a type predicate function to allow TypeScript to narrow it to something we can work with. Add the following type predicate function beneath the component:

```
function isError(error: any): error is { statusText:
string } {
  return "statusText" in error;
}
```

The function checks whether the error object has a `statusText` property and if so, gives it a type with this property.

8.   We can now use this function to render the information in the `statusText` property:

```
return (
  <>
    <Header />
    <div className="text-center p-5 text-xl">
      <h1 className="text-xl text-slate-900">
        Sorry, an error has occurred
      </h1>
      {isError(error) && (
        <p className="text-base text-slate-700">
          {error.statusText}
        </p>
      )}
    </div>
  </>
);
```

9.   In the running app, the information about the error appears on the error page as an invalid path:

Figure 6.12 – Error page containing information about the error

That completes this section on error pages. The key point is to use an `errorElement` prop on a route to catch and display errors. Specific error information can be obtained using the `useRouteError` hook.

For more information on `errorElement`, see the following link: `https://reactrouter.com/en/main/route/error-element`. For more information on the `useRouteError` hook, see the following link: `https://reactrouter.com/en/main/hooks/use-route-error`.

Next, we will learn about index routes.

Using index routes

Currently, the app's root path displays nothing other than the header. In this section, we will learn about index routes to display a nice welcome message in the root path.

Understanding index routes

An **index route** can be thought of as a default child route. In React Router, if no children match a parent route, it will display an index route if one is defined. An index route has no path and instead has an `index` Boolean property, as in the following example:

```
{
  path: "/",
  element: <App />,
  children: [
    {
      index: true,
      element: <HomePage />,
    },
    ...,
  ]
}
```

Next, we will add a home page using an index route in our app.

Using an index route in the app

Carry out the following steps to add a home page using an index route in our app:

1. Create a new file in the `src/pages` folder called `HomePage.tsx` with the following content:

    ```
    export function HomePage() {
      return (
        <div className="text-center p-5 text-xl">
          <h1 className="text-xl text-slate-900">Welcome to
            React Tools!</h1>
        </div>
      );
    }
    ```

    The page displays a welcome message.

2. Open `Routes.tsx` and import the home page we just created:

```
import { HomePage } from './pages/HomePage';
```

3. Add the home page as an index page for the root path as follows:

```
const router = createBrowserRouter([
  {
    path: '/',
    element: <App />,
    errorElement: <ErrorPage />,
    children: [
      {
        index: true,
        element: <HomePage />,
      },
      ...
    ]
  }
]);
```

4. We will add links to the logo and app title in the header to go to the home page. Open `Header.tsx` and import the `Link` component from React Router:

```
import { NavLink, Link } from 'react-router-dom';
```

5. Wrap links to the root page around the logo and title as follows:

```
<header ...>
  <Link to="">
    <img src={logo} ... />
  </Link>
  <Link to="">
    <h1 ...>React Tools</h1>
  </Link>
  <nav>
    ...
  </nav>
</header>
```

6. In the running app, click the app title to go to the root page, and you will see the welcome message displayed:

Welcome to React Tools!

Figure 6.13 – Welcome page

That completes this section on index routes.

To recap, an index route is a default child route and is defined using an `index` Boolean property.

For more information on index routes, see the following link: `https://reactrouter.com/en/main/route/route#index`.

Next, we will learn about search parameters.

Using search parameters

In this section, we will learn about search parameters in React Router and use them to implement a search feature in the app.

Understanding search parameters

Search parameters are part of a URL that comes after the ? character and separated by the & character. Search parameters are sometimes referred to as **query parameters**. In the following URL, `type` and `when` are search parameters: `https://somewhere.com/?type=sometype&when=recent`.

React Router has a hook that returns functions for getting and setting search parameters called `useSearchParams`:

```
const [searchParams, setSearchParams] = useSearchParams();
```

`searchParams` is a JavaScript `URLSearchParams` object. There is a `get` method on `URLSearchParams`, which can be used to get the value of a search parameter. The following example gets the value of a search parameter called `type`:

```
const type = searchParams.get('type');
```

`setSearchParams` is a function used to set search parameter values. The function parameter is an object as in the following example:

```
setSearchParams({ type: 'sometype', when: 'recent' });
```

Next, we will add search functionality to our app.

Adding search functionality to the app

We will add a search box to the header of the app. Submitting a search will take the user to the products list page and list a filtered set of products matching the search criteria. Carry out the following steps:

1. Open `Header.tsx` and add `useSearchParams` to the React Router import. Also, add an `import` statement for the `FormEvent` type from React:

    ```
    import { FormEvent } from 'react';
    import {
      NavLink,
      Link,
      useSearchParams
    } from 'react-router-dom';
    ```

2. Use the `useSearchParams` hook to destructure functions to get and set search parameters before the `return` statement:

    ```
    export function Header() {
      const [searchParams, setSearchParams] =
    useSearchParams();
      return ...
    }
    ```

3. Add the following search form above the logo:

    ```
    <header ...>
      <form
        className="relative text-right"
        onSubmit={handleSearchSubmit}
      >
        <input
          type="search"
          name="search"
          placeholder="Search"
    ```

```
          defaultValue={searchParams.get('search') ?? ''}
          className="absolute right-0 top-0 rounded py-2 px-3
            text-gray-700"
        />
      </form>
      <Link to="">
        <img src={logo} ... />
      </Link>
      ...
    </header>
```

The form contains a search box with its default value as the value of a `search` parameter. `searchParams.get` returns `null` if the parameter doesn't exist, so a **nullish coalescing operator** (`??`) is used to set the search box's default value to an empty string in this case.

> **Note**
>
> The **nullish coalescing operator** (`??`) returns the right operand if the left operand is `null` or `undefined`; otherwise, it returns the left operand. For more information, see the following link: `https://developer.mozilla.org/en-US/docs/Web/JavaScript/Reference/Operators/Nullish_coalescing`.

The form submission calls a `handleSearchSubmit` function, which we'll implement in the next step.

4. Add a `handleSearchSubmit` function as follows, just above the `return` statement:

```
export function Header() {
  const [searchParams, setSearchParams] =
    useSearchParams();
  function handleSearchSubmit(e:
    FormEvent<HTMLFormElement>) {
    e.preventDefault();
    const formData = new FormData(e.currentTarget);
    const search = formData.get('search') as string;
    setSearchParams({ search });
  }
  return ...
}
```

The submit handler parameter is typed using FormEvent. FormEvent is a generic type that takes in the type of the element, which is HTMLFormElement for a form submit handler.

We use the preventDefault method on submit handler parameters to prevent the form from being submitted to the server because we handle all the logic in this function.

We use the JavaScript FormData interface to get the value of the search field. Then, we use a type assertion to set the type of the search field value to a string.

The last line of code in the submit handler sets the value of the search parameter. This will update the browser's URL to have this search parameter.

> **Note**
>
> We will learn a lot more about forms in React in *Chapter 7, Working with Forms.*

5. Now, we need to filter the products list with the value of the search parameter. Open ProductsPage.tsx and add useSearchParams to the import statement:

```
import { Link, useSearchParams } from 'react-router-dom';
```

6. At the top of the ProductsPage component, destructure searchParams from useSearchParams as follows:

```
export function ProductsPage() {
  const [searchParams] = useSearchParams();
  return ...
}
```

7. Add the following function just before the return statement to filter the products list by the search value:

```
const [searchParams] = useSearchParams();
function getFilteredProducts() {
  const search = searchParams.get('search');
  if (search === null || search === "") {
    return products;
  } else {
    return products.filter(
      (product) =>
        product.name
          .toLowerCase()
```

```
        .indexOf(search.toLowerCase()) > -1
    );
  }
}
return ...
```

The function starts by getting the value of the `search` parameter. The full product list is returned if there is no search parameter or if the value is an empty string. Otherwise, the product list is filtered using the array's `filter` function, checking that the search value is contained within the product name irrespective of the case.

8. Use the function we just created in the JSX to output the filtered products. Replace the reference to `products` with a call to `getFilteredProducts` as follows:

```
<ul className="list-none m-0 p-0">
  {getFilteredProducts().map((product) => (
    <li
      key={product.id}
      className="p-1 text-base text-slate-800"
    >
      <Link
        to={`${product.id}`}
        className="p-1 text-base text-slate-800
          hover:underline"
      >
        {product.name}
      </Link>
    </li>
  ))}
</ul>
```

9. In the running app, whilst on the home page, enter some search criteria in the search box and press *Enter* to submit the search.

The search parameter is added to the URL in the browser. However, it doesn't navigate to the products list page. Don't worry about this because we'll address this issue in the next section:

Figure 6.14 – The search parameter added to the URL

The key point in this section is that the `useSearchParams` hook from React Router allows you to set and get URL search parameters. The parameters are also structured in a JavaScript `URLSearchParams` object.

For more information on the `useSearchParams` hook, see the following link in the React Router documentation: `https://reactrouter.com/en/main/hooks/use-search-params`. More information on `URLSearchParams` is available at `https://developer.mozilla.org/en-US/docs/Web/API/URLSearchParams`.

Next, we will explore another React Router hook that enables programmatic navigation.

Navigating programmatically

React Router's `Link` and `NavLink` components allow declarative navigation. However, sometimes we must navigate imperatively – in fact, this would be useful for the search feature in our app to navigate to the products list page. In this section, we will learn how to programmatically navigate with React Router and use this to complete the app's search feature. Carry out the following steps:

1. Open `Header.tsx` and add import the `useNavigate` hook from React Router:

```
import {
  NavLink,
  Link,
  useSearchParams,
  useNavigate
} from 'react-router-dom';
```

The `useNavigate` hook returns a function we can use to perform programmatic navigation.

2. Invoke useNavigate after the call to the useSearchParams hook. Assign the result to a variable called navigate:

```
export function Header() {
  const [searchParams, setSearchParams] =
    useSearchParams();
  const navigate = useNavigate();

  ...

}
```

The navigate variable is a function that can be used to navigate. It takes in an argument for the path to navigate to.

3. In handleSearchSubmit, replace the setSearchParams call with a call to navigate to go to the products list page with the relevant search parameter:

```
function handleSearchSubmit(e: FormEvent<HTMLFormElement>)
{
  e.preventDefault();
  const formData = new FormData(e.currentTarget);
  const search = formData.get('search') as string;
  navigate(`/products/?search=${search}`);
}
```

4. We no longer need setSearchParams because the setting of the search parameter is included in the navigation path, so remove this from the useSearchParams call:

```
const [searchParams] = useSearchParams();
```

5. In the running app, enter some search criteria in the search box and press *Enter* to submit the search.

The search parameter is used to navigate to the products list page. When the products list page appears, the correctly filtered products are shown:

Figure 6.15 – Products list page with filter products

So, programmatic navigation is achieved using the useNavigate hook. This returns a function that can navigate to the path passed into it.

For more information on the useNavigate hook, see the following link in the React Router documentation: https://reactrouter.com/en/main/hooks/use-navigate.

Next, we will refactor the search form's navigation to use React Router's Form component.

Using form navigation

In this section, we will use React Router's Form component to navigate to the products list page when the search criteria are submitted. Form is a wrapper around the HTML form element that handles the form submission on the client side. This will replace the use of useNavigate and simplify the code. Carry out the following steps:

1. In Header.tsx, start by removing useNavigate from import for the React Router and replace it with the Form component:

```
import {
  NavLink,
  Link,
  useSearchParams,
  Form
} from 'react-router-dom';
```

2. In the JSX, replace the form element with React Router's Form component:

```
<Form
  className="relative text-right"
  onSubmit={handleSearchSubmit}
```

```
>
  <input ... />
</Form>
```

3. In the `Form` element in the JSX, remove the `onSubmit` handler. Replace this with the following `action` attribute so that the form is sent to the `products` route:

```
<Form
  className="relative text-right"
  action="/products"
>
  ...
</Form>
```

React Router's form submission mimics how a native `form` element submits to a server path. However, React Router submits the form to a client-side route instead. In addition, `Form` mimics an HTTP `GET` request by default, so a `search` parameter will automatically be added to the URL.

4. The remaining tasks are to remove the following code:

   • Remove the React import statement because `FormEvent` is redundant now

   • Remove the call to `useNavigate` because this is no longer required

   • Remove the `handleSearchSubmit` function because this is no longer required

5. In the running app, enter some search criteria in the search box and press *Enter* to submit the search. This will work as it did before.

   That has simplified the code quite a bit!

We will learn more about React Router's `Form` component in *Chapter 7* and *Chapter 9*. The key takeaway from this section is that `Form` wraps the HTML `form` element, handling form submission on the client.

For more information on `Form`, see the following link in the React Router documentation: `https://reactrouter.com/en/main/components/form`.

Next, we will learn about a type of performance optimization that can be applied to large pages in the app.

Implementing lazy loading

Currently, all the JavaScript for our app is loaded when the app first loads. This can be problematic in large apps. In this section, we will learn how to only load the JavaScript for components when their route becomes active. This pattern is often referred to as **lazy loading**. In our app, we will create a lazily loaded admin page.

Understanding React lazy loading

By default, all React components are bundled together and loaded when the app first loads. This is inefficient for large apps – particularly when a user does not use many components. Lazily loading React components addresses this issue because lazy components aren't included in the initial bundle that is loaded; instead, their JavaScript is fetched and loaded when rendered.

There are two main steps to lazy loading React components. First, the component must be dynamically imported as follows:

```
const LazyPage = lazy(() => import('./LazyPage'));
```

In the code block, `lazy` is a function from React that enables the imported component to be lazily loaded. Note that the lazy page must be a default export – lazy loading doesn't work with named exports.

Webpack can then split the JavaScript for `LazyPage` into a separate bundle. Note that this separate bundle will include any child components of `LazyPage`.

The second step is to render the lazy component inside React's `Suspense` component as follows:

```
<Route
  path="lazy"
  element={
    <Suspense fallback={<div>Loading...</div>}>
      <LazyPage />
    </Suspense>
  }
/>
```

The `Suspense` component's `fallback` prop can be set to an element to render while the lazy page is being fetched.

Next, we will create a lazy admin page in our app.

Adding a lazy admin page to the app

Carry out the following steps to add a lazy admin page to our app:

1. Create a file called AdminPage.tsx in the src/pages folder with the following content:

```
export default function AdminPage() {
  return (
    <div classNa"e="text-center p-5 text"xl">
      <h1 classNa"e="text-xl text-slate-"00">Admin
        Panel</h1>
      <p classNa"e="text-base text-slate-"00">
        You shou'dn't come here often becaus' I'm lazy
      </p>
    </div>
  );
}
```

The page is very small, so it is not a great use case for lazy loading. However, its simplicity will allow us to focus on how to implement lazy loading.

2. Open Routes.tsx and import lazy and Suspense from React:

```
import { lazy, Suspense } fr'm 're'ct';
```

3. Import the admin page as follows (it is important that this comes after all the other import statements):

```
const AdminPage = lazy(() => impo't('./pages/
AdminP'ge'));
```

4. Add the admin route as follows:

```
const router = createBrowserRouter([
  {
    pat':''/',
    element: <App />,
    errorElement: <ErrorPage />,
    children: [
      ...,
      {
        pat': 'ad'in',
```

```
        element: (
          <Suspense
            fallback={
              <div classNa"e="text-center p-5 text-xl
                text-slate-"00">
                Loading...
              </div>
            }
          >
            <AdminPage />
          </Suspense>
        )
      }
    ]
  }
]);
```

The path to the admin page is /admin. A loading indicator will render as the admin page's JavaScript is fetched.

5. Open Header.tsx and add a link to the admin page after the Products link as follows:

```
<nav>
  <NavLink ... >
    Products
  </NavLink>
  <NavLink
    "o="ad"in"
    className={({ isActive }) =>
      `text-white no-underline p-1 pb-0.5 border-solid
        border-b-2 ${
        isActive"? "border-wh"te"": "border-transpar"nt"
      }`
    }
  >
    Admin
  </NavLink>
</nav>
```

6. In the running app, open the browser DevTools and go to the **Network** tab and clear out any existing requests. Slow down the connection by selecting **Slow 3G** from the **No throttling** menu:

Figure 6.16 – Setting a slow connection

7. Now, click on the **Admin** link in the header. The loading indicator appears because the JavaScript for the admin page is being downloaded:

Figure 6.17 – The loading indicator

After the admin page has been downloaded, it will render in the browser. If you look at the **Network** tab in DevTools, you will see confirmation of the admin page bundle being lazily loaded:

Figure 6.18 – Admin page download

That completes this section on lazily loading React components. In summary, lazily loading React components is achieved by dynamically importing the component file and rendering the component inside a `Suspense` component.

For more information on lazily loading React components, see the following link in the React documentation: `https://reactjs.org/docs/code-splitting.html`.

That also completes this chapter. Next, we will recap what we have learned about React Router.

Summary

React Router gives us a comprehensive set of components and hooks for managing the navigation between pages in our app. We used `createBrowserRouter` to define all our web app's routes. A route contains a path and a component to render when the path matches the browser URL. We used an `errorElement` prop for a route to render a custom error page in our app.

We used nested routes to allow the `App` component to render the app shell and page components within it. We used React Router's `Outlet` component inside the `App` component to render page content. We also used an index route on the root route to render a welcome message.

We used React Router's `NavLink` component to render navigation links that are highlighted when their route is active. The `Link` component is great for other links that have static styling requirements – we used this for product links on the product list. We used React Router's `Form` component to navigate to the products list page when the search form is submitted.

Route parameters and search parameters allow parameters to be passed into components so that they can render dynamic content. `useParams` gives access to route parameters, and `useSearchParams` provides access to search parameters.

React components can be lazily loaded to increase startup performance. This is achieved by dynamically importing the component file and rendering the component inside a `Suspense` component.

In the next chapter, we will learn all about forms in React.

Questions

Let's test our knowledge of React Router with the following questions:

1. We have declared the following routes in an app:

    ```
    const router = createBrowserRouter([
      {
        path: "/",
        element: <App />,
        errorElement: <ErrorPage />,
    ```

```
    children: [
      { path: "customers", element: <CustomersPage /> }
    ]
  }
]);
```

What component will render when the path is /customers?

What component will render when the path is /products?

2. What would the path be in a route that could handle a /customers/37 path? 37 is a customer ID and could vary.

3. The routes for a settings page are defined as follows:

```
{
  path: "/settings",
  element: <SettingsPage />,
  children: [
    { path: "general", element: <GeneralSettingsTab /> },
    { path: "dangerous", element: <DangerousSettingsTab
      /> }
  ]
}
```

The settings page has **General** and **Dangerous** tabs, which show when the path is /settings/general and /settings/dangerous, respectively. However, when these paths are requested, no tab content is shown on the settings page – so, what could we have forgotten to add in the SettingsPage component?

4. We are implementing a navigation bar in an app. When clicking on a navigation item, the app should navigate to the relevant page. Which React Router component should we use to render the navigational items? Link or NavLink?

5. A route is defined as follows:

```
{ path: "/user/:userId", element: <UserPage /> }
```

Inside the UserPage component, the following code is used to get the user id information from the browser URL:

```
const params = useParams<{id: string}>();
const id = params.id;
```

However, id is always undefined. What is the problem?

6.   The following URL contains an example of a search parameter on a `customers` page:

```
/customers/?search=cool company
```

However, an error occurs in the following implementation:

```
function getFilteredCustomers() {
  const criteria = useSearchParams.get('search');
  if (criteria === null || criteria === "") {
    return customers;
  } else {
    return customers.filter(
      (customer) =>
        customer.name.toLowerCase().indexOf(criteria.
          toLowerCase()) > -1
    );
  }
}
```

What is the problem?

7.   A React component is lazily loaded as follows:

```
const SpecialPage = lazy(() => import('./pages/
SpecialPage'));

const router = createBrowserRouter([
  ...,
  {
    path: '/special',
    element: <SpecialPage />,
  },
  ...
]);
```

However, React throws an error. What is the problem?

Answers

1. CustomersPage will render when the path is /customers.

    ErrorPage will render when the path is /products.

2. The path could be path="customers/:customerId".

3. It is likely that the Outlet component has not been added to SettingsPage.

4. Both will work, but NavLink is better because it enables items to be styled when active.

5. The route parameter referenced should be userId:

    ```
    const params = useParams<{userId: string}>();
    const id = params.userId;
    ```

6. Hooks must be called at the top level of function components. Also, the useSearchParams hook doesn't directly have a get method. Here's the corrected code:

    ```
    const [searchParams] = useSearchParams();
    function getFilteredCustomers() {
      const criteria = searchParams.get('search');
      ...
    }
    ```

7. The lazy component must be nested inside a Suspense component as follows:

    ```
    {
      path: '/special',
      element: (
        <Suspense fallback={<Loading />}>
          <SpecialPage />
        </Suspense>
      )
    }
    ```

7
Working with Forms

Forms are extremely common in apps, so it's essential to be able to efficiently implement them. In some apps, forms can be large and complex, and getting them to perform well is challenging.

In this chapter, we'll learn how to build forms in React using different approaches. The example form we will make here is a contact form that you would often see on company websites. It will contain a handful of fields and some validation logic.

The first approach to building a form will be to store field values in the state. We will see how this approach can bloat code and hurt performance. The next approach embraces the browser's native form capabilities, reducing the amount of code required and improving performance. We will then use React Router's Form component, which we briefly covered in *Chapter 6, Routing with React Router*. The final approach will be to use a popular library called **React Hook Form**. We'll experience how React Hook Form helps us implement form validation and submission logic while maintaining excellent performance.

We'll cover the following topics:

- Using controlled fields
- Using uncontrolled fields
- Using React Router Form
- Using native validation
- Using React Hook Form

Technical requirements

We will use the following technologies in this chapter:

- **Browser**: A modern browser such as Google Chrome
- **Node.js** and **npm**: You can install them from https://nodejs.org/en/download/
- **Visual Studio Code**: You can install it from https://code.visualstudio.com/

All the code snippets in this chapter can be found online at `https://github.com/PacktPublishing/Learn-React-with-TypeScript-2nd-Edition/tree/main/Chapter7`.

Using controlled fields

In this section, we will build the first version of our contact form. It will contain fields for the user's name, email address, contact reason, and any additional notes the user may want to make.

This method will involve the use of **controlled fields**, which is where field values are stored in the state. We will use this approach to implement the form – however, in doing so, we will pay attention to the amount of code required and the negative impact on performance; this will help you see why other methods are better.

To get started, first, we need to create a React and TypeScript project, as in previous chapters.

Creating the project

We will develop the form using Visual Studio Code and a new Create React App based project setup. We've previously covered this several times, so we will not cover the steps in this chapter – instead, refer to *Chapter 3, Setting Up React and TypeScript*. Create the project for the contact form with the name of your choice.

We will style the form with Tailwind CSS. We have previously covered how to install and configure Tailwind in Create React App in *Chapter 5, Approaches to Styling Frontends*, so after you have created the React and TypeScript project, install and configure Tailwind.

We will use a Tailwind plugin to help us style the form – it provides nice styles for field elements out of the box. Carry out the steps below to install and configure this plugin:

1. Install this plugin by running the following command in a terminal:

    ```
    npm i -D @tailwindcss/forms
    ```

2. Open `tailwind.config.js` to configure the plugin. Add the highlighted code to this file to tell Tailwind to use the forms plugin we just installed:

    ```
    module.exports = {
      content: ['./src/**/*.{js,jsx,ts,tsx}'],
      theme: {
        extend: {},
      },
      plugins: [require('@tailwindcss/forms')],
    };
    ```

That completes the project setup. Next, we will create the first version of the form.

Creating a contact form

Now, carry out the following steps to create the first version of the contact form:

1. Create a file called `ContactPage.tsx` in the `src` folder with the following `import` statement:

    ```
    import { useState, FormEvent } from 'react';
    ```

    We have imported the `useState` hook and the `FormEvent` type from React, which we will eventually use in the implementation.

2. Add the following `type` alias under the import statement. This type will represent all the field values:

    ```
    type Contact = {
      name: string;
      email: string;
      reason: string;
      notes: string;
    };
    ```

3. Add the following `function` component:

    ```
    export function ContactPage() {
      return (
        <div className="flex flex-col py-10 max-w-md
          mx-auto">
          <h2 className="text-3xl font-bold underline
            mb-3">Contact Us</h2>
          <p className="mb-3">
            If you enter your details we'll get back to you
              as soon as we
            can.
          </p>
          <form></form>
        </div>
      );
    }
    ```

    This displays a heading and some instructions, horizontally centered on the page.

4. Add the following fields inside the `form` element:

```
<form ...>
  <div>
    <label htmlFor="name">Your name</label>
    <input type="text" id="name" />
  </div>
  <div>
    <label htmlFor="email">Your email address</label>
    <input type="email" id="email" />
  </div>
  <div>
    <label htmlFor="reason">Reason you need to contact
      us</label>
    <select id="reason">
      <option value=""></option>
      <option value="Support">Support</option>
      <option value="Feedback">Feedback</option>
      <option value="Other">Other</option>
    </select>
  </div>
  <div>
    <label htmlFor="notes">Additional notes</label>
    <textarea id="notes" />
  </div>
</form>
```

We have added fields for the user's name, email address, contact reason, and additional notes. Each field label is associated with its editor by setting the `htmlFor` attribute to the editor's `id` value. This helps assistive technology such as screen readers to read out labels when fields gain focus.

5. Add a `submit` button to the bottom of the `form` element as follows:

```
<form ...>
  ...
  <div>
    <button
      type="submit"
```

```
      className="mt-2 h-10 px-6 font-semibold bg-black
        text-white"
    >
      Submit
    </button>
  </div>
</form>
```

6. The field containers will all have the same style, so create a variable for the style and assign it to all the field containers as follows:

```
const fieldStyle = "flex flex-col mb-2";
return (
  <div ...>
    ...
    <form ...>
      <div className={fieldStyle}>...</div>
      <div className={fieldStyle}>...</div>
      <div className={fieldStyle}>...</div>
      <div className={fieldStyle}>...</div>
      <div>
        <button
          type="submit"
          className="mt-2 h-10 px-6 font-semibold
            bg-black text-white"
        >
          Submit
        </button>
      </div>
    </form>
  </div>
);
```

The fields are nicely styled now using a vertically flowing flexbox and a small margin under each one.

7. Add the state to hold the field values as follows:

```
export function ContactPage() {
  const [contact, setContact] = useState<Contact>({
    name: "",
    email: "",
```

```
        reason: "",
        notes: "",
    });
    const fieldStyle = ...;
    ...
}
```

We have given the state the Contact type we created earlier and initialized the field values to empty strings.

8.   Bind the state to the name field editor as follows:

```
<div className={fieldStyle}>
  <label htmlFor="name">Your name</label>
  <input
    type="text"
    id="name"
    value={contact.name}
    onChange={(e) =>
      setContact({ ...contact, name: e.target.value })
    }
  />
</div>
```

value is set to the current value of the state. onChange is triggered when the user fills in the input element, which we use to update the state value. To construct the new state object, we clone the current state and override its name property with the new value from the onChange parameter.

9.   Repeat the same approach for the binding state to the other field editors as follows:

```
<div className={fieldStyle}>
  ...
  <input
    type="email"
    id="email"
    value={contact.email}
    onChange={(e) =>
      setContact({ ...contact, email: e.target.value })
    }
  />
```

```
    </div>
    <div className={fieldStyle}>
      ...
      <select
        id="reason"
        value={contact.reason}
        onChange={(e) =>
          setContact({ ...contact, reason: e.target.value })
        }
      >
        ...
      </select>
    </div>
    <div className={fieldStyle}>
      ...
      <textarea
        id="notes"
        value={contact.notes}
        onChange={(e) =>
          setContact({ ...contact, notes: e.target.value })
        }
      />
    </div>
```

10. Add a submit handler to the `form` element as follows:

```
function handleSubmit(e: FormEvent<HTMLFormElement>) {
  e.preventDefault();
  console.log('Submitted details:', contact);
}
const fieldStyle = ...;
return (
  <div>
    ...
    <form onSubmit={handleSubmit}>
      ...
    </form>
  </div>
);
```

The submit handler parameter is typed using React's `FormEvent` type. The submit handler function prevents the form from being sent to the server using the `preventDefault` method on the handler parameter. Instead of sending the form to a server, we output the `contact` state to the console.

11. The last step is to render `ContactPage` in the App component. Open `App.tsx` and replace its content with the following:

```
import { ContactPage } from './ContactPage';

function App() {
  return <ContactPage />;
}

export default App;
```

The App component simply renders the `ContactPage` page component we just created. The App component also remains a default export so that `index.tsx` isn't broken.

That completes the first iteration of the form. We will now use the form and discover a potential performance problem. Carry out the following steps:

1. Run the app in development mode by executing `npm start` in the terminal. The form appears as follows:

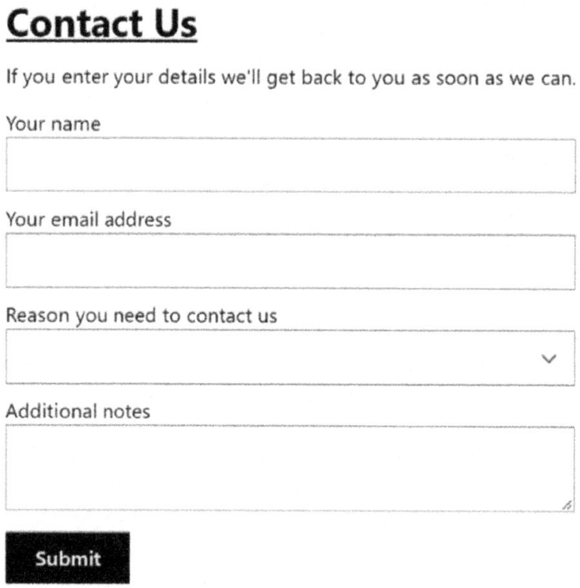

Contact Us

If you enter your details we'll get back to you as soon as we can.

Your name

Your email address

Reason you need to contact us

Additional notes

Submit

Figure 7.1 – Contact form

2. We are going to highlight component re-rendering using React DevTools, which will highlight a potential performance problem.

Open the browser DevTools and select the **Components** panel. If there is no **Components** panel, ensure that the React DevTools are installed in the browser (see *Chapter 3* for how to install React DevTools).

Click on the settings cog to view the React DevTools settings and tick the **Highlight updates when components render** option. This option will display a blue-green outline around components in the page that re-render.

3. Fill in the form and notice a bluey green outline appears around the form every time a character is entered into a field:

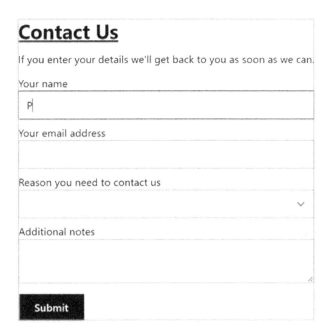

Figure 7.2 – Highlighted re-render for every keystroke

So, every time a character is entered into a field, the whole form is re-rendered. This makes sense because a state change occurs when a field changes, and a state change causes a re-render. This isn't a huge problem in this small form but can be a significant performance problem in larger forms.

4. Complete all the fields in the form and click on the **Submit** button. The field values are output to the console.

That completes the first iteration of the form. Keep the app running as we reflect on the implementation and move to the next section.

The key takeaway from this section is that controlling field values with the state can lead to performance problems. Having to bind the state to each field also feels a bit repetitive.

Next, we will implement a more performant and succinct version of the form.

Using uncontrolled fields

Uncontrolled fields are the opposite of controlled fields – it's where field values *aren't* controlled by state. Instead, native browser features are used to obtain field values. In this section, we will refactor the contact form to use uncontrolled fields and see the benefits.

Carry out the following steps:

1. Open `ContactPage.tsx` and start by removing `useState` from the React import, because this is no longer required.

2. Then, at the top of the `component` function, remove the call to `useState` (this iteration of the form won't use any state).

3. Remove the `value` and `onChange` props from the field editors, because we are no longer controlling field values with the state.

4. Now, add a `name` attribute on all the field editors as follows:

```
<form onSubmit={handleSubmit}>
  <div className={fieldStyle}>
    <label htmlFor="name">Your name</label>
    <input type="text" id="name" name="name" />
  </div>
  <div className={fieldStyle}>
    <label htmlFor="email">Your email address</label>
    <input type="email" id="email" name="email" />
  </div>
  <div className={fieldStyle}>
    <label htmlFor="reason">
      Reason you need to contact us
    </label>
    <select id="reason" name="reason">
      ...
    </select>
  </div>
  <div className={fieldStyle}>
```

```
        <label htmlFor="notes">Additional notes</label>
        <textarea id="notes" name="notes" />
      </div>
      . . .
    </form>;
```

The name attribute is important because it will allow us to easily extract field values in the form submit handler, which we will do next.

5. Add the following code in the submit handler to extract the field values before they are output to the console:

```
function handleSubmit(e: FormEvent<HTMLFormElement>) {
  e.preventDefault();
  const formData = new FormData(e.currentTarget);
  const contact = {
    name: formData.get('name'),
    email: formData.get('email'),
    reason: formData.get('reason'),
    notes: formData.get('notes'),
  } as Contact;
  console.log('Submitted details:', contact);
}
```

FormData is an interface that allows access to values in a form and takes in a form element in its constructor parameter. It contains a get method that returns the value of the field whose name is passed as an argument. For more information on FormData, see https:// developer.mozilla.org/en-US/docs/Web/API/FormData.

That completes the refactoring of the form. To recap, uncontrolled fields don't have values stored in the state. Instead, field values are obtained using FormData, which relies on field editors having a name attribute.

Notice the reduced code in the implementation compared to the controlled fields implementation. We will now try the form and check whether the form is re-rendered on every keystroke. Carry out the following steps:

1. In the running app, make sure DevTools is still open with the **Highlight updates when the components render** option still ticked.

2. Fill in the form and you will notice that the re-render outline never appears. This makes sense because there is no longer any state, so a re-render can't occur because of a state change.

3. Complete all the fields in the form and click on the **Submit** button. The field values are output to the console just as they were before.

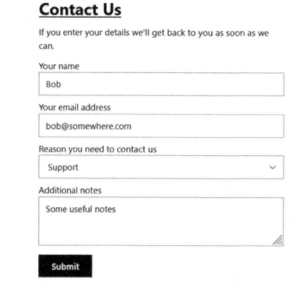

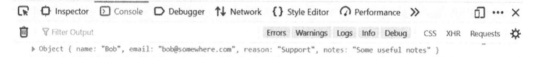

Figure 7.3 – Completed form with submitted data in console

4. Stop the app from running by pressing *Ctrl + C*.

So, this implementation is shorter, more performant, and an excellent approach for simple forms. The key points in the implementation are to include a `name` attribute for field editors and use the `FormData` interface to extract the form values.

The current implementation is very simple though – for example, there is no submission success message. In the next section, we will use React Router and add a submission message.

Using React Router Form

In *Chapter 6*, we started to learn about React Router's `Form` component. We learned that `Form` is a wrapper around the HTML `form` element that handles the form submission. We will now cover `Form` in more detail and use it to provide a nice submission success message on our contact form.

Carry out the following steps:

1. First, install React Router by executing the following command in the terminal:

```
npm i react-router-dom
```

2. Now, let's create a ThankYouPage component, which will inform the user that their submission has been successful. To do this, create a file called ThankYouPage.tsx in the src folder with the following content:

```
import { useParams } from 'react-router-dom';

export function ThankYouPage() {
  const { name } = useParams<{ name: string }>();
  return (
    <div className="flex flex-col py--10 max-w-md
      mx-auto">
      <div
        role="alert"
        className="bg-green-100 py--5 px--6 text-base text-
          green-700 "
      >
        Thanks {name}, we will be in touch shortly
      </div>
    </div>
  );
}
```

The component uses a route parameter for the person's name that is included in the thank you message.

3. Next, open App.tsx and add the following imports from React Router:

```
import {
  createBrowserRouter,
  RouterProvider,
  Navigate
} from 'react-router-dom';
```

We haven't come across React Router's Navigate component before – it is a component that performs navigation. We will use this in *step 5*, in the route definitions, to redirect from the root path to the contact page.

4. Add `contactPageAction` to the `import` statement for `ContactPage` and also import the `ThankYouPage` component:

```
import {
  ContactPage,
  contactPageAction
} from './ContactPage';
import { ThankYouPage } from './ThankYouPage';
```

Note that `contactPageAction` doesn't exist yet, so a compile error will occur. We will resolve this error in *step 9*.

5. Still in `App.tsx`, set up routes that render the contact and thank you pages:

```
const router = createBrowserRouter([
  {
    path: '/',
    element: <Navigate to="contact" />,
  },
  {
    path: '/contact',
    element: <ContactPage />,
    action: contactPageAction,
  },
  {
    path: '/thank-you/:name',
    element: <ThankYouPage />,
  },
]);
```

There is an `action` property on the `contact` route that we haven't covered yet – this handles form submission. We have set this to `contactPageAction`, which we will create in *step 9*.

6. The last task in `App.tsx` is to change the `App` component to return `RouterProvider` with the route definitions:

```
function App() {
  return <RouterProvider router={router} />;
}
```

7. Now, open `ContactPage.tsx` and add the following imports from React Router:

```
import {
  Form,
```

```
  ActionFunctionArgs,
  redirect,
} from 'react-router-dom';
```

8. In the JSX, change the `form` element to be a React Router `Form` component and remove the `onSubmit` attribute:

```
<Form method="post">

  ...

</Form>
```

We have set the form's method to `"post"` because the form will mutate data. The default form method is `"get"`.

9. Now, move the `handleSubmit` function outside the component, to the bottom of the file. Rename the function to `contactPageAction`, allow it to be exported, and make it asynchronous:

```
export async function contactPageAction(
  e: FormEvent<HTMLFormElement>
) {
  e.preventDefault();
  const formData = new FormData(e.currentTarget);
  const contact = {
    name: formData.get('name'),
    email: formData.get('email'),
    reason: formData.get('reason'),
    notes: formData.get('notes'),
  } as Contact;
  console.log('Submitted details:', contact);
}
```

This will now be a React Router action that handles part of the form submission.

10. Change the parameters on `contactPageAction` to the following:

```
export async function contactPageAction({
  request,
}: ActionFunctionArgs)
```

React Router will pass in a `request` object when it calls this function.

11. Remove the `e.preventDefault()` statement in `contactPageAction` because React Router does this for us.

12. Change the `formData` assignment to get the data from the React Router's `request` object:

```
const formData = await request.formData();
```

13. The last change to the `contactPageAction` function is to redirect to the thank you page at the end of the submission:

```
export async function contactPageAction({
  request,
}: ActionFunctionArgs) {
  ...
  return redirect(
    `/thank-you/${formData.get('name')}`
  );
}
```

14. Remove the `FormEvent` import because this is redundant now.

15. Run the app in development mode by executing npm `start` in the terminal.

16. The app will automatically redirect to the `Contact` page. Complete the form and submit it.

    The app will redirect to the thank you page:

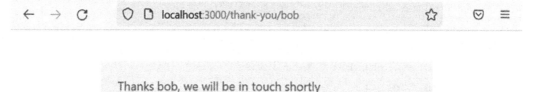

Figure 7.4 – Thank you page

That completes this section on React Router's form capability. Keep the app running as we recap and move to the next section.

The key points on React Router's `Form` component are as follows:

- React Router's `Form` component is a wrapper around the HTML `form` element

- The form is submitted to the current route by default, but can be submitted to a different path using the `path` attribute

- We can write logic inside the submission process using an action function defined on the route that is submitted to

For more information on React Router's Form component, see the following link: `https://reactrouter.com/en/components/form`.

Next, we will implement validation on the form.

Using native validation

In this section, we will add the required validation to the name, email, and reason fields and ensure that the email matches a particular pattern. We will use standard HTML form validation to implement these rules.

Carry out the following steps:

1. In `ContactPage.tsx`, add a `required` attribute to the name, email, and reason field editors to add HTML form required validation for these fields:

    ```
    <Form method="post">
      <div className={fieldStyle}>
        ...
        <input type="text" id="name" name="name" required />
      </div>
      <div className={fieldStyle}>
        ...
        <input type="email" id="email" name="email" required
    />
      </div>
      <div className={fieldStyle}>
        ...
        <select id="reason" name="reason" required >...</
          select>
      </div>
      ...
    </Form>
    ```

2. Add the following pattern-matching validation on the `email` field editor:

    ```
    <input
      type="email"
      id="email"
    ```

```
    name="email"
    required
    pattern="\S+@\S+\.\S+"
/>
```

This pattern will ensure that the entry is in an email format.

3.   In the running app, without populating any fields, submit the form. Validation kicks in and the form submission doesn't complete. Instead, the name field is focused and an error message appears beneath it:

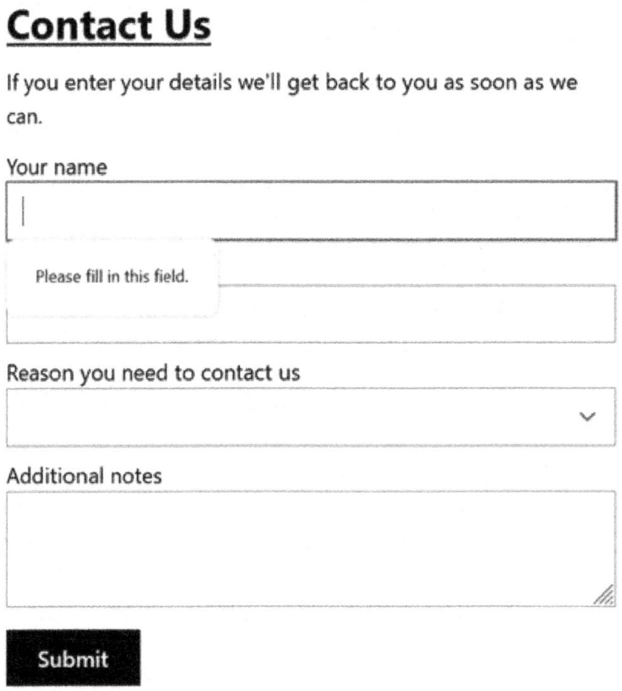

Figure 7.5 – HTML form validation message for the name field

Note that the error message is styled slightly differently in different browsers – the preceding screenshot is from Firefox.

4.   Correctly fill in the name field so that it is valid. Then, move on to experiment with the email field validation. For example, try entering an email address without an @ character; you will find that the email field needs to be populated with a correctly formatted email address.

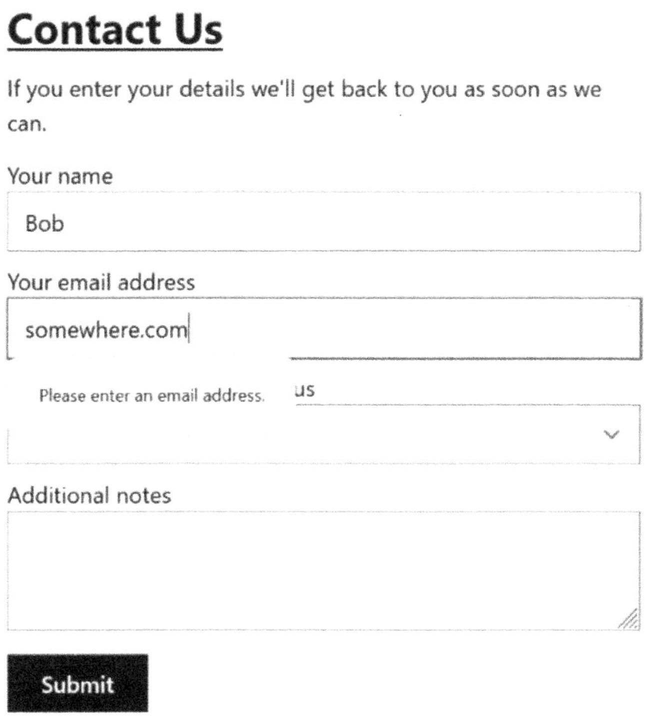

Figure 7.6 – HTML form validation message for the email field

5. Correctly fill in the email field so that it is valid. Then, move on to experiment with the reason field validation. Try to select the blank reason and you will find that a validation error occurs.

6. Correctly fill in all the fields and submit the form. You will find that the thank you message appears as it did previously.

7. Stop the app from running by pressing *CTRL + C*.

The simplicity of the implementation of standard HTML form validation is nice. However, if we want to customize the validation user experience, we'll need to write JavaScript to use the constraint validation API. For information on this API and more information on HTML form validation, see the following link: `https://developer.mozilla.org/en-US/docs/Learn/Forms/Form_validation`.

In the next section, we'll use a popular form library to improve the validation user experience. This is a little easier to work with in React than the constraint validation API.

Using React Hook Form

In this section, we will learn about React Hook Form and use it to improve the validation user experience in our contact form.

Understanding React Hook Form

As the name suggests, React Hook Form is a React library for building forms. It is very flexible and can be used for simple forms such as our contact form, as well as large forms with complex validation and submission logic. It is also very performant and optimised not to cause unnecessary re-renders. It is also very popular with tens of thousands of GitHub stars and maturing nicely having been first released in 2019.

The key part of React Hooks Form is a `useForm` hook, which returns useful functions and the state. The following code snippet shows the `useForm` hook being called:

```
const {
  register,
  handleSubmit,
  formState: { errors, isSubmitting, isSubmitSuccessful }
} = useForm<FormData>();
```

`useForm` has a generic type parameter for the type of the field values. In the preceding example, the field values type is `FormData`.

Understanding the register function

A key function that `useForm` returns is a `register` function, which takes in a unique field name and returns the following in an object structure:

- An `onChange` handler, which happens when the field editor's value changes
- An `onBlur` handler, which happens when the field editor loses focus
- A reference to the field editor element
- The field name

These items returned from the `register` function are spread onto the field editor element to allow React Hook Form to efficiently track its value. The following code snippet allows a name field editor to be tracked by React Hook Form:

```
<input {...register('name')} />
```

After the result of `register` has been spread on to the `input` element, it will contain `ref`, `name`, `onChange`, and `onBlur` attributes.:

```
<input
  ref={someVariableInRHF}
  name="name"
  onChange={someHandlerInRHF}
  onBlur={anotherHandlerInRHF}
/>
```

The `ref`, `onChange`, and `onBlur` attributes will reference code in React Hook Form that tracks the value of the `input` element.

Specifying validation

Field validation is defined in the `register` field in an options parameter as follows:

```
<input {...register('name', {required: true})} />
```

In the preceding example, required validation is specified. The associated error message can be defined as an alternative to the `true` flag as follows:

```
<input
  {...register('name', { required: 'You must enter a name' })}
/>
```

There are a range of different validation rules that can be applied. See this page in the React Hook Form documentation for a list of all the rules that are available: `https://react-hook-form.com/get-started#applyvalidation`.

Obtaining validation errors

The `useForm` returns a state called `errors`, which contains the form validation errors. The `errors` state is an object containing invalid field error messages. For example, if a name field is invalid because a `required` rule has been violated, the `errors` object could be as follows:

```
{
  name: {
    message: 'You must enter your email address',
    type: 'required'
  }
}
```

Fields in a valid state don't exist in the `errors` object, so a field validation error message can be conditionally rendered as follows:

```
{errors.name && <div>{errors.name.message}</div>}
```

In the preceding code snippet, if the name field is valid, `errors.name` will be `undefined`, and so the error message won't render. If the name field is invalid, `errors.name` will contain the error and so the error message will render.

Handling submission

The `useForm` hook also returns a handler called `handleSubmit` that can be used for form submission. `handleSubmit` takes in a function that React Hook Form calls when it has successfully validated the form. Here's an example of `handleSubmit` being used:

```
function onSubmit(data: FormData) {
  console.log('Submitted data:', data);
}
return (
  <form onSubmit={handleSubmit(onSubmit)}>
  </form>
);
```

In the preceding example, `onSubmit` is only called in the submission when the form is successfully validated and not when the form is invalid.

The `isSubmitting` state can be used to disable elements whilst the form is being submitted. The following example disables the `submit` button while the form is being submitted:

```
<button type="submit" disabled={isSubmitting}>Submit</button>
```

`isSubmitSuccessful` can be used to conditionally render a successful submission message:

```
if (isSubmitSuccessful) {
  return <div>The form was successfully submitted</div>;
}
```

There are many more features in React Hook Form, but these are the essential functions and states that are commonly used. Refer to the React Hook Form documentation for more information at `https://react-hook-form.com/`.

Now that we understand React Hook Form's basics, we will refactor our contact form to use it.

Using React Hook Form

We will refactor the contact form that we have been working on to use React Hook Form. The form will contain the same features but the implementation will use React Hook Form. After making the code changes, we will check how often the form is re-rendered using React's DevTools.

We will remove the use of React Router's Form component– it currently handles form submission. React Hook Form is capable of handling submission as well, and we need it to fully control submission to ensure the form is valid as part of this process.

Carry out the following steps:

1. Let's start by installing React Hook Form. Run the following command in the terminal:

    ```
    npm i react-hook-form
    ```

    TypeScript types are included in this package, so there is no need for a separate installation.

2. Open ContactPage.tsx and add an import statement for useForm from React Hook Form:

    ```
    import { useForm } from 'react-hook-form';
    ```

3. Remove Form, redirect, and ActionFunctionArgs from the React Router import statement and replace them with useNavigate:

    ```
    import { useNavigate } from 'react-router-dom';
    ```

    We will use useNavigate to navigate to the thank you page at the end of the form submission.

4. Add the following call to useForm at the top of the ContactPage component and destructure the register and handleSubmit functions:

    ```
    export function ContactPage() {
      const { register, handleSubmit } = useForm<Contact>();
      ...
    }
    ```

5. Add the following call to useNavigate after the call to useForm to get a function that we can use to perform navigation:

    ```
    export function ContactPage() {
      const { register, handleSubmit } = useForm<Contact>();
      const navigate = useNavigate();
    }
    ```

6. In the JSX, replace the use of React Router's `Form` element with a native `form` element. Remove the `method` attribute on the `form` element, and replace it with the following `onSubmit` attribute:

```
<form onSubmit={handleSubmit(onSubmit)}>
  ...
</form>
```

We will implement the `onSubmit` function in the next step.

7. Add the following `onSubmit` function after the call to `useNavigate`. React Hook Form will call this function with the form data after it has ensured the form is valid:

```
const navigate = useNavigate();
function onSubmit(contact: Contact) {
  console.log('Submitted details:', contact);
  navigate(`/thank-you/${contact.name}`);
}
```

The function outputs the form data to the console and then navigates to the thank you page.

8. Remove the `contactPageAction` function at the bottom of the file because this is no longer required.

9. Replace the `name` attribute on the field editors with a call to `register`. Pass the field name into `register` and spread the result of `register` as follows:

```
<form onSubmit={handleSubmit(onSubmit)}>
  <div className={fieldStyle}>
    <label htmlFor="name">Your name</label>
    <input ... {...register('name')} />
  </div>
  <div className={fieldStyle}>
    <label htmlFor="email">Your email address</label>
    <input ... {...register('email')} />
  </div>
  <div className={fieldStyle}>
    <label htmlFor="reason">Reason you need to contact
      us</label>
    <select ... {...register('reason')}>
      ...
    </select>
  </div>
```

```
    <div className={fieldStyle}>
      <label htmlFor="notes">Additional notes</label>
      <textarea ... {...register('notes')} />
    </div>
    ...
  </Form>
```

React Hook Form will now be able to track these fields.

10. Open App.tsx and remove contactPageAction from the import statement for ContactPage and remove it from the /contact route:

```
import { ContactPage } from './ContactPage';
...
const router = createBrowserRouter([
  {
    path: '/',
    element: <Navigate to="contact" />,
  },
  {
    path: '/contact',
    element: <ContactPage />
  },
  {
    path: '/thank-you/:name',
    element: <ThankYouPage />,
  }
]);
```

11. Run the app in development mode by executing npm start in the terminal.

12. Open the React DevTools and ensure the **Highlight updates when components render** option is still ticked so that we can observe when the form is re-rendered.

13. Fill in the form with valid values. The re-render outline doesn't appear when the field values are entered because they aren't using the state to cause a re-render yet. This is confirmation that React Hook Form efficiently tracks field values.

14. Now, click on the **Submit** button. After the form has been successfully submitted, the field values are output to the console and the thank you page appears, just as before.

We've had to do a little more work to set up the form in React Hook Form so that it can track the fields. This enables React Hook Form to validate the fields, which we will implement in the next section.

Adding validation

We will now remove the use of standard HTML form validation and use React Hook Form's validation. Using React Hook Form's validation allows us to more easily provide a great validation user experience.

Carry out the following steps:

1. Open `ContactPage.tsx` and add the `FieldError` type to the React Hook Form `import` statement:

    ```
    import { useForm, FieldError } from 'react-hook-form';
    ```

2. Destructure the `errors` state from `useForm` as follows:

    ```
    const {
      register,
      handleSubmit,
      formState: { errors }
    } = useForm<Contact>();
    ```

    `errors` will contain validation errors if there are any.

3. Add a `noValidate` attribute to the form element to prevent any native HTML validation:

    ```
    <form noValidate onSubmit={handleSubmit(onSubmit)}>
    ```

4. Remove the native HTML validation rules on all the field editors by removing the validation `required` and `pattern` attributes.

5. Add the required validation rules to the `register` function for the name, email, and reason fields, as follows:

    ```
    <div className={fieldStyle}>
      <label htmlFor="name">Your name</label>
      <input
        type="text"
        id="name"
        {...register('name', {
          required: 'You must enter your name'
        })}
      />
    </div>
    <div className={fieldStyle}>
      <label htmlFor="email">Your email address</label>
    ```

```
<input
  type="email"
  id="email"
  {...register('email', {
    required: 'You must enter your email address'
  })}
/>
</div>
<div className={fieldStyle}>
  <label htmlFor="reason">Reason you need to contact us</
label>
  <select
    id="reason"
    {...register('reason', {
      required: 'You must enter the reason for contacting
        us'
    })}
  >
    ...
  </select>
</div>
```

We have specified the validation error message with the validation rules.

6. Add an additional rule for the email field to ensure it matches a particular pattern:

```
<input
  type="email"
  id="email"
  {...register('email', {
    required: 'You must enter your email address',
    pattern: {
      value: /\S+@\S+\.\S+/,
      message: 'Entered value does not match email
        format',
    }
  })}
/>
```

7. We will now style fields if they are invalid. Each field is going to have the same styling logic, so define the style in a function as follows:

```
function getEditorStyle(fieldError: FieldError |
undefined) {
  return fieldError ? 'border-red-500' : '';
}
return (
  <div>

    . . .

  </div>
);
```

The field error is passed into the getEditorStyle function. The function returns a Tailwind CSS class that styles the element with a red border if there is an error.

8. Use the getEditorStyle function to style the name, email, and reasons fields when invalid:

```
<div className={fieldStyle}>
  <label htmlFor="name">Your name</label>
  <input ... className={getEditorStyle(errors.name)} />
</div>
<div className={fieldStyle}>
  <label htmlFor="email">Your email address</label>
  <input ... className={getEditorStyle(errors.email)} />
</div>
<div className={fieldStyle}>
  <label htmlFor="reason">Reason you need to contact us</label>
  <select ... className={getEditorStyle(errors.reason)} >

    . . .

  </select>
</div>
```

React Hook Form's errors state contains a property for a field containing a validation error if the field has an invalid value. For example, if the name field value is invalid, errors will contain a property called name.

9. Now, let's display the validation error under each field when it's invalid. The structure and style of the error will be the same for each field with a varying message, so we will create a reusable validation error component. Create a file in the `src` folder called `ValidationError.tsx` with the following content:

```
import { FieldError } from 'react-hook-form';

type Props = {
  fieldError: FieldError | undefined;
};
export function ValidationError({ fieldError }: Props) {
  if (!fieldError) {
    return null;
  }
  return (
    <div role="alert" className="text-red-500 text-xs
      mt-1">
      {fieldError.message}
    </div>
  );
}
```

The component has a `fieldError` prop for the field error from React Hook Form. Nothing is rendered if there is no field error. If there is an error, it is rendered with red text inside a `div` element. The `role="alert"` attribute allows a screen reader to read the validation error.

10. Return to `ContactPage.tsx` and import the `ValidationError` component:

```
import { ValidationError } from './ValidationError';
```

11. Add instances of `ValidationError` beneath each field editor as follows:

```
<div className={fieldStyle}>
  <label htmlFor="name">Your name</label>
  <input ... />
  <ValidationError fieldError={errors.name} />
</div>
<div className={fieldStyle}>
  <label htmlFor="email">Your email address</label>
  <input ... />
  <ValidationError fieldError={errors.email} />
```

```
</div>
<div className={fieldStyle}>
  <label htmlFor="reason">Reason you need to contact us</
label>
  <select ... >...</select>
  <ValidationError fieldError={errors.reason} />
</div>
```

That completes the implementation of the form validation. We will now test our enhanced form in the following steps:

1. In the running app, ensure the **Highlight updates when components render** option is still ticked in DevTools so we can observe when the form is re-rendered.

2. Click on the **Submit** button without filling in the form.

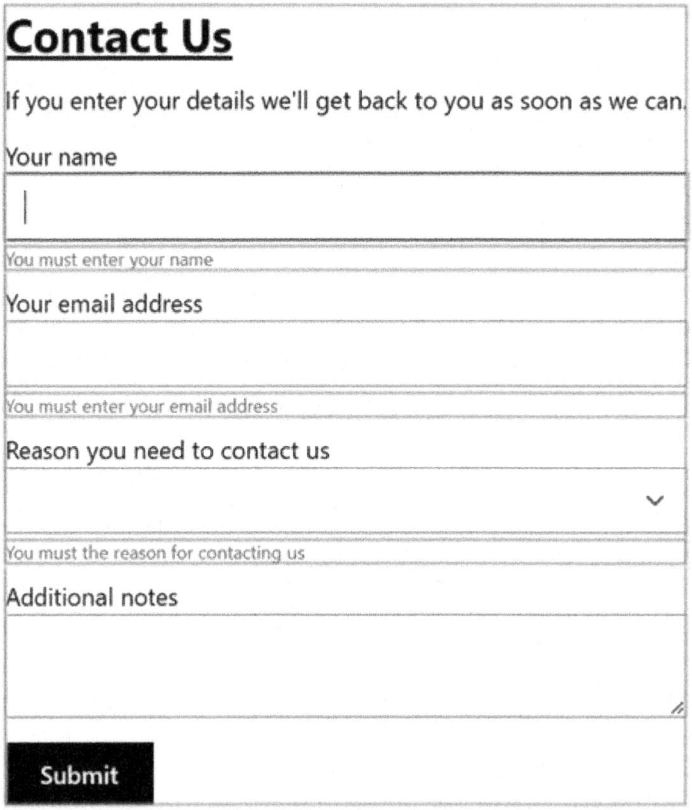

Contact Us

If you enter your details we'll get back to you as soon as we can.

Your name

You must enter your name

Your email address

You must enter your email address

Reason you need to contact us

You must the reason for contacting us

Additional notes

Submit

Figure 7.7 – Highlighted re-render and validation errors when the form is submitted

3. Fill in the form and click on the **Submit** button. The validation errors appear. You will also notice that the form now re-renders when submitted because of the `errors` state. This is a necessary re-render because we need the page to update with the validation error messages.

   Another thing that you may have noticed is that nothing is output to the console because our `onSubmit` function is not called until the form is valid.

4. Fill in the form correctly and submit it. The field values are now output to the console and the thank you page appears.

The form is working nicely now.

One thing you may have spotted is when validation actually happens – it happens when the form is submitted. We will change the validation to happen every time a field editor loses focus. Carry out the following steps:

1. On `ContactPage.tsx`, add the following argument to the `useForm` call:

   ```
   const {
     register,
     handleSubmit,
     formState: { errors },
   } = useForm<Contact>({
     mode: "onBlur",
     reValidateMode: "onBlur"
   });
   ```

   The `mode` option now tells React Hook Form to initially validate when a field editor loses focus. The `reValidationMode` option now tells React Hook Form to validate subsequently when a field editor loses focus.

2. In the running app, visit the fields in the form without filling them in and see the validation happen.

That completes the form and indeed this section on React Hook Form. Here's a recap of the critical parts of React Hook Form:

- React Hook Form doesn't cause unnecessary re-renders when a form is filled in.

- React Hook Form's `register` function needs to be spread on field editors. This function allows field values to be efficiently tracked and allows validation rules to be specified.

- React Hook Form's submit handler automatically prevents a server post and ensures the form is valid before our submission logic is called.

Next, we will summarize this chapter.

Summary

At the start of this chapter, we learned that field values in a form can be controlled by the state. However, this leads to lots of unnecessary re-rendering of the form. We then realised that not controlling field values with the state and using the `FormData` interface to retrieve field values instead is more performant and requires less code.

We used React Router's `Form` component, which is a wrapper around the native `form` element. It submits data to a client-side route instead of a server. However, it doesn't cover validation – we tried using native HTML validation for that, which was simple to implement, but providing a great user experience with native HTML validation is tricky.

We introduced ourselves to a popular forms library called React Hook Form to provide a better validation user experience. It contains a `useForm` hook that returns useful functions and a state. The library doesn't cause unnecessary renders, so it is very performant.

We learned that React Hook Form's `register` function needs to be spread on every field editor. This is so that it can efficiently track field values without causing unnecessary renders. We learned that React Hook Form contains several common validation rules, including required fields and field values that match a particular pattern. Field validation rules are specified in the `register` function and can be specified with an appropriate validation message. `useForm` returns an `errors` state variable, which can be used to render validation error messages conditionally.

We explored the submit handler that React Hook Form provides. We learned that it prevents a server post and ensures that the form is valid. This submit handler has an argument for a function that is called with the valid form data.

In the next chapter, we will focus on state management in detail.

Questions

Answer the following questions to check what you have learned about forms in React:

1. How many times will the following form render after the initial render when `Bob` is entered into the name field?

```
function ControlledForm () {
  const [name, setName] = useState('');
  return (
    <form
      onSubmit={(e) => {
        e.preventDefault();
        console.log(name);
      }}
```

```
    >
      <input
        placeholder="Enter your name"
        value={name}
        onChange={(e) => setName(e.target.value)}
      />
    </form>
  );
}
```

2. How many times will the following form render after the initial render when `Bob` is entered into the name field?

```
function UnControlledForm() {
  return (
    <form
      onSubmit={(e) => {
        e.preventDefault();
        console.log(
          new FormData(e.currentTarget).get('name')
        );
      }}
    >
      <input placeholder="Enter your name" name="name" />
    </form>
  );
}
```

3. The following form contains an uncontrolled search field. When search criteria is entered into it and submitted, `null` appears in the console rather than the search criteria. Why is that so?

```
function SearchForm() {
  return (
    <form
      onSubmit={(e) => {
        e.preventDefault();
        console.log(
          new FormData(e.currentTarget).get('search')
        );
      }}
    >
```

```
        <input type="search" placeholder="Search ..." />
      </form>
    );
  }
```

4. The following component is a search form implemented using React Hook Form. When search criteria are entered into it and submitted, an empty object appears in the console, rather than an object containing the search criteria. Why is that so?

```
function SearchReactHookForm() {
  const { handleSubmit } = useForm();
  return (
    <form
      onSubmit={handleSubmit((search) => console.
        log(search))}
    >
      <input type="search" placeholder="Search ..." />
    </form>
  );
}
```

5. The following component is another search form implemented using React Hook Form. The form does function correctly but a type error is raised on the onSubmit parameter. How can the type error be resolved?

```
function SearchReactHookForm() {
  const { handleSubmit, register } = useForm();
  async function onSubmit(search) {
    console.log(search.criteria);
    // send to web server to perform the search
  }
  return (
    <form onSubmit={handleSubmit(onSubmit)}>
      <input
        type="search"
        placeholder="Search ..."
        {...register('criteria')}
      />
    </form>
  );
}
```

6. Continuing with the search form from the last question, how can we disable the `input` element while the search is being performed on the web server?

7. Continuing with the search form from the last question, how can we prevent a search from executing if the criteria is blank?

Answers

1. The form will render three times when `Bob` is entered into the name field. This is because each change of value causes a re-render because the value is bound to the state.

2. The form will never re-render when `Bob` is entered into the name field because its value isn't bound to the state.

3. The `FormData` interface requires the name attribute to be on the `input` element or it won't be able to find it and it will return `null`:

```
<input type="search" placeholder="Search ..."
name="search" />
```

4. For React Hook Form to track the field, the `register` function needs to be spread on the `input` element as follows:

```
function SearchReactHookForm() {
  const { handleSubmit, register } = useForm();
  return (
    <form
      onSubmit={handleSubmit((search) => console.
        log(search))}
    >
      <input
        type="search"
        placeholder="Search ..."
        {...register('criteria')}
      />
    </form>
  );
}
```

5. A type for field values can be defined and specified in the call to `useForm` and also the `onSubmit` search parameter:

```
type Search = {
  criteria: string;
```

```
};
function SearchReactHookForm() {
  const { handleSubmit, register } = useForm<Search>();
  async function onSubmit(search: Search) {
    ...
  }
  return ...
}
```

6. React Hook Form's isSubmitting state can be used to disable the input element while the search is being performed on the web server:

```
function SearchReactHookForm() {
  const {
    handleSubmit,
    register,
    formState: { isSubmitting },
  } = useForm<Search>();
  ...
  return (
    <form onSubmit={handleSubmit(onSubmit)}>
      <input
        type="search"
        placeholder="Search ..."
        {...register('criteria')}
        disabled={isSubmitting}
      />
    </form>
  );
}
```

7. The required validation can be added to the search form to prevent a search from executing if the criteria are blank:

```
<input
  type="search"
  placeholder="Search ..."
  {...register('criteria', { required: true })}
  disabled={isSubmitting}
/>
```

Part 3: Data

This part covers different approaches for interacting with both REST and GraphQL APIs and the benefits of each approach. We will learn about different approaches for efficiently managing the data from these APIs in states, including using several popular third-party libraries.

This part includes the following chapters:

- *Chapter 8, State Management*
- *Chapter 9, Interacting with RESTful APIs*
- *Chapter 10, Interacting with GraphQL APIs*

8

State Management

In this chapter, we'll learn about **shared state**, which is state that is used by several different components. We will explore three approaches to managing shared state, discussing the pros and cons of each approach.

To do this, we will build a simple app containing a header that displays the user's name, with the main content also referencing the user's name. The user's name will be stored in state that needs to be accessed by several components.

We will start with the simplest state solution. This is to use one of React's state hooks to store the state and pass it to other components using props. This approach is often referred to as **prop drilling**.

The second approach we will learn about is a feature in React called **context**. We will learn how to create a context containing a state and let other components access it.

The last approach we will cover is a popular library called **Redux**. We will take the time to understand what Redux is and its concepts before refactoring the app to use it.

So, we'll cover the following topics:

- Creating the project
- Using prop drilling
- Using React context
- Using Redux

Technical requirements

We will use the following technologies in this chapter:

- **Node.js** and **npm**: You can install them from `https://nodejs.org/en/download/`
- **Visual Studio Code**: You can install it from `https://code.visualstudio.com/`

All the code snippets in this chapter can be found online at `https://github.com/PacktPublishing/Learn-React-with-TypeScript-2nd-Edition/tree/main/Chapter8`.

Creating the project

We will develop our form using Visual Studio Code and a new Create React App-based project setup. We've previously covered this several times, so we will not cover the steps in this chapter – instead, see *Chapter 3, Setting Up React and TypeScript*.

We will style the form with Tailwind CSS. We also previously covered how to install and configure Tailwind in Create React App in *Chapter 5, Approaches to Styling Frontends*. So, after you have created the React and TypeScript project, install and configure Tailwind.

We will also use the @tailwindcss/forms plugin to style the form. So, install this plugin as well – see *Chapter 7, Working with Forms*, for information on how to do this.

The app we will build will contain a header and some content beneath it. Here is the component structure we will create:

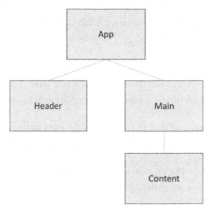

Figure 8.1 – App component structure

The header will have a **Sign in** button to authenticate and authorize a user to get their name and permissions. Once authenticated, the user's name will be displayed in the app header, and the user will be welcomed in the content. If the user has admin permissions, important content will be shown.

So, carry out the following steps to create the initial versions of the files that we need in the app without any statement management (some of the code snippets are lengthy – don't forget you can copy them from https://github.com/PacktPublishing/Learn-React-with-TypeScript-2nd-Edition/tree/main/Chapter8/prop-drilling):

1. We will start by creating a file containing a function to authenticate a user. Create a folder called api in the src folder. Then, create a file called authenticate.ts in the api folder with the following content:

    ```
    export type User = {
      id: string;
    ```

```
  name: string;
};
export function authenticate(): Promise<User | undefined>
{
  return new Promise((resolve) =>
    setTimeout(() => resolve({ id: "1", name: "Bob" }),
      1000)
  );
}
```

The function simulates successful authentication for a user called Bob.

2. Next, we will create a file containing a function to authorize a user. So, create a file called
   authorize.ts in the api folder with the following content:

```
export function authorize(id: string): Promise<string[]>
{
  return new Promise((resolve) =>
    setTimeout(() => resolve(["admin"]), 1000)
  );
}
```

The function simulates a user being authorized to have admin permissions.

3. Next, we will create a component for the app header. Create a file called Header.tsx in the
   src folder with the following content:

```
import { User } from './api/authenticate';

type Props = {
  user: undefined | User;
  onSignInClick: () => void;
  loading: boolean;
};
```

The component has a prop for the user, which will be undefined if the user isn't authenticated yet. The component also has a prop called onSignInClick for a **Sign in** button click handler. The last component prop is called loading and it determines whether the app is in a loading state when the user is authenticated or authorized.

4. Add the following component implementation into `Header.tsx`:

```tsx
export function Header({
  user,
  onSignInClick,
  loading,
}: Props) {
  return (
    <header className="flex justify-between items-center
      border-b-2 border-gray-100 py-6">
      {user ? (
        <span className="ml-auto font-bold">
          {user.name} has signed in
        </span>
      ) : (
        <button
          onClick={onSignInClick}
          className="whitespace-nowrap inline-flex items-
            center justify-center ml-auto px-4 py-2 w-36
            border border-transparent rounded-md
            shadow-sm text-base font-medium text-white
            bg-indigo-600 hover:bg-indigo-700"
          disabled={loading}
        >
          {loading ? '...' : 'Sign in'}
        </button>
      )}
    </header>
  );
}
```

The component informs the user that they have signed in if they have been authenticated. If the user is unauthenticated, the component displays a **Sign in** button.

5. Next, we will implement a component for the main app content. Create a file called `Main.tsx` in the `src` folder with the following content:

```tsx
import { User } from './api/authenticate';
import { Content } from './Content';

type Props = {
```

```
    user: undefined | User;
    permissions: undefined | string[];
};
```

The component has a prop for the user and their permissions. We have imported a component called Content, which we will create in *step 7*.

6. Now, add the following component implementation in Main.tsx:

```
export function Main({ user, permissions }: Props) {
    return (
        <main className="py-8">
            <h1 className="text-3xl text-center font-bold
                underline">Welcome</h1>
            <p className="mt-8 text-xl text-center">
                {user ? `Hello ${user.name}!` : "Please sign in"}
            </p>
            <Content permissions={permissions} />
        </main>
    );
}
```

The component instructs the user to sign in if they are unauthenticated or shows a **Hello** message if they are authenticated. The content also references a Content component passing it the user's permissions.

7. The last file to create in the src folder is called Content.tsx. Add the following content to the file:

```
type Props = {
    permissions: undefined | string[];
};
export function Content({ permissions }: Props) {
    if (permissions === undefined) {
        return null;
    }

    return permissions.includes('admin') ? (
        <p className="mt-4 text-l text-center">
            Some important stuff that only an admin can do
        </p>
```

```
    ) : (
      <p className="mt-4 text-l text-center">
        Insufficient permissions
      </p>
    );
  }
```

If the user is unauthorized, the component displays nothing. If the user has admin permissions, it displays some important stuff. Otherwise, it informs the user that they lack permissions.

That completes the project setup. The app will compile and run but won't show any of the components we created yet because we haven't referenced them in the App component. We will do this next when we share the user and permission information across several components.

Using prop drilling

In this first state management approach, we will store the user, permissions, and loading state in the App component. The App component will then pass this state to the Header and Main components using props.

So, this approach uses React features that we are already aware of. The approach is referred to as **prop drilling** because the state is passed down the component tree using props.

Carry out the following steps to rework the App component to store the user, permissions, and loading state, and pass this state down to the Header and Main components:

1. Open App.tsx and start by removing all the existing code and adding the following import statements:

```
import { useReducer } from 'react';
import { Header } from './Header';
import { Main } from './Main';
import { authenticate, User } from './api/authenticate';
import { authorize } from './api/authorize';
```

We have imported useReducer from React to store the state. We have also imported the Header and Main components so that we can render them with the state values. Lastly, we've imported the authenticate and authorize functions because we will create the **Sign in** handler in this component.

2. After the import statements, add a type for the state and create a variable for the initial state values:

```
type State = {
  user: undefined | User,
```

```
    permissions: undefined | string[],
    loading: boolean,
  };
  const initialState: State = {
    user: undefined,
    permissions: undefined,
    loading: false,
  };
```

3. Next, create a type for the different actions that can update the state:

```
type Action =
  | {
      type: "authenticate",
    }
  | {
      type: "authenticated",
      user: User | undefined,
    }
  | {
      type: "authorize",
    }
  | {
      type: "authorized",
      permissions: string[],
    };
```

The "authenticate" action will start the authentication process, and "authenticated" happens when it has been completed. Likewise, the "authorize" action will start the authorization process, and "authorized" happens when it has been completed.

4. Next, add a reducer function that updates the state:

```
function reducer(state: State, action: Action): State {
  switch (action.type) {
    case "authenticate":
      return { ...state, loading: true };
    case "authenticated":
      return { ...state, loading: false, user: action.
        user };
```

```
      case "authorize":
        return { ...state, loading: true };
      case "authorized":
        return {
          ...state,
          loading: false,
          permissions: action.permissions,
        };
      default:
        return state;
    }
  }
```

The function takes in the existing state and the action as parameters. The function uses a switch statement on the action type to create a new version of the state in each branch.

5. Now, let's define the App component as follows:

```
function App() {
  const [{ user, permissions, loading }, dispatch] =
    useReducer(reducer, initialState);

  return (
    <div className="max-w-7xl mx-auto px-4">
      <Header
        user={user}
        onSignInClick={handleSignInClick}
        loading={loading}
      />
      <Main user={user} permissions={permissions} />
    </div>
  );
}


export default App;
```

The component uses useReducer with the reducer function and the initialState variable we defined earlier. We have destructured the user, permissions, and loading state values from useReducer. In the JSX, we have rendered both the Header and Main components passing the appropriate state values as props.

6. The `Header` element in the JSX references a handler called `handleSignInClick`, which needs implementation. Create this above the return statement as follows:

```
async function handleSignInClick() {
  dispatch({ type: "authenticate" });
  const authenticatedUser = await authenticate();
  dispatch({
    type: "authenticated",
    user: authenticatedUser,
  });
  if (authenticatedUser !== undefined) {
    dispatch({ type: "authorize" });
    const authorizedPermissions = await authorize(
      authenticatedUser.id
    );
    dispatch({
      type: "authorized",
      permissions: authorizedPermissions,
    });
  }
}
```

The sign-in handler authenticates and authorizes the user and dispatches the necessary actions along the way.

7. Run the app in development mode by running `npm start` in the terminal. The app appears as shown in the screenshot:

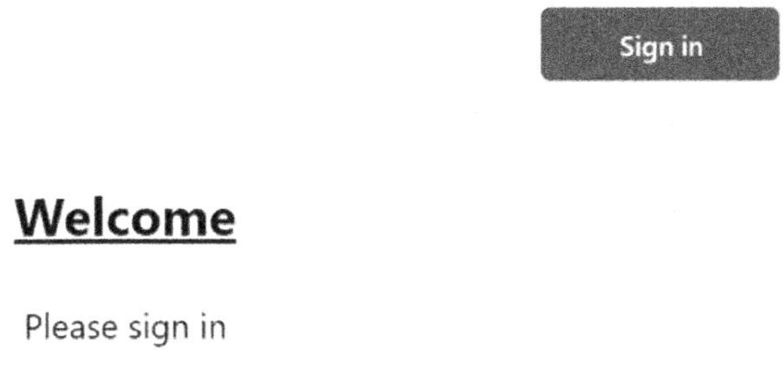

Welcome

Please sign in

Figure 8.2 – App before signing in

8. Click the **Sign in** button. The authentication and authorization processes then happen, and after a couple of seconds, the following screen appears:

Bob has signed in

<u>Welcome</u>

Hello Bob!

Some important stuff that only an admin can do

Figure 8.3 – App after signing in

That completes the prop drilling approach.

A nice thing about this approach is that it is simple and uses React features we are already familiar with. A downside of this approach is that it forces all components between the component providing state and components accessing the state to have a prop for that state. So, some components that do not need access to the state are forced to access it. An example is the Main component – the permissions state is forced to pass through it to the Content component.

The key point in this section is that it is fine to share state across a few adjacent components using props but isn't ideal for sharing across lots of components far apart in the component tree.

Next, keep the app running, and we will look at a more appropriate solution for sharing state across many components.

Using React context

In this section, we will learn a feature in React called **context**. We will then refactor the app from the last section to use React context.

Understanding React context

React context is an object that can be accessed by components. This object can contain state values, so it provides a mechanism for sharing state across components.

A context is created using a createContext function as follows:

```
const SomeContext = createContext<ContextType>(defaultValue);
```

A default value for the context must be passed into createContext. It also has a generic type parameter for the type that represents the object created by createContext.

The context also contains a `Provider` component that needs to be placed above components requiring access to the context object in the component tree. A provider wrapper component can be created that stores the shared state and passes it to the context `Provider` component as follows:

```
export function SomeProvider({ children }: Props) {
  const [someState, setSomeState] = useState(initialState);
  return (
    <SomeContext.Provider value={{ someState }}>
      {children}
    </SomeContext.Provider>
  );
}
```

`useState` has been used for the state in the preceding example, but `useReducer` could also be used.

The provider wrapper component can then be placed appropriately in the component tree, above components requiring the shared state:

```
function App() {
  return (
    <SomeProvider>
      <Header />
      <Main />
    </SomeProvider>
  );
}
```

React also contains a `useContext` hook that can be used so that the context values can be consumed as a hook, as follows:

```
const { someState } = useContext(SomeContext);
```

The context must be passed into `useContext` and properties from the context object can be destructured from its result.

So, components that want access to the shared state can access it using `useContext` as follows:

```
export function SomeComponent() {
  const { someState } = useContext(SomeContext);
  return <div>I have access to {someState}</div>;
}
```

For more information on React context, see the following link: `https://reactjs.org/docs/context.html`.

Now that we understand React context, we will use it in the app we created in the previous section.

Using React context

We will refactor the app from the last section to use React context. We will start by creating a file containing the context and the provider wrapper. Then, we will use `useReducer` in the provider wrapper to store the state. We will also create a wrapper for `useContext` to make consuming it easy.

So, to do this, carry out the following steps:

1. Start by creating a file called `AppContext.tsx` in the `src` folder. This will contain the context, the provider wrapper, and the `useContext` wrapper.

2. Add the following import statements to `AppContext.tsx`:

    ```
    import {
      createContext,
      useContext,
      useReducer,
      ReactNode,
    } from 'react';
    import { User } from './api/authenticate';
    ```

    We have imported all the functions we need from React along with the `ReactNode` type that we will need for the provider wrapper `children` prop. We have also imported the `User` type, which we will need for the user state type.

3. We need to add a type for the state and a variable for the initial state values. We already have these in `App.tsx`, so the following lines can be moved from `App.tsx` to `AppContext.tsx`:

    ```
    type State = {
      user: undefined | User,
      permissions: undefined | string[],
      loading: boolean,
    };
    const initialState = {
      user: undefined,
      permissions: undefined,
      loading: false,
    };
    ```

4. Similarly, the `Action` type and the `reducer` function can be moved from `App.tsx` to `AppContext.tsx`. Here are the lines to move:

```
type Action =
  | {
      type: "authenticate",
    }
  | {
      type: "authenticated",
      user: User | undefined,
    }
  | {
      type: "authorize",
    }
  | {
      type: "authorized",
      permissions: string[],
    };

function reducer(state: State, action: Action): State {
  switch (action.type) {
    case "authenticate":
      return { ...state, loading: true };
    case "authenticated":
      return { ...state, loading: false, user: action.
        user };
    case "authorize":
      return { ...state, loading: true };
    case "authorized":
      return { ...state, loading: false, permissions:
        action.permissions };
    default:
      return state;
  }
}
```

Note that the `App.tsx` file will raise a compile error after moving this function. We will resolve this in the next set of instructions.

5. Next, we will create a type for the context in `AppContext.tsx`:

```
type AppContextType = State & {
  dispatch: React.Dispatch<Action>,
};
```

The context will consist of the state values and a `dispatch` function to dispatch actions.

6. Now we can create the context as follows:

```
const AppContext = createContext<AppContextType>({
  ...initialState,
  dispatch: () => {},
});
```

We have called the context `AppContext`. We use the `initialState` variable and a dummy `dispatch` function as the default context value.

7. Next, we can implement the provider wrapper as follows:

```
type Props = {
  children: ReactNode;
};
export function AppProvider({ children }: Props) {
  const [{ user, permissions, loading }, dispatch] =
    useReducer(reducer, initialState);
  return (
    <AppContext.Provider
      value={{
        user,
        permissions,
        loading,
        dispatch,
      }}
    >
      {children}
    </AppContext.Provider>
  );
}
```

We have called the component `AppProvider`, and it returns the context's `Provider` component with the state values and the `dispatch` function from `useReducer`.

8. The last thing to do in `AppContext.tsx` is to create a wrapper for `useContext` as follows:

```
export const useAppContext = () =>
useContext(AppContext);
```

That completes the work we need to do in `AppContext.tsx`.

So, `AppContext.tsx` exports an `AppProvider` component that can be placed above `Header` and `Main` in the component tree so that they can access the user and permissions information. `AppContext.tsx` also exports `useAppContext` so that the `Header`, `Main`, and `Content` components can use it to get access to the user and permissions information.

Now, carry out the following steps to make the necessary changes to the `App`, `Header`, `Main`, and `Content` components to access the user and permissions information from `AppContext`:

1. We will start with `Header.tsx`. Begin by importing the `authenticate`, `authorize`, and `useAppContext` functions. Also, remove the `User` type and the props for the `Header` component:

```
import { authenticate } from './api/authenticate';
import { authorize } from './api/authorize';
import { useAppContext } from './AppContext';

export function Header() {
  return ...
}
```

2. `Header` will now handle the sign-in process instead of App. So, move the `handleSignInClick` handler from App in `App.tsx` to `Header.tsx` and place it above the return statement as follows:

```
export function Header() {
  async function handleSignInClick() {
    dispatch({ type: 'authenticate' });
    const authenticatedUser = await authenticate();
    dispatch({
      type: 'authenticated',
      user: authenticatedUser,
    });
    if (authenticatedUser !== undefined) {
      dispatch({ type: 'authorize' });
      const authorizedPermissions = await authorize(
```

```
        authenticatedUser.id
    );
    dispatch({
      type: 'authorized',
      permissions: authorizedPermissions,
    });
  }
}
return ...
}
```

3. Update the sign-in click handler to reference the function we just added:

```
<button
  onClick={handleSignInClick}
  className=...
  disabled={loading}
>
  {loading ? '...' : 'Sign in'}
</button>
```

4. The last thing to do in Header.tsx is to get user, loading, and dispatch from the context. Add the following call to useAppContext at the top of the component:

```
export function Header() {
  const { user, loading, dispatch } = useAppContext();
  ...
}
```

5. Let's move on to Main.tsx. Remove the import statement for the User type and add an import statement for useAppContext:

```
import { Content } from './Content';
import { useAppContext } from './AppContext';
```

6. Remove the props for the Main component and get user from useAppContext:

```
export function Main() {
  const { user } = useAppContext();
  return ...
}
```

7. In the JSX in Main, remove the permissions attribute on the Content element:

```
<Content />
```

8. Now, open Content.tsx and add an import statement for useAppContext:

```
import { useAppContext } from './AppContext';
```

9. Remove the props for the Content component and get permissions from useAppContext:

```
export function Content() {
  const { permissions } = useAppContext();
  if (permissions === undefined) {
    return null;
  }
  return ...
}
```

10. Lastly, we will modify App.tsx. Remove the import statements except for Header and Main, and add an import statement for AppProvider:

```
import { Header } from './Header';
import { Main } from './Main';
import { AppProvider } from './AppContext';
```

11. Still in App.tsx, remove the call to useReducer and remove all the attributes passed to Header and Main:

```
function App() {
  return (
    <div className="max-w-7xl mx-auto px-4">
      <Header />
      <Main />
    </div>
  );
}
```

12. Wrap AppProvider around Header and Main so that they can access the context:

```
function App() {
  return (
    <div className="max-w-7xl mx-auto px-4">
```

```
          <AppProvider>
            <Header />
            <Main />
          </AppProvider>
        </div>
      );
    }
```

The compile errors will now be resolved and the running app will look and behave like before.

13. Stop the app running by pressing *Ctrl + C*.

That completes the refactoring of the app to use React context instead of prop drilling.

In comparison to prop drilling, React context requires more code to be written. However, it allows components to access shared state using a hook rather than passing it through components using props. It's an elegant, shared-state solution, particularly when many components share state.

Next, we will learn about a popular third-party library that can be used to share state.

Using Redux

In this section, we will learn about Redux before using it to refactor the app we have been working on to use it.

Understanding Redux

Redux is a mature state management library that was first released in 2015. It was released before React context and became a popular approach for shared state management.

Creating a store

In Redux, the state lives in a centralized immutable object referred to as a **store**. There is only a single store for the whole app. Like `useReducer`, the state in a store is updated by dispatching an **action**, which is an object containing the type of change and any data required to make the change. An action is handled by a `reducer` function, which creates a new version of the state.

In the past, a lot of code was needed to set up a Redux store and consume it in a React component. Today, a companion library called Redux Toolkit reduces the code required to use Redux. A Redux store can be created using the Redux Toolkit's `configureStore` function as follows:

```
export const store = configureStore({
  reducer: {
    someFeature: someFeatureReducer,
```

```
      anotherFeature: anotherFeatureReducer
    },
  });
```

The `configureStore` function takes in the store's reducers. Each feature in the app can have its own area of state and reducer to change the state. The different areas of state are often referred to as **slices**. In the preceding example, there are two slices called `someFeature` and `anotherFeature`.

The Redux Toolkit has a function to create slices, called `createSlice`:

```
export const someSlice = createSlice({
  name: "someFeature",
  initialState,
  reducers: {
    someAction: (state) => {
      state.someValue = "something";
    },
    anotherAction: (state) => {
      state.someOtherValue = "something else";
    },
  },
});
```

The `createSlice` function takes in an object parameter containing the slice name, the initial state, and functions to handle the different actions and update the state.

The slice created from `createSlice` contains a `reducer` function that wraps the action handlers. This `reducer` function can be referenced in the `reducer` property of `configureStore` when the store is created:

```
export const store = configureStore({
  reducer: {
    someFeature: someSlice.reducer,
    ...
  },
});
```

In the preceding code snippet, the reducer from `someSlice` has been added to the store.

Providing the store to React components

The Redux store is defined in the component tree using its `Provider` component. The value of the Redux store (from `configureStore`) needs to be specified on the `Provider` component. The `Provider` component must be placed above the components requiring access to the store:

```
<Provider store={store}>
  <SomeComponent />
  <AnotherComponent />
</Provider>
```

In the preceding example, `SomeComponent` and `AnotherComponent` have access to the store.

Accessing the store from a component

Components can access state from the Redux store using a `useSelector` hook from React Redux. A function that selects the relevant state in the store is passed into `useSelector`:

```
const someValue = useSelector(
  (state: RootState) => state.someFeature.someValue
);
```

In the preceding example, `someValue` is selected from the `someFeature` slice in the store.

Dispatching actions to the store from a component

React Redux also has a `useDispatch` hook that returns a `dispatch` function that can be used to dispatch actions. The action is a function from the slice created using `createSlice`:

```
const dispatch = useDispatch();
return (
  <button onClick={() => dispatch(someSlice.actions.
someAction())}>
    Some button
  </button>
);
```

In the preceding example, `someAction` in `someSlice` is dispatched when the button is clicked.

For more information on Redux, see the following link: `https://redux.js.org/`. And for more information on the Redux Toolkit, see the following link: `https://redux-toolkit.js.org/`.

Now that we understand Redux, we will use it in the app we created in the previous section.

Installing Redux

First, we must install Redux and the Redux Toolkit into our project. Run the following command in the terminal:

```
npm i @reduxjs/toolkit react-redux
```

This will install all the Redux bits we need, including its TypeScript types.

Using Redux

Now, we can refactor the app to use Redux instead of React context. First, we will create a Redux slice for the user information before creating a Redux store with this slice. We will then move on to add the store to the React component tree and consume it in the Header, Main, and Content components.

Creating a Redux Slice

We will start by creating a Redux slice for the state for a user. Carry out the following steps:

1.   Create a folder called store in the src folder and then a file called userSlice.ts within it.

2.   Add the following import statements to userSlice.ts:

```
import { createSlice } from '@reduxjs/toolkit';
import type { PayloadAction } from '@reduxjs/toolkit';
import { User } from '../api/authenticate';
```

We will eventually use createSlice to create the Redux slice. PayloadAction is a type that we can use for action objects. We will need the User type when defining the type for the state.

3.   Copy the following State type and initial state value from AppContext.tsx into userSlice. ts:

```
type State = {
  user: undefined | User;
  permissions: undefined | string[];
  loading: boolean;
};
const initialState: State = {
  user: undefined,
  permissions: undefined,
  loading: false,
};
```

4. Next, start to create the slice in `userSlice.ts`, as follows:

```
export const userSlice = createSlice({
  name: 'user',
  initialState,
  reducers: {


  }
});
```

We have named the slice user and passed in the initial state value. We export the slice so that we can use it later to create the Redux store.

5. Now, define the following action handlers inside the `reducers` object:

```
reducers: {
  authenticateAction: (state) => {
    state.loading = true;
  },
  authenticatedAction: (
    state,
    action: PayloadAction<User | undefined>
  ) => {
    state.user = action.payload;
    state.loading = false;
  },
  authorizeAction: (state) => {
    state.loading = true;
  },
  authorizedAction: (
    state,
    action: PayloadAction<string[]>
  ) => {
    state.permissions = action.payload;
    state.loading = false;
  }
}
```

Each action handler updates the required state. `PayloadAction` is used for the type of the action parameters. `PayloadAction` is a generic type with a parameter for the type of the action payload.

6. Lastly, export the action handlers and the `reducer` function from the slice:

```
export const {
   authenticateAction,
   authenticatedAction,
   authorizeAction,
   authorizedAction,
} = userSlice.actions;


export default userSlice.reducer;
```

A default export has been used for the `reducer` function so the consumer can name it as required.

That completes the implementation of the Redux slice.

Creating the Redux store

Next, let's create the Redux store. Carry out the following steps:

1. Create a file called `store.ts` in the `store` folder containing the following import statements:

```
import { configureStore } from '@reduxjs/toolkit';
import userReducer from './userSlice';
```

2. Next, use the `configureStore` function to create the store referencing the reducer from the slice we created earlier:

```
export const store = configureStore({
   reducer: { user: userReducer }
});
```

We export the `store` variable so that we can later use it on React Redux's `Provider` component.

3. The last thing to do in `store.ts` is export the type for Redux's full state object, which we will eventually require in the `useSelector` hook in components consuming the Redux store:

```
export type RootState = ReturnType<typeof store.
getState>;
```

ReturnType is a standard TypeScript utility type that returns the return type of the function type passed into it. The getState function in the Redux store returns the full state object. So, we use ReturnType to infer the type of the full state object rather than explicitly defining it.

That completes the implementation of the Redux store.

Adding the Redux store to the component tree

Next, we will add the store at an appropriate place in the component tree using the Provider component from React Redux. Follow these steps:

1.   Open App.tsx and remove the AppContext import statement. Remove the AppContext.tsx file as well because this is no longer required.

2.   Add an import statement for the Provider component from React Redux and the Redux store we created:

```
import { Provider } from 'react-redux';
import { store } from './store/store';
```

3.   Replace AppProvider with Provider in the JSX, as follows:

```
<div className="max-w-7xl mx-auto px-4">
  <Provider store={store}>
    <Header />
    <Main />
  </Provider>
</div>
```

We pass the imported Redux store into Provider.

The Redux store is now accessible to the Header, Main, and Content components.

Consuming the Redux store in the components

We will now integrate the Redux store into the Header, Main, and Content components. This will replace the previous React context consumption code. Follow these steps:

1.   Start by opening Header.tsx and remove the AppContext import statement.

2.   Add the following import statements to Header.tsx:

```
import { useSelector, useDispatch } from 'react-redux';
import type { RootState } from './store/store';
import {
  authenticateAction,
```

```
    authenticatedAction,
    authorizeAction,
    authorizedAction,
  } from './store/userSlice';
```

We will be referencing state from Redux as well as dispatching actions, so we have imported both useSelector and useDispatch. The RootState type is required in the function we will eventually pass to useSelector. We have also imported all the actions from the slice we created because we will need them in the revised sign-in handler.

3. Inside the Header component, replace the useAppContext call with useSelector calls to get the required state:

```
export function Header() {
  const user = useSelector(
    (state: RootState) => state.user.user
  );
  const loading = useSelector(
    (state: RootState) => state.user.loading
  );
  async function handleSignInClick() {
    ...
  }
  return ...
}
```

4. Also, call useDispatch to get a dispatch function:

```
export function Header() {
  const user = useSelector(
    (state: RootState) => state.user.user
  );
  const loading = useSelector(
    (state: RootState) => state.user.loading
  );
  const dispatch = useDispatch();
  async function handleSignInClick() {
    ...
  }
  return ...
}
```

5. The last thing to do in Header.tsx is to modify handleSignInClick to reference the action functions from the Redux slice:

```
async function handleSignInClick() {
  dispatch(authenticateAction());
  const authenticatedUser = await authenticate();
  dispatch(authenticatedAction(authenticatedUser));
  if (authenticatedUser !== undefined) {
    dispatch(authorizeAction());
    const authorizedPermissions = await authorize(
      authenticatedUser.id
    );
    dispatch(authorizedAction(authorizedPermissions));
  }
}
```

6. Now, open Main.tsx and replace the AppContext import statement with import statements for useSelector and the RootState type:

```
import { useSelector } from 'react-redux';
import { RootState } from './store/store';
```

7. Replace the call to useAppContext with a call to useSelector to get the user state value:

```
export function Main() {
  const user = useSelector(
    (state: RootState) => state.user.user
  );
  return ...
}
```

8. Next, open Content.tsx and replace the AppContext import statement with import statements for useSelector and the RootState type:

```
import { useSelector } from 'react-redux';
import { RootState } from './store/store';
```

9. Replace the call to `useAppContext` with a call to `useSelector` to get the `permissions` state value:

```
export function Content() {
  const permissions = useSelector(
    (state: RootState) => state.user.permissions
  );
  if (permissions === undefined) {
    return null;
  }
  return ...
}
```

10. Run the app by running `npm start` in the terminal. The app will look and behave just as it did before.

That completes the refactoring of the app to use Redux rather than React context.

Here's a recap of the key points for using Redux:

- State is stored in a central store

- State is updated by dispatching actions that are handled by reducers

- A `Provider` component needs to be placed appropriately in the component tree to give components access to the Redux store

- Components can select state using a `useSelector` hook and dispatch actions using a `useDispatch` hook

As you have experienced, even using the Redux Toolkit requires many steps when using Redux to manage state. It is overkill for simple state management requirements but shines when there is a lot of shared application-level state.

Summary

In this chapter, we built a small one-page app that contained components that needed to share state. We started by using our existing knowledge and used props to pass the state between the components. We learned that a problem with this approach was that components not needing access to the state are forced to access it if its child components do need access to it.

We moved on to learn about React context and refactored the app to use it. We learned that React context can store state using `useState` or `useReducer`. The state can then be provided to components in the tree using the context's `Provider` component. Components then access the context state via the `useContext` hook. We found that this was a much nicer solution than passing the state via props, particularly when many components need access to the state.

Next, we learned about Redux, which is similar to React context. A difference is that there can only be a single Redux store containing the state, but there can be many React contexts. We learned that a `Provider` component needs to be added to the component tree to give components access to the Redux store. Components select state using the `useSelector` hook and dispatch actions using the `useDispatch` hook. Reducers handle actions and then update the state accordingly.

In the next chapter, we will learn how to work with REST APIs in React.

Questions

Answer the following questions to check what you have learned in this chapter:

1. We have a context defined as follows to hold the theme state for an app:

    ```
    type Theme = {
      name: string;
      color: 'dark' | 'light';
    };
    type ThemeContextType = Theme & {
      changeTheme: (
        name: string,
        color: 'dark' | 'light'
      ) => void;
    };
    const ThemeContext = createContext<ThemeContextType>();
    ```

    The code doesn't compile though; what is the problem?

2. The context from question 1 has a provider wrapper called `ThemeProvider`, which is added to the component tree as follows:

    ```
    <ThemeProvider>
      <Header />
      <Main />
    </ThemeProvider>
    <Footer />
    ```

    The theme state is `undefined` when destructured from `useContext` in the `Footer` component. What is the problem?

3. Is it possible to have two React contexts in an app?

4. Is it possible to have two Redux stores in an app?

5. The following code dispatches an action to change the theme:

```
function handleChangeTheme({ name, color }: Theme) {
  useDispatch(changeThemeAction(name, color));
}
```

There is a problem with this code. What is this problem?

6. In a React component, is it possible to use state only required by this component using `useState` as well as state from a Redux store?

7. In this chapter, when we implemented the Redux slice, the action handlers appeared to directly update the state, as in the following example:

```
authorizedAction: (
  state,
  action: PayloadAction<string[]>
) => {
  state.permissions = action.payload;
  state.loading = false;
}
```

Why are we allowed to mutate the state? I thought that state in React had to be immutable?

Answers

1. `createContext` must be passed a default value when using it with TypeScript. Here's the corrected code:

```
const ThemeContext = createContext<ThemeContextType>({
  name: 'standard',
  color: 'light',
  changeTheme: (name: string, color: 'dark' | 'light') =>
{},
});
```

2. `Footer` must be placed inside `ThemeProvider` as follows:

```
<ThemeProvider>
  <Header />
  <Main />
```

```
    <Footer />
  </ThemeProvider>
```

3. Yes, there is no limit on the number of React contexts in an app.

4. No, only a single Redux store can be added to an app.

5. useDispatch can't be used directly to dispatch an action – it returns a function that can be used to dispatch an action:

```
const dispatch = useDispatch();
function handleChangeTheme({ name, color }: Theme) {
    dispatch(changeThemeAction(name, color));
}
```

6. Yes, local state defined using useState or useReducer can be used alongside shared state from a Redux store.

7. The Redux Toolkit uses a library called **immer** to allow developers to directly update the state object without mutating it. For more information on *immer*, see the following link: https://github.com/immerjs/immer.

9

Interacting with RESTful APIs

In this chapter, we will build a page that lists blog posts fetched from a REST API, as well as also a form to submit blog posts to the REST API. Through this, we will learn about various approaches to interacting with a REST API from a React component.

The first approach will be using React's `useEffect` hook with the browser's `fetch` function. As part of this process, we learn how to use a type assertion function to strongly type the data from a REST API. We will then use the data loading capability of **React Router** and experience its benefits. After that, we will move on to use a popular library called **React Query** and experience its benefits, before using React Query and React Router together to get the best of both these libraries.

So, in this chapter, we'll cover the following topics:

- Getting set up
- Using the effect hook with fetch
- Posting data with fetch
- Using React Router
- Using React Query
- Using React Router with React Query

Technical requirements

We will use the following technologies in this chapter:

- **Node.js** and **npm**: You can install them from `https://nodejs.org/en/download/`
- **Visual Studio Code**: You can install it from `https://code.visualstudio.com/`

All the code snippets in this chapter can be found online at `https://github.com/PacktPublishing/Learn-React-with-TypeScript-2nd-Edition/tree/main/Chapter9`.

Creating the project

In this section, we will start by creating the project for the app we will build. We will then create a REST API for the app to consume.

Setting up the project

We will develop the app using Visual Studio Code and require a new Create React App-based project setup. We've previously covered this several times, so we will not cover the steps in this chapter – instead, see *Chapter 3, Setting Up React and TypeScript*.

We will style the app with Tailwind CSS. We have previously covered how to install and configure Tailwind in Create React App in *Chapter 5, Approaches to Styling Frontends*. So, after you have created the React and TypeScript project, install and configure Tailwind.

We will use React Router to load data, so see *Chapter 6, Routing with React Router,* for information on how to do this.

We will use **React Hook Form** to implement the form that creates blog posts, and the `@tailwindcss/forms` plugin to style the form. See *Chapter 7, Working with Forms,* for a reminder of how to implement these.

Understanding the component structure

The app will be a single page containing a form for adding new posts above a list of all the existing posts. The app will be structured into the following components:

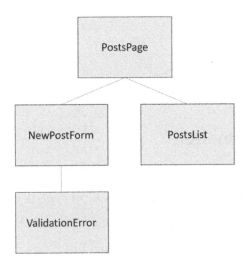

Figure 9.1 – App component structure

Here's a description of these components:

- `PostsPage` will render the whole page by referencing the `NewPostForm` and `PostsLists` components. It will also interact with the REST API.

- `NewPostForm` will render a form that allows a user to enter a new blog post. This will use the `ValidationError` component to render validation error messages. The `ValidationError` component will be the same as the one created in *Chapter 7*.

- `PostsList` will render the list of blog posts.

Right, now we know the component structure, let's create the REST API.

Creating a REST API

We will create a REST API using a tool called **JSON Server**, which allows a REST API to be quickly created. Install JSON Server by running the following command:

```
npm i -D json-server
```

We then define the data behind the API in a JSON file. Create a file called `db.json` in the root of the project containing the following:

```json
{
  "posts": [
    {
      "title": "Getting started with fetch",
      "description": "How to interact with backend APIs using
        fetch",
      "id": 1
    },
    {
      "title": "Getting started with useEffect",
      "description": "How to use React's useEffect hook for
        interacting with backend APIs",
      "id": 2
    }
  ]
}
```

The preceding JSON means that the data behind the API will initially contain two blog posts (this code snippet can be copied from `https://github.com/PacktPublishing/Learn-React-with-TypeScript-2nd-Edition/blob/main/Chapter9/useEffect-fetch/db.json`).

Now we need to define an npm script to start the JSON server and handle requests. Open `package.json` and add a script called `server` as follows:

```
{
  ...,
  "scripts": {
    ...,
    "server": "json-server --watch db.json --port 3001 --delay
      2000"
  },
  ...
}
```

The script starts the JSON server and watches the JSON file we just created. We have specified that the API runs on port 3001 so that it doesn't clash with the app running on port 3000. We have also slowed down the API responses by adding a 2-second delay, which will help us see when data is being fetched from the React app.

In a terminal, start the API by running the script we just created, as follows:

```
npm run server
```

After a few seconds, the API starts. To check that the API is working correctly, open a browser and enter the following address: `http://localhost:3001/posts`. The blog post data should appear in the browser as follows:

Figure 9.2 – Blog posts REST API

For more information on JSON Server, see the following link: `https://github.com/typicode/json-server`.

Now that the project is set up with a REST API, keeping the API running, next, we will learn how to interact with the REST API using `useEffect`.

Using the effect hook with fetch

In this section, we will create a page that lists the blog posts returned from the REST API we just created. We will use the browser's `fetch` function and React's `useEffect` hook to interact with the REST API.

Getting blog posts using fetch

We will start by creating a function that gets blog posts from the REST API using the browser's `fetch` function; we will store the API URL in an environment variable. To do this, carry out the following steps:

1. The same URL will be used to get, as well as save, new blog posts to the REST API. We will store this URL in an environment variable. So, create a file called `.env` in the root of the project containing this variable, as follows:

   ```
   REACT_APP_API_URL = http://localhost:3001/posts/
   ```

   This environment variable is injected into the code at build time and can be accessed by code using `process.env.REACT_APP_API_URL`. Environment variables in Create React App projects must be prefixed with `React_APP_`. For more information on environment variables, see the following link: `https://create-react-app.dev/docs/adding-custom-environment-variables/`.

2. Now, create a folder called `posts` in the `src` folder for all the files for the blog post feature.

3. Create a file called `getPosts.ts` in the `posts` folder. In this file, add the following function that gets the blog posts:

   ```
   export async function getPosts() {
     const response = await fetch(
       process.env.REACT_APP_API_URL!
     );
     const body = await response.json()
     return body;
   }
   ```

The fetch function has an argument for the URL to the REST API. We have used the REACT_APP_API_URL environment variable to specify this URL. Environment variable values can be undefined, but we know this isn't the case, so we have added a **not null assertion** (!) after it.

> **Note**
>
> A not null assertion operator is a special operator in TypeScript. It is used to inform the TypeScript compiler that the expression before it can't be null or undefined.

fetch returns a Response object and we call its json method to get the response body in JSON format. The json method is asynchronous, so we need to await it.

For more information on fetch, see the following link: https://developer.mozilla.org/en-US/docs/Web/API/Fetch_API.

That completes an initial version of getPosts. However, the return value type from getPosts is currently any, which means no type checking will occur on it. We will improve this next.

Strongly typing response data

In *Chapter 2, Introducing TypeScript*, we learned how to make unknown data strongly typed using the unknown type and type predicates. We will use the unknown type with a slightly different TypeScript feature called a **type assertion function** to type the response data in the getPosts function. Carry out the following steps:

1. Add a type assertion to the JSON response so that the body variable has a type of unknown:

```
export async function getPosts() {
  const response = await fetch(postsUrl);
  const body = (await response.json()) as unknown;
  return body;
}
```

2. Next, add the following type assertion function beneath getPosts:

```
export function assertIsPosts(
  postsData: unknown
    ): asserts postsData is PostData[] {
}
```

Notice the return type annotation: asserts postsData is PostData[]. This is called an **assertion signature** and specifies that the postsData parameter is of the PostData[] type if no error occurs in the function execution.

Don't worry about the compile error where PostData is referenced – we will create the PostData type in *step 8*.

3. Let's carry on with the implementation of assertIsPosts. It will be a series of checks on the postsData parameter and it will throw an exception if a check fails. Start the implementation by checking that postsData is an array:

```
export function assertIsPosts(
  postsData: unknown
): asserts postsData is PostData[] {
  if (!Array.isArray(postsData)) {
    throw new Error("posts isn't an array");
  }
  if (postsData.length === 0) {
    return;
  }
}
```

4. Now, let's do a check on the array items to see whether they have an id property:

```
export function assertIsPosts(
  postsData: unknown
): asserts postsData is PostData[] {
  ...
  postsData.forEach((post) => {
    if (!('id' in post)) {
      throw new Error("post doesn't contain id");
    }
    if (typeof post.id !== 'number') {
      throw new Error('id is not a number');
    }
  });
}
```

We loop around all the posts using the array's forEach method. Inside the loop, we check that the id property exists using the in operator. We also check that the id value is of the number type using the typeof operator.

5. We can do similar checks for the `title` and `description` properties:

```
export function assertIsPosts(
  postsData: unknown
): asserts postsData is PostData[] {
  ...
  postsData.forEach((post) => {
    . . .
    if '!('ti'le' in post)) {
      throw new Err"r("post do'sn't contain ti"le");
    }
    if (typeof post.title !'= 'str'ng') {
      throw new Err'r('title is not a str'ng');
    }
    if '!('descript'on' in post)) {
      throw new Err"r("post do'sn't contain
        descript"on");
    }
    if (typeof post.description !'= 'str'ng') {
      throw new Err'r('description is not a str'ng');
    }
  });
}
```

That completes the implementation of the type assertion function.

6. Moving back to `getPosts`, add a call to the `assert` function:

```
export async function getPosts() {
  const response = await fetch(postsUrl);
  const body = (await response.json()) as unknown;
  assertIsPosts(body);
  return body;
}
```

The `body` variable will now be of the `PostData[]` type after a successful call to `assertIsPosts`. You can hover over the `body` variable in the return statement to confirm this.

7. The final steps are to add the `PostData` type. Add an import statement at the top of `getPosts. ts` as follows to import `PostData`:

    ```
    import { PostData } from './types';
    ```

    The file will still have compile errors because the `types` file doesn't exist yet – we'll do this in the next step.

8. Add a file called `types.ts` in the `posts` folder with the following definition for the `PostData` type:

    ```
    export type PostData = {
      id: number;
      title: string;
      description: string;
    };
    ```

    This type represents a blog post from the REST API.

Now, we have a strongly typed function that gets blog posts from the REST API. Next, we will create a React component that lists the blog posts.

Creating a blog posts list component

We will create a React component that takes in the blog post data and renders it in a list. Carry out the following steps:

1. Create a file called `PostsList.tsx` in the `posts` folder with the following import statement:

    ```
    import { PostData } from './types';
    ```

2. Next, start to implement the component as follows:

    ```
    type Props = {
      posts: PostData[];
    };
    export function PostsList({ posts }: Props) {

    }
    ```

    The component has a prop called `posts` that will contain the blog posts.

3. Now, render the blog posts in an unordered list, as follows:

    ```
    export function PostsList({ posts }: Props) {
      return (
    ```

```
      <ul className="list-none">
        {posts.map((post) => (
          <li key={post.id} className="border-b py-4">
            <h3 className="text-slate-900 font-bold">
              {post.title}
            </h3>
            <p className=" text-slate-900 ">{post.
description}</p>
          </li>
        ))}
      </ul>
    );
  }
```

The Tailwind CSS classes add gray lines between the blog posts with bold titles.

That completes the `PostsList` component. Next, we will create a page component that references the `PostsList` component.

Creating a blog posts page component

We will create a blog posts page component that gets blog post data using the `getPosts` function and renders it using the `PostsList` component we just created. Carry out the following steps:

1. Create a file called `PostsPage.tsx` in the `posts` folder components with the following import statements:

    ```
    import { useEffect, useState } from 'react';
    import { getPosts } from './getPosts';
    import { PostData } from './types';
    import { PostsList } from './PostsList';
    ```

    We have imported the `getPosts` function, the `PostList` component, and the `PostData` type we created in the last section. We have also imported the `useState` and `useEffect` hooks from React. We will use React state to store the blog posts and use `useEffect` to call `getPosts` when the page component is mounted.

2. Start the implementation of the page component by defining the state for the blog posts and whether they are being fetched:

    ```
    export function PostsPage() {
      const [isLoading, setIsLoading] = useState(true);
      const [posts, setPosts] = useState<PostData[]>([]);
    }
    ```

3. Next, call the `getPosts` function using the `useEffect` hook as follows:

```
export function PostsPage() {
  ...
  useEffect(() => {
    let cancel = false;
    getPosts().then((data) => {
      if (!cancel) {
        setPosts(data);
        setIsLoading(false);
      }
    });
    return () => {
      cancel = true;
    };
  }, []);
}
```

We use the older promise syntax when calling `getPosts` because the newer `async/await` syntax can't be directly used within `useEffect`.

If the `PostsPage` component is unmounted while the call to `getPosts` is still in progress, the setting of the `data` and `isLoading` state variables will result in an error. For this reason, we have used a `cancel` flag to ensure that the component is still mounted when the `data` and `isLoading` state variables are set.

We have also specified an empty array as the effect dependencies so that the effect only runs when the component is mounted.

4. Add a loading indicator while the data is being fetched after the call to `useEffect`:

```
export function PostsPage() {
  . . .
  useEffect(...);
  if (isLoading) {
    return (
      <div className="w-96 mx-auto mt-6">
        Loading ...
      </div>
    );
  }
}
```

The Tailwind CSS classes position the loading indicator horizontally in the center of the page with a bit of margin above it.

5. Finally, render a page title and the posts list after the conditional loading indicator:

```
export function PostsPage() {
  ...
  if (isLoading) {
    return (
      <div className="w-96 mx-auto mt--6">
        Loading ...
      </div>
    );
  }
  return (
    <div className="w-96 mx-auto mt--6">
      <h2 className="text-xl text-slate-900 font-
bold">Posts</h2>
      <PostsList posts={posts} />
    </div>
  );
}
```

The Tailwind CSS classes position the list in the center of the page with a bit of margin above. A large **Posts** title is also rendered above the list in a dark gray color.

6. Now, open App.tsx and replace its contents with the following so that it renders the page component we just created:

```
import { PostsPage } from './posts/PostsPage';

function App() {
  return <PostsPage />;
}
export default App;
```

7. Run the app by running `npm start` in a new terminal separate from the one running the REST API. The loading indicator will appear briefly as the data is being fetched:

Figure 9.3 – Loading indicator

The blog post list will then appear as follows:

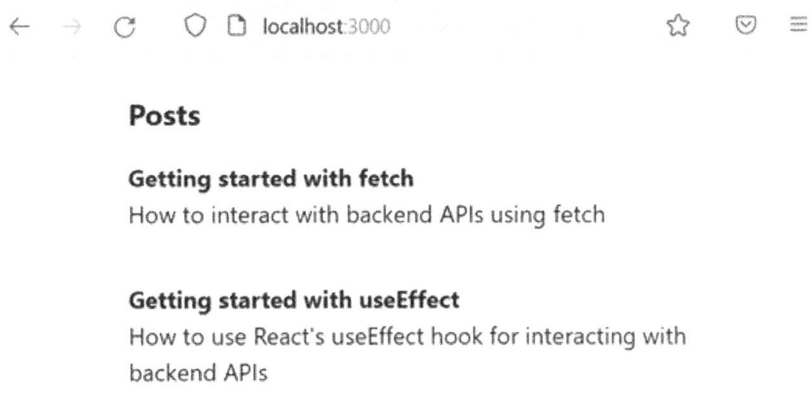

Figure 9.4 – Blog posts list

That completes this version of the `PostsPage` component.

Here are the key points we learned in this section on interacting with HTTP GET requests in a REST API using `fetch` and `useEffect`:

- `fetch` will make the actual HTTP request that has the REST API's URL as a parameter
- A type assertion function can be used to strongly type response data
- `useEffect` can trigger the `fetch` call when the component that holds the data in state is mounted
- A flag can be used inside `useEffect` to check that the component hasn't been unmounted during the HTTP request before the data state is set

Still keeping the app and REST API running, in the next section, we will learn how to post data to a REST API using `fetch`.

Posting data with fetch

In this section, we will create a form that submits a new blog post to our REST API. We will create a function that uses `fetch` to post to the REST API. That function will be called in the form's submit handler.

Creating new blog posts using fetch

We will start by creating the function that sends a new blog post to the REST API. This will use the browser's `fetch` function, but this time, using an HTTP POST request. Carry out the following steps:

1. We will start by opening `types.ts` in the `posts` folder and adding the following two types:

    ```
    export type NewPostData = {
      title: string;
      description: string;
    };

    export type SavedPostData = {
      id: number;
    };
    ```

    The first type represents a new blog post, and the second type represents the data from the API when the blog post is successfully saved.

2. Create a new file called `savePost.ts` in the `posts` folder and add the following import statement:

    ```
    import { NewPostData, SavedPostData } from './types';
    ```

    We have also imported the types we just created.

3. Start to implement the `savePost` function as follows:

    ```
    export async function savePost(
      newPostData: NewPostData
    ) {
      const response = await fetch(
        process.env.REACT_APP_API_URL!,
        {
          method: 'POST',
          body: JSON.stringify(newPostData),
          headers: {
    ```

```
        'Content-Type': 'application/json',
      },
    }
  );
}
```

The savePost function has a parameter, newPostData, containing the title and description for the new blog post, and sends it to the REST API using fetch. A second argument has been specified in the fetch call to specify that an HTTP POST request should be used and that the new blog post data should be included in the request body. The request body has also been declared as being in JSON format.

4. Next, strongly type the response body as follows:

```
export async function savePost(newPostData: NewPostData)
{
  const response = await fetch( ... );
  const body = (await response.json()) as unknown;
  assertIsSavedPost(body);
}
```

We set the response body as having the unknown type and then use a type assertion function to give it a specific type. This will raise a compile error until we implement assertIsSavedPost in *step 6*.

5. Finish the implementation of savePost by merging the blog post ID from the response with the blog post title and description supplied to the function:

```
export async function savePost(newPostData: NewPostData)
{
  . . .
  return { ...newPostData, ...body };
}
```

So, the object returned from the function will be a new blog post with the ID from the REST API.

6. The last step is to implement the type assertion function:

```
function assertIsSavedPost(
  post: any
): asserts post is SavedPostData {
  if (!('id' in post)) {
    throw new Error("post doesn't contain id");
```

```
    }
    if (typeof post.id !== 'number') {
      throw new Error('id is not a number');
    }
  }
```

The function checks whether the response data contains a numeric `id` property, and if it does, it asserts that the data is of the `SavedPostData` type.

That completes the implementation of the `savePost` function. Next, we will add a form component that allows the user to enter new blog posts.

Creating a blog post form component

We will create a component that contains a form that captures a new blog post. When the form is submitted, it will call the `savePost` function we just created.

We will use React Hook Form to implement the form along with a `ValidationError` component. We covered React Hook Form and the `ValidationError` component in detail in *Chapter 7*, so the implementation steps won't be covered in much detail.

Carry out the following steps:

1. We will start by creating a `ValidationError` component that will render form validation errors. Create a file called `ValidationError.tsx` in the `posts` folder with the following content:

    ```
    import { FieldError } from 'react-hook-form';

    type Props = {
      fieldError: FieldError | undefined,
    };
    export function ValidationError({ fieldError }: Props) {
      if (!fieldError) {
        return null;
      }
      return (
        <div role="alert" className="text-red-500 text-xs
          mt-1">
          {fieldError.message}
        </div>
      );
    }
    ```

2. Create a new file in the `posts` folder called `NewPostForm.tsx`. This will contain a form to capture the title and description for a new blog post. Add the following import statements to the file:

```
import { FieldError, useForm } from 'react-hook-form';
import { ValidationError } from './ValidationError';
import { NewPostData } from './types';
```

3. Start to implement the form component as follows:

```
type Props = {
  onSave: (newPost: NewPostData) => void;
};
export function NewPostForm({ onSave }: Props) {
}
```

The component has a prop for saving a new blog post so that the interaction with the REST API can be handled outside of this form component.

4. Now, destructure the `register` and `handleSubmit` functions and useful state variables from React Hook Form's `useForm` hook:

```
type Props = {
  onSave: (newPost: NewPostData) => void;
};
export function NewPostForm({ onSave }: Props) {
  const {
    register,
    handleSubmit,
    formState: { errors, isSubmitting, isSubmitSuccessful
  },
  } = useForm<NewPostData>();
}
```

We pass the type for the new post data into the `useForm` hook so it knows the shape of the data to capture.

5. Create a variable for the field container style and a function for the editor style:

```
export function NewPostForm({ onSave }: Props) {
  ...
  const fieldStyle = 'flex flex-col mb-2';
  function getEditorStyle(
```

```
        fieldError: FieldError | undefined
    ) {
        return fieldError ? 'border-red-500' : '';
    }
}
```

6. Render `title` and `description` fields in a `form` element as follows:

```
export function NewPostForm({ onSave }: Props) {
    ...
    return (
        <form
            noValidate
            className="border-b py-4"
            onSubmit={handleSubmit(onSave)}
        >
            <div className={fieldStyle}>
                <label htmlFor="title">Title</label>
                <input
                    type="text"
                    id="title"
                    {...register('title', {
                        required: 'You must enter a title',
                    })}
                    className={getEditorStyle(errors.title)}
                />
                <ValidationError fieldError={errors.title} />
            </div>
            <div className={fieldStyle}>
                <label htmlFor="description">Description</label>
                <textarea
                    id="description"
                    {...register('description', {
                        required: 'You must enter the description',
                    })}
                    className={getEditorStyle(errors.description)}
                />
```

```
            <ValidationError fieldError={errors.description}
              />
          </div>
        </form>
      );
    }
```

7. Lastly, render a Save button and the success message:

```
<form
  noValidate
  className="border-b py-4"
  onSubmit={handleSubmit(onSave)}
>
  <div className={fieldStyle}> ... </div>
  <div className={fieldStyle}> ... </div>
  <div className={fieldStyle}>
    <button
      type="submit"
      disabled={isSubmitting}
      className="mt-2 h-10 px-6 font-semibold bg-black
        text-white"
    >
      Save
    </button>
    {isSubmitSuccessful && (
      <div
        role="alert"
        className="text-green-500 text-xs mt-1"
      >
        The post was successfully saved
      </div>
    )}
  </div>
</form>
```

That completes the implementation of the NewPostForm component.

8. Now open PostPage.tsx and import the NewPostForm component and the savePost function we created earlier. Also, import the NewPostData type:

```
import { useEffect, useState } from 'react';
import { getPosts } from './getPosts';
import { PostData, NewPostData } from './types';
import { PostsList } from './PostsList';
import { savePost } from './savePost';
import { NewPostForm } from './NewPostForm';
```

9. In the PostPage JSX, add the NewPostForm form above the PostsList:

```
<div className="w-96 mx-auto mt--6">
  <h2 className="text-xl text-slate-900 font-
    bold">Posts</h2>
  <NewPostForm onSave={handleSave} />
  <PostsList posts={posts} />
</div>;
```

10. Add the save handler function just below the effect that gets blog posts:

```
useEffect(() => {
  ...
}, []);
async function handleSave(newPostData: NewPostData) {
  const newPost = await savePost(newPostData);
  setPosts([newPost, ...posts]);
}
```

11. The hander calls savePost with the data from the form. After the post has been saved, it is added to the start of the posts array.

12. In the running app, the new blog post form will appear above the blog post list, as follows:

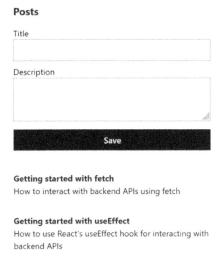

Figure 9.5 – New blog post form above the posts list

13. Fill in the form with a new blog post and press the **Save** button. The new post should appear at the top of the list after a couple of seconds.

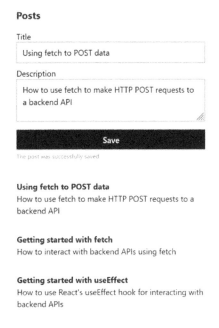

Figure 9.6 – New blog post added to posts list

That completes the implementation of the form and its integration into the blog posts page.

Here are a couple of key points we learned in this section on posting data with `fetch`:

- The second parameter in the `fetch` function allows the HTTP method to be specified. In this section, we used this parameter to make an HTTP POST request.

- The second parameter in `fetch` also allows the request body to be supplied.

Once again, keeping the app and REST API running, in the next section, we will use React Router's data-fetching capabilities to simplify our data-fetching code.

Using React Router

In this section, we will learn about how React Router can integrate with the data-fetching process. We will use this knowledge to simplify the code that fetches blog posts in our app.

Understanding React Router data loading

React Router data loading is similar to React Router forms, which we learned about in *Chapter 7*. Instead of defining an action that handles form submission, we define a **loader** that handles data loading. The following code snippet defines a loader on a `some-page` route:

```
const router = createBrowserRouter([
  ...,
  {
    path: '/some-page',
    element: <SomePage />,
    loader: async () => {
      const response = fetch('https://somewhere');
      return await response.json();
    }
  },
  ...
]);
```

React Router calls the loader to get the data before it renders the component defined on the route. The data is then available in the component via a `useLoaderData` hook:

```
export function SomePage() {
  const data = useLoaderData();
  ...
}
```

This approach is efficient as the route component is only rendered once because the data is available on the first render.

For more information on React Router loaders, see the following link: `https://reactrouter.com/en/main/route/loader`. For more information on the `useLoaderData` hook, see the following link: `https://reactrouter.com/en/main/hooks/use-loader-data`.

Now that we are starting to understand data loading in React Router, we will use this in our app.

Using React Router for data loading

Carry out the following steps to use a React Router data loader in our app:

1. Open `App.tsx` and add the following import statement:

    ```
    import {
      createBrowserRouter,
      RouterProvider
    } from 'react-router-dom';
    ```

2. Also, import the `getPosts` function:

    ```
    import { getPosts } from './posts/getPosts';
    ```

    `getPosts` will be the loader function.

3. Add the following router definition above the App component:

    ```
    const router = createBrowserRouter([
      {
        path: "/",
        element: <PostsPage />,
        loader: getPosts
      }
    ]);
    ```

4. In the App component, replace `PostsPage` with `RouterProvider`:

    ```
    function App() {
      return <RouterProvider router={router} />;
    }
    ```

5. Open `PostsPage.tsx` and remove the React import statement, as this is no longer required in this component.

6. Also, add `assertIsPosts` to the `getPosts` import statement and remove `getPosts`:

    ```
    import { assertIsPosts } from './getPosts';
    ```

    We will eventually need `assertIsPosts` to type the data.

7. Still in `PostsPage.tsx`, add the following import statement for a hook in React Router that allows us to access the loader data:

    ```
    import { useLoaderData } from 'react-router-dom';
    ```

8. Inside the `PostsPage` component, remove the `isLoading` and `posts` state definitions. These won't be needed because we will get the data from React Router without having to do any waiting.

9. Remove the call to `useEffect` that currently gets the data.

10. Remove the second line of the `handleSave` function that sets the `posts` state. `handleSave` should now read as follows:

    ```
    async function handleSave(newPostData: NewPostData) {
      await savePost(newPostData);
    }
    ```

11. Remove the loading indicator as well.

12. Now at the top of the `PostsPage` component, make a call to `useLoaderData` and assign the result to a `posts` variable:

    ```
    export function PostsPage() {
      const posts = useLoaderData();

      ...
    }
    ```

13. Unfortunately, `posts` is of the `unknown` type, so there is a type error where it is passed to the `PostsLists` component. Use the `assertsIsPosts` function to type the data with `PostData[]`:

    ```
    const posts = useLoaderData();
    assertIsPosts(posts);
    ```

    The type errors are now resolved.

    Note that `PostData` from the `types` import statement is unused. Leave it intact because we will use this again in the next section.

14. The running app should look and behave similarly to how it previously did. One thing you may notice is that when a new blog post is added using the form, it doesn't appear in the list – you have to manually refresh the page for it to appear. This will be resolved when we use React Query later in this chapter.

Notice how much code we just removed – this indicates that the code is much simpler now. Another benefit of using React Router to load the data is that `PostsPage` isn't re-rendered after the data is fetched – the data is fetched before `PostsPage` is rendered.

Next, we will improve the user experience of the data-fetching process.

Deferred React Router data fetching

If the data-fetching process is slow, there will be a noticeable delay before a component is rendered by React Router. Fortunately, there is a solution to this using React Router's `defer` function and `Await` component, along with React's `Suspense` component. Carry out the following steps to add these to our app:

1. Start by opening `App.tsx` and add the `defer` function to the React Router import statement:

```
import {
  createBrowserRouter,
  RouterProvider,
  defer
} from 'react-router-dom';
```

2. Update the `loader` function as follows in the route definition:

```
const router = createBrowserRouter([
  {
    path: "/",
    element: ...,
    loader: async () => defer({ posts: getPosts() })
  }
]);
```

React Router's `defer` function takes in an object of promised data. The property name in the object is a unique key for the data, which is `posts` in our case. The value is the function that fetches the data, which is `getPosts` in our case.

Notice that we don't await `getPosts` because we want the loader to complete and `PostsPage` to immediately render.

3. Open `PostsPage.tsx` and add an import statement for React's `Suspense` component:

    ```
    import { Suspense } from 'react';
    ```

4. Add the `Await` component to the React Router import statement:

    ```
    import { useLoaderData, Await } from 'react-router-dom';
    ```

5. In the component, update the call to `useLoaderData` to assign the result to a `data` variable instead of `posts`:

    ```
    const data = useLoaderData();
    ```

    The shape of the loader data is a little different now – it will be an object containing a `posts` property containing the blog posts. The blog posts also won't immediately be there as they previously were – the `data.posts` property will contain a promise for the blog posts instead.

6. Also, remove the call to `assertIsPosts` – we will use this later in *step 9*.

7. The `data` variable is of the `unknown` type, so add a type assertion function beneath the component that can be used to strongly type it:

    ```
    type Data = {
      posts: PostData[];
    };
    export function assertIsData(
      data: unknown
    ): asserts data is Data {
      if (typeof data !== 'object') {
        throw new Error("Data isn't an object");
      }
      if (data === null) {
        throw new Error('Data is null');
      }
      if (!('posts' in data)) {
        throw new Error("data doesn't contain posts");
      }
    }
    ```

    The type assertion function checks that the `data` parameter is an object containing a `posts` property.

8. We can now use the assertion function to type the `data` variable in the component:

```
const data = useLoaderData();
assertIsData(data);
```

9. In the JSX, wrap `Suspense` and `Await` around `PostsList` as follows:

```
<Suspense fallback={<div>Fetching...</div>}>
  <Await resolve={data.posts}>
    {(posts) => {
      assertIsPosts(posts);
      return <PostsList posts={posts} />;
    }}
  </Await>
</Suspense>
```

`Suspense` and `Await` work together to only render `PostsLists` when the data has been fetched. We use `Suspense` to render a **Fetching...** message while the data is being fetched. We also use `assertIsPosts` to ensure that `posts` is typed correctly.

10. In the running app, you will now notice the **Fetching...** message when the page loads:

Figure 9.7 – Fetching message during data fetching

11. Stop the app from running by pressing *Ctrl* + *C* in the terminal that is running the app but keep the API running.

The great thing about this solution is that a re-render still doesn't occur when `PostsPage` is rendered because of the use of `Suspense` and `Await`.

We will now quickly recap what we have learned with React Router's data-fetching capabilities:

- React Router's `loader` allows us to efficiently load fetched data into a route component
- React Router's `defer` allows the route component not to be blocked from rendering the component while data is being fetched
- React Router's `useLoaderData` hook allows a component to access a route's loader data
- React's `Suspense` and React Router's `Await` allow a component to render while data is still being fetched

For more information on deferred data in React Router, see the following link: `https://reactrouter.com/en/main/guides/deferred`.

In the next section, we will use another popular library for managing server data to further improve the user experience.

Using React Query

React Query is a popular library for interacting with REST APIs. The key thing it does is manage the state surrounding REST API calls. One thing that it does that React Router doesn't is that it maintains a cache of the fetched data, which improves the perceived performance of an app.

In this section, we will refactor the app to use React Query rather than React Router's loader capability. We will then refactor the app again to use both React Query and React Router's loader to get the best of both these worlds.

Installing React Query

Our first job is to install React Query, which we can do by running the following command in a terminal:

```
npm i @tanstack/react-query
```

This library includes TypeScript types, so no additional package is required to be installed.

Adding the React Query provider

React Query requires a provider component in the component tree above the components that need access to the data it manages. Eventually, React Query will hold the blog post data in our app. Carry out the following steps to add the React Query provider component to the `App` component:

1. Open `App.tsx` and add the following import statement:

    ```
    import {
      QueryClient,
    ```

```
  QueryClientProvider,
} from '@tanstack/react-query';
```

`QueryClient` provides access to the data. `QueryClientProvider` is the provider component we need to place in the component tree.

2. Wrap `QueryClientProvider` around `RouterProvider` as follows:

```
const queryClient = new QueryClient();
const router = createBrowserRouter( ... );
function App() {
  return (
    <QueryClientProvider client={queryClient}>
      <RouterProvider router={router} />
    </QueryClientProvider>
  );
}
```

`QueryClientProvider` requires an instance of `QueryClient` to be passed into it, so we create this instance outside of the App component. We place the `queryClient` variable above the router definition because we will eventually use it in the router definition.

The `PostsPage` component now has access to React Query. Next, we will use React Query in `PostsPage`.

Getting data using React Query

React Query refers to a request to fetch data as a **query** and has a `useQuery` hook to carry out this. We will use React Query's `useQuery` hook in the `PostsPage` component to call the `getPosts` function and store the data it returns. This will temporarily replace the use of React Router's loader. Carry out the following steps:

1. Import `useQuery` from React Query:

    ```
    import { useQuery } from '@tanstack/react-query';
    ```

2. Add `getPosts` to the `getPosts` import statement:

    ```
    import { assertIsPosts, getPosts } from './getPosts';
    ```

    We will eventually use `getPosts` to fetch data and store it within React Query.

3. In the `PostPage` component, comment out the `data` variable:

    ```
    // const data = useLoaderData();
    // assertIsData(data);
    ```

We are commenting these lines out rather than removing them because we will use them again in the next section when we use React Router and React Query together.

4. Now, add a call to `useQuery` as follows:

```
export function PostsPage() {
  const {
    isLoading,
    isFetching,
    data: posts,
  } = useQuery(['postsData'], getPosts);
  // const data = useLoaderData();
  // assertIsData(data);
  ...
}
```

The first argument passed to `useQuery` is a unique key for the data. This is because React Query can store many datasets and uses the key to identify each one. The key is an array containing the name given to the data in our case. However, the key array could include things like the ID of a particular record we want to fetch or a page number if we want to only fetch a page of records.

The second argument passed to `useQuery` is the fetching function, which is our existing `getPosts` function.

We have destructured the following state variables:

-   `isLoading` – Whether the component is being loaded for the first time.

-   `isFetching` – Whether the fetching function is being called. React Query will refetch data when it thinks it is stale. We will experience refetching later when we play with the app.

-   `data` – The data that has been fetched. We have aliased this `posts` variable to match the previous `posts` state value. Keeping the same name minimizes the changes required in the rest of the component.

> **Note**
>
> There are other useful state variables that can be destructured from `useQuery`. An example is `isError`, which indicates whether the `fetch` function errored. See the following link for more information: `https://tanstack.com/query/v4/docs/reference/useQuery`.

5. Add a loading indicator above the return statement:

```
if (isLoading || posts === undefined) {
  return (
    <div className="w-96 mx-auto mt--6">
```

```
        Loading ...
      </div>
    );
  }
  return ...
```

The check for the `posts` state being `undefined` means that the TypeScript compiler knows that `posts` isn't `undefined` when referenced in the JSX.

6. In the JSX, comment out `Suspense` and its children:

```
return (
  <div className="w-96 mx-auto mt-6">
    <h2 className="text-xl text-slate-900 font-
      bold">Posts</h2>
    <NewPostForm onSave={mutate} />
    {/* <Suspense fallback={<div>Fetching ...</div>}>
        <Await resolve={data.posts}
          errorElement={<p>Error!</p>}>
          {(posts) => {
            assertIsPosts(posts);
            return <PostsList posts={posts} />;
          }}
        </Await>
      </Suspense> */}
  </div>
);
```

We have commented this block out rather than removing it because we will revert to it in the next section when we use React Router and React Query together.

7. When data is being fetched, display a fetching indicator and render the blog posts when the data has been fetched:

```
<div className="w-96 mx-auto mt-6">
  <h2 className="text-xl text-slate-900 font-
    bold">Posts</h2>
  <NewPostForm onSave={handleSave} />
  {isFetching ? (
    <div>Fetching ...</div>
  ) : (
```

```
        <PostsList posts={posts} />
      )}
      . . .
    </div>
```

8. Run the app by running npm start in the terminal. The blog post page will appear the same as it did before. A technical difference is that the PostsPage is re-rendered after the data has been fetched.

9. Leave the browser window and set the focus to a different window, such as your code editor. Now, set your focus back on the browser window and notice that the fetching indicator appears for a split second:

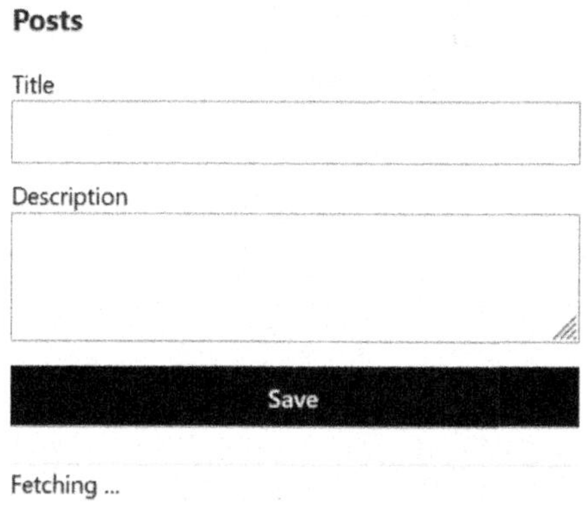

Posts

Title

Description

Save

Fetching ...

Figure 9.8 – Fetching indicator when data is refetched

This is because React Query, by default, assumes that data is stale when the browser regains focus. For more information on this behavior, see the following link in the React Query documentation: https://tanstack.com/query/v4/docs/guides/window-focus-refetching.

10. A great feature of React Query is that it maintains a cache of the data. This allows us to render components with data from the cache while fresh data is being fetched. To experience this, in the PostsPage JSX, remove the isFetching condition for when PostsList is rendered:

```
    <PostsList posts={posts} />
```

So, PostsList will now render even if the data is stale.

11. In the running app, press *F5* to refresh the page. Then, leave the browser window and set the focus to a different window. Set your focus back on the browser window and notice that no fetching indicator appears and the blog posts list remains intact.

12. Repeat the previous step but this time, observe the **Network** tab in the browser's DevTools. Notice that a second network request is made when the app is refocused:

Figure 9.9 – Two API requests for blog posts

So, React Query seamlessly allows the component to render the old data and re-renders it with the new data after it has been fetched.

Next, we will continue to refactor the posts page to use React Query when a new blog post is sent to the API.

Updating data using React Query

React Query can update data using a feature called **mutations** using a useMutation hook. Carry out the following steps in PostsPage.tsx to change the saving of a new blog post to use a React Query mutation:

1. Update the React Query import as follows:

    ```
    import {
      useQuery,
      useMutation,
      useQueryClient,
    } from '@tanstack/react-query';
    ```

The useMutation hook allows us to carry out a mutation. The useQueryClient hook will enable us to get the instance of queryClient that the component is using and access and update the cached data.

2. Add a call to useMutation after the call to useQuery as follows:

```
const {
  isLoading,
  data: posts,
  isFetching,
} = useQuery(['postsData'], getPosts);

const { mutate } = useMutation(savePost);
```

We pass useMutation the function that performs the REST API HTTP POST request. We destructure the mutate function from the return value of useMutation, which we will use in *step 4* to trigger the mutation.

> **Note**
>
> There are other useful state variables that can be destructured from useMutation. An example is isError, which indicates whether the fetch function errored. See the following link for more information: https://tanstack.com/query/v4/docs/reference/useMutation.

3. When the mutation has successfully been completed, we want to update the posts cache to contain the new blog post. Make the following highlighted changes to implement this:

```
const queryClient = useQueryClient();
const { mutate } = useMutation(savePost, {
  onSuccess: (savedPost) => {
    queryClient.setQueryData<PostData[]>(
      ['postsData'],
      (oldPosts) => {
        if (oldPosts === undefined) {
          return [savedPost];
        } else {
          return [savedPost, ...oldPosts];
        }
      }
    );
```

```
    },
  });
```

The second argument on useMutation allows the mutation to be configured. The onSuccess configuration option is a function called when the mutation has been successfully completed.

useQueryClient returns the query client that the component is using. This query client has a method called setQueryData, which allows the cached data to be updated. setQueryData has arguments for the key of the cached data and the new copy of data to be cached.

4. We can trigger the mutation when the new post is saved by calling the destructured mutate function in the onSave prop on the NewPostForm JSX element:

```
<NewPostForm onSave={mutate} />
```

5. Now, we can remove the handleSave function because this is now redundant.

6. The imported NewPostData type can be removed as well. This type's import statement should now be as follows:

```
import { PostData } from './types';
```

7. In the running app, if you enter and save a new blog post, it will appear in the list as in the previous implementation:

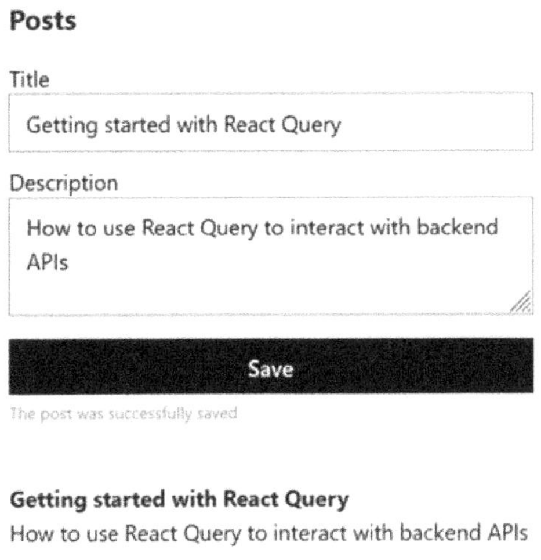

Figure 9.10 – New blog post added to posts list

That completes the refactoring of saving new blog posts to use a React Query mutation. That also completes this section on React Query – here's a recap of the key points:

- React Query is a popular library that manages data from a backend API in a cache, helping to improve performance
- React Query doesn't actually make the HTTP requests – the browser's `fetch` function can be used to do this
- React Query's `QueryClientProvider` component needs to be placed high in the component tree above where backend data is needed
- React Query's `useQuery` hook allows data to be fetched and cached in state
- React Query's `useMutation` hook allows data to be updated

For more information on React Query, visit the library's documentation site: `https://tanstack.com/query`.

Next, we will learn how to integrate React Query into React Router's data-fetching capabilities.

Using React Router with React Query

So far, we have experienced the benefits of both React Router and React Query data fetching. React Router reduces the number of re-renders, while React Query provides a client-side cache of the data. In this section, we will use these libraries together in our app so that it has both these benefits.

Carry out the following steps:

1. Start by opening `App.tsx` and change the loader function on the route definition to the following:

```
const router = createBrowserRouter([
  {
    path: '/',
    element: ...,
    loader: async () => {
      const existingData = queryClient.getQueryData([
        'postsData',
      ]);
      if (existingData) {
        return defer({ posts: existingData });
      }
      return defer({
        posts: queryClient.fetchQuery(
```

```
        ['postsData'],
        getPosts
      )
    });
  }
 }
])
```

Inside the loader, we use React Query's `getQueryData` function on the query client to get the existing data from its cache. If there is cached data, it is returned; otherwise, the data is fetched, deferred, and added to the cache.

2. Open `PostsPage.tsx` and remove the use of React Query's `useQuery` because the React Router loader manages the data loading process now.

3. Remove the `getPosts` function from the `getPosts` import statement because this is used in the React Router loader now.

4. Also, remove the loading indicator because we will revert to using React Suspense in *step 6*.

5. The data will be retrieved using React Router's `useLoaderData` hook again, so uncomment those two lines of code:

```
export function PostsPage() {
  const queryClient = useQueryClient();
  const { mutate } = useMutation( ... );
  const data = useLoaderData();
  assertIsData(data);
  return ...
}
```

6. Also, reinstate the use of `Suspense` and `Await` in the JSX. The JSX should be as follows now:

```
<div className="w-96 max-w-xl mx-auto mt-6">
  <h2 className="text-xl text-slate-900 font-bold">
    Posts
  </h2>
  <NewPostForm onSave={mutate} />
  <Suspense fallback={<div>Fetching ...</div>}>
    <Await resolve={data.posts}>
      {(posts) => {
        assertIsPosts(posts);
```

```
        return <PostsList posts={posts} />;
    }}
    </Await>
    </Suspense>
</div>
```

7. The running app will appear and display the blog posts just as before, but a second render of `PostsPage` will no longer occur when the app is first loaded. However, after adding a new blog post using the form, it doesn't appear in the list. We will resolve this in the next step.

8. After the new blog post has been saved, we need to cause the route component to re-render in order to get the latest data. We can do this by causing the router to navigate to the page we are already on, as follows:

```
import {
  useLoaderData,
  Await,
  useNavigate
} from 'react-router-dom';
...
export function PostsPage() {
  const navigate = useNavigate();
  const queryClient = useQueryClient();
  const { mutate } = useMutation(savePost, {
    onSuccess: (savedPost) => {
      queryClient.setQueryData<PostData[]>(
        ['postsData'],
        (oldPosts) => {
          if (oldPosts === undefined) {
            return [savedPost];
          } else {
            return [savedPost, ...oldPosts];
          }
        }
      );
      navigate('/');
    },
  });
  ...
}
```

We perform the navigation after the blog post has been saved and added to the cache. This means the route's loader will execute and populate its data from the cache. `PostsPage` will then be rendered with `useLoaderData` returning the up-to-date data.

That completes this final revision of the app and this section on using React Router with React Query. By integrating these two libraries, we get the following key benefits of each library:

- React Router's data loader prevents an unnecessary re-render when data is loaded onto a page
- React Query's cache prevents unnecessary calls to the REST API

The way these two libraries integrate is to get and set data in the React Query cache, in the React Router loader.

Summary

In this chapter, we used the browser's `fetch` function to make HTTP `GET` and `POST` requests. The request's URL is the first argument on the `fetch` function. The second argument on `fetch` allows the request options to be specified, such as the HTTP method and body.

A type assertion function can be used to strongly type the data in the response body of an HTTP request. The function takes in the data having an unknown type. The function then carries out checks to validate the type of data and throws an error if it is invalid. If no errors occur, the asserted type for the data is specified in the functions assertion signature.

React's `useEffect` hook can be used to execute a call to fetch data from a backend API and store the data in the state when the component is mounted. A flag can be used inside `useEffect` to ensure the component is still mounted after the HTTP request before the data state is set.

React Query and React Router replace the use of `useEffect` and `useState` in the data-fetching process and simplify our code. React Router's loader function allows data to be fetched and passed into the component route removing an unnecessary re-render. React Query contains a cache that can be used in components to render data optimistically while up-to-date data is being fetched. React Query also contains a `useMutation` hook to enable data to be updated.

In the next chapter, we will cover how to interact with GraphQL APIs.

Questions

Answer the following questions to check what you have learned in this chapter:

1. The following effect attempts to fetch data from a REST API and store it in the state:

```
useEffect(async () => {
  const response = await fetch('https://some-rest-api/');
```

```
    const data = await response.json();
    setData(data);
  }, []);
```

What are the problems with this implementation?

2. The following fetching function returns an array of first names:

```
export async function getFirstNames() {
  const response = await fetch('https://some-
    firstnames/');
  const body = await response.json();
  return body;
}
```

However, the return type of the function is any. So, how can we improve the implementation to have a return type of string[]?

3. In the fetch function argument, what should be specified in the method option for it to make an HTTP PUT request?

```
fetch(url, {
  method: ???,
  body: JSON.stringify(data),
});
```

4. How do you specify a bearer token in an HTTP Authorization header when making an HTTP request to a protected resource using fetch?

5. A component uses React Query's useQuery to fetch data but the component errors with the following error:

Uncaught Error: No QueryClient set, use QueryClientProvider to set one

What do you think the problem is?

6. What state variable can be destructured from React Query's useMutation to determine whether the HTTP request has returned an error?

Answers

1. There are two problems with the implementation:

    - useEffect doesn't support top-level async/await

    - If the component is umounted during the HTTP request, an error will occur when the data state is set

Here is an implementation with those issues resolved:

```
useEffect(() => {
  let cancel = false;
  fetch('https://some-rest-api/')
    .then((response) => data.json())
    .then((data) => {
      if (!cancel) {
        setData(data);
      }
    });
  return () => {
    cancel = true;
  };
}, []);
```

2. An assert function can be used on the response body object as follows:

```
export async function getFirstNames() {
  const response = await fetch('https://some-
    firstnames/');
  const body = await response.json();
  assertIsFirstNames(body);
  return body;
}


function assertIsFirstNames(
  firstNames: unknown
): asserts firstNames is string[] {
  if (!Array.isArray(firstNames)) {
    throw new Error('firstNames isn't an array');
  }
  if (firstNames.length === 0) {
    return;
  }
  firstNames.forEach((firstName) => {
    if (typeof firstName !== 'string') {
      throw new Error('firstName is not a string');
```

```
        }
    });
}
```

3. The method option should be `'PUT'`:

```
fetch(url, {
    method: 'PUT',
    body: JSON.stringify(data),
});
```

4. The `headers.Authorization` option can be used to specify a bearer token when making an HTTP request to a protected resource using `fetch`:

```
fetch(url, {
    headers: {
        Authorization: 'Bearer some-bearer-token',
        'Content-Type': 'application/json',
    },
});
```

5. The problem is that React Query's `QueryClientProvider` hasn't been placed above the component using `useQuery` in the component tree.

6. The `isError` state variable can be destructured from React Query's `useMutation` to determine whether the HTTP request has returned an error. Alternatively, the `status` state variable can be checked for a value of `'error'`.

10

Interacting with GraphQL APIs

GraphQL APIs are web APIs that have a special language for interacting with them. These APIs are a very popular alternative to REST APIs with React frontends.

In this chapter, we'll first understand the special GraphQL language, executing some basic queries on the GitHub GraphQL API. We will then build a React app that allows users to search for a GitHub repository and star it, experiencing the benefits of GraphQL over REST.

The app will use the browser's `fetch` function with React Query to interact with the GitHub GraphQL API. We will then refactor the implementation of the app to use a specialized GraphQL client called **Apollo Client**.

We'll cover the following topics:

- Understanding the GraphQL syntax
- Getting set up
- Using the React Query with fetch
- Using Apollo Client

Technical requirements

We will use the following technologies in this chapter:

- **Node.js** and **npm**: You can install them at `https://nodejs.org/en/download/`.
- **Visual Studio Code**: You can install it at `https://code.visualstudio.com/`.
- **GitHub**: You'll need a GitHub account. If you haven't got an account, you can sign up at the following link: `https://github.com/join`.
- **GitHub GraphQL API Explorer**: We'll use this tool to play with the syntax of GraphQL queries and mutations. The tool can be found at `https://docs.github.com/en/graphql/overview/explorer`.

All the code snippets in this chapter can be found online at `https://github.com/PacktPublishing/Learn-React-with-TypeScript-2nd-Edition/tree/main/Chapter10`.

Understanding the GraphQL syntax

Like React Query, GraphQL refers to a request to fetch data as a **query**. In the following subsections, we'll learn how to write a basic GraphQL query that returns data from a couple of fields. These fields will have primitive values and so the result will be flat. We'll then learn how to write a more advanced query containing object-based field values that have their own properties. Lastly, we will learn how to make queries more reusable using parameters.

Returning flat data

Carry out the following steps to use the GitHub GraphQL API Explorer to get information about your GitHub user account:

1. Open the following URL in a browser to open the GitHub GraphQL API Explorer: `https://docs.github.com/en/graphql/overview/explorer`.

2. Sign in using the **Sign in with GitHub** button if you aren't signed in already. A GraphQL API Explorer page appears, as follows:

Figure 10.1 – GitHub GraphQL API Explorer

3. In the top-left panel of the GraphQL API Explorer, enter the following query:

```
query {
  viewer {
    name
  }
}
```

The query starts with the `query` keyword to specify that the operation is a query to fetch data (rather than update data). It is worth noting that the `query` keyword is optional because the operation defaults to a query.

After the operation, the data to be returned is specified by specifying the required objects and fields. In our example, we have specified that the `name` field in the `viewer` object is returned.

4. Click the **Execute Query** button, which is the round button containing the black triangle.

The query result appears to the right of the query as follows:

GraphiQL ▶ Prettify | History | Explorer

```
1 ▾ query {
2       viewer {
3         name
4       }
5  }
```

```
{
  data": {
    "viewer": {
      "name": "Carl Rippon"
    }
  }
}
```

QUERY VARIABLES   REQUEST HEADERS

1

Figure 10.2 – GitHub GraphQL

The data we requested is returned as a JSON object. The `name` field value should be your name stored in your GitHub account.

5. On the right-hand side of the query results is **Documentation Explorer**. Expand this panel if it's not already expanded:

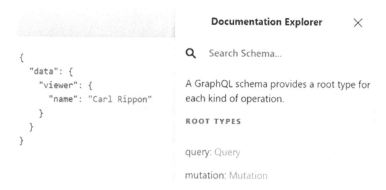

Figure 10.3 – Documentation Explorer

6. Click on the **Query** link in **Documentation Explorer**. All the objects are shown that can be queried, including viewer, which is the one we just queried. The object type appears to the right of the object name, and the object description appears underneath.

> **Note**
>
> Like many languages, GraphQL's fields have types – there are built-in types such as String, Int, and Boolean, as well as the ability to create custom types. See the following link for more information: https://graphql.org/learn/schema/#type-language.

7. Scroll down to the viewer object in **Documentation Explorer** (it should be right at the bottom):

topic(name: String!): Topic
Look up a topic by name.

user(login: String!): User
Lookup a user by login.

viewer: User!
The currently authenticated user.

Figure 10.4 – viewer object in Documentation Explorer

8. Click on the User type next to the viewer object name in **Documentation Explorer**. All the fields available in the User type are listed:

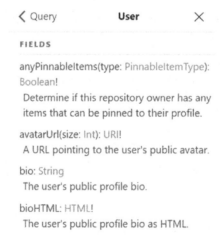

Figure 10.5 – Fields in the User type

9. Let's add `avatarUrl` to our query, as this is an additional field available to us:

```
query {
  viewer {
    name
    avatarUrl
  }
}
```

We simply add the `avatarUrl` field inside the `viewer` object with a carriage return between the `name` and `avatarUrl` fields.

10. The `avatarUrl` field is added to the JSON result if you execute the query. This should be a path to an image of you:

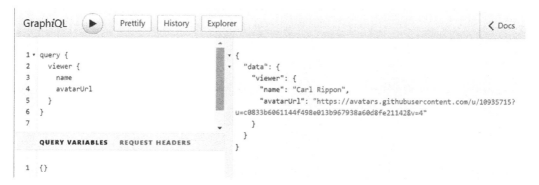

Figure 10.6 – Updated query result with avatarUrl

That completes our first graphQL query.

11. We are already seeing how flexible GraphQL is with being able to specify which fields we want to be returned in the response. Next, we'll create another query that returns a hierarchical structure.

Returning hierarchical data

We will make a more complex query now by returning an object-based field rather than just fields with primitive values. This will mean the result will have a hierarchical structure rather than being flat. We'll query for a GitHub repository, returning its name, description, and the number of stars it has. So, carry out the following steps:

1. Start by entering the following query into the query panel of the GitHub GraphQL API explorer:

```
query {
  repository (owner:"facebook", name:"react") {
```

```
        id
        name
        description
      }
   }
```

The query asks for the `id`, `name`, and `description` fields in the `repository` object. After the `repository` object is specified, two parameters for the `owner` and name of the repository are specified.

2. Let's now request the number of stars against the repository. To do this, add the `totalCount` field within the `stargazers` object as follows:

```
query {
   repository (owner:"facebook", name:"react") {
      id
      name
      description
      stargazers {
        totalCount
      }
   }
}
```

3. If you execute the query, the result will appear like the following screenshot:

Figure 10.7 – Query for a specific repository

That completes our second GraphQL query.

So, GraphQL allows us to make a single web request for different bits of data, returning just the fields that we require. Doing a similar thing with a REST API would probably require multiple requests and we'd get a lot more data than we need to return. It is in these types of queries where GraphQL shines over REST.

Next, we will learn how to allow query parameter values to vary.

Specifying query parameters

The query we have just made already has parameters for the repository name and owner. However, the `owner` parameter is hardcoded to have a value of `"facebook"`, and the `name` parameter to have a value of `"react"`.

You may have noticed the **QUERY VARIABLES** panel under the query panel. This allows query parameter values to be specified. The query parameters then reference variable names instead of hardcoded values.

Carry out the following steps to adjust the repository query so that the query parameters can vary:

1. Add the following query variables in the **QUERY VARIABLES** panel:

   ```
   {
     "owner": "facebook",
     "name": "react"
   }
   ```

   As you can see, the variables are specified using JSON syntax. We have named the variable for the repository owner, `owner`, and the variable for the repository name, `name`.

2. Update the query to reference the query variables as follows:

   ```
   query ($owner: String!, $name: String!) {
     repository (owner:$owner, name:$name) {
       . . .
     }
   }
   ```

   The query parameters are specified in parentheses after the `query` keyword. The parameter names must be prefixed with a dollar sign (`$`). The type for each parameter is specified after a colon (`:`) – both parameters are `String` in our case. The exclamation mark (`!`) after the type means it is a required query parameter. The parameters can then be referenced within the query, which, in our case, is where we request the repository object.

3. If we execute the query, the JSON result will be the same as the query with the hardcoded repository owner and name criteria.

4. Now, change the variable values to target a different repository and rerun the query. The JSON result will contain the same fields but with values for the repository requested. The following is the query and result for the TypeScript repository:

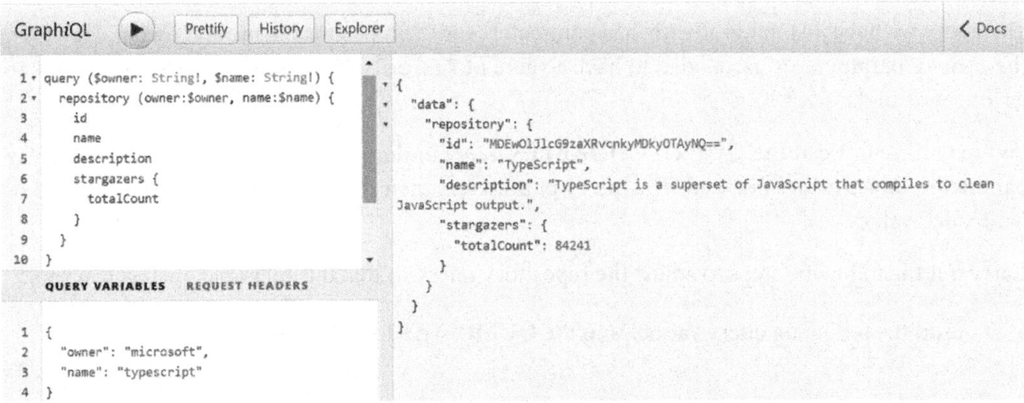

Figure 10.8 – Query with parameters for the TypeScript repository

5. We are now getting comfortable with reading data from a GraphQL server. Next, we'll learn how to request changes to GraphQL data.

GraphQL mutations

A change to data in GraphQL is referred to as a **mutation**. Starring a repository is a change to the underlying data, so we can class this as an example of a mutation.

Carry out the following steps to create a mutation that stars a GitHub repository:

1. In order to star a repository, we need the repository ID. So, copy the repository ID of the last query result into your clipboard. The following is the ID of the TypeScript repository:

```
"MDEwOlJlcG9zaXRvcnkyMDkyOTAyNQ=="
```

2. Replace the query variables with a variable for the repository ID we want to star:

```
{
    "repoId": "MDEwOlJlcG9zaXRvcnkyMDkyOTAyNQ=="
}
```

3. Replace the content in the query panel with the following mutation:

```
mutation ($repoId: ID!) {
    addStar(input: { starrableId: $repoId }) {
        starrable {
```

```
      stargazers {
        totalCount
      }
    }
  }
}
```

Let's break down this code:

- We prefix a mutation with the `mutation` keyword.

- We put parameters to be passed into the mutation after the `mutation` keyword in parentheses. In our case, we have a single parameter for the repository ID we want to star.

- `addStar` is the mutation function we call, which has a parameter called `input` that we need to pass.

- `input` is actually an object that has a field called `starrableId` that we need to include. The value of this is the repository ID we want to star, so we set it to our `$repoId` repository ID variable.

- After the mutation parameters, we specify what we want to return in the response. In our case, we want to return the number of stars on the repository.

4. If we execute the mutation, the star will be added to the repository, and the new total number of stars will be returned:

Figure 10.9 – Mutation to star the repository

That completes this section on getting comfortable with the GraphQL syntax. To recap, here are some key points:

- A GraphQL query fetches data, and a mutation changes data. These operations are specified with the `query` and `mutation` keywords, respectively.
- The data required in the response can be specified in the query/mutation, which helps the backend interactions be efficient.
- Query parameter variables can be specified to allow a query/mutation to be reusable.

Next, we will set up a React project that will eventually interact with the GitHub GraphQL API.

Setting up the project

In this section, we will start by creating the project for the app we will build. We will build a React app that allows users to search for a GitHub repository and star it. It will use the GitHub GraphQL API, so we will generate a **personal access token** (**PAT**) for this and store it in an environment variable.

Creating the project

We will develop the app using Visual Studio Code and a new Create React App-based project setup. We've previously covered this several times, so we will not cover the steps in this chapter – instead, see *Chapter 3, Setting Up React and TypeScript*.

We will style the app with Tailwind CSS. We have previously covered how to install and configure Tailwind in a Create React App in *Chapter 5, Approaches to Styling Frontends*. So, after you have created the React and TypeScript project, install and configure Tailwind.

We will use React Hook Form to implement the form that creates blog posts, and the `@tailwindcss/forms` plugin to style the form. So, install the `@tailwindcss/forms` plugin and React Hook Form (see *Chapter 7, Working with Forms,* if you can't remember how to do this).

Now that the project is set up, next, we will gain access to the GitHub GraphQL API.

Creating a PAT for the GitHub GraphQL API

The GitHub GraphQL API is protected by a PAT, which is a string of characters and is a common mechanism for protecting web APIs. Carry out the following steps to generate a PAT:

1. In a browser, go to GitHub: `https://github.com/`.
2. Sign in to your GitHub account if you aren't already signed in. You can create a GitHub account if you haven't got one by using the **Sign Up** button.
3. Now, open the menu under your avatar and click **Settings**.

4. Next, access the **Developer Settings** option at the bottom of the left-hand bar.

5. Go to the **Personal access tokens** page on the left-hand bar.

6. Click the **Generate new token** button to start creating the PAT. You will likely be prompted to input your password after clicking the button.

7. Before the token is generated, you will be asked to specify the scopes. Enter a token description, tick the repo and user scopes, and then click the **Generate token** button.

The token is then generated and displayed on the page. Take a copy of this because we'll need this in the next section when building our app.

Creating environment variables

Before writing code that interacts with the GitHub GraphQL API, we will create environment variables for the API URL and the PAT:

1. Let's start by creating an environment file to store the URL for the GitHub GraphQL API. Create a file called `.env` in the root of the project containing this variable, as follows:

    ```
    REACT_APP_GITHUB_URL = https://api.github.com/graphql
    ```

    This environment variable is injected into the code at build time and can be accessed by code using `process.env.REACT_APP_GITHUB_URL`. Environment variables in Create React App projects must be prefixed with `React_APP_`.

    For more information on environment variables, see the following link: `https://create-react-app.dev/docs/adding-custom-environment-variables/`.

2. Now, we will create a second environment variable for the GitHub PAT token. However, we don't want to commit this file to source code control, so place it in a file called `.env.local` at the root of the project:

    ```
    REACT_APP_GITHUB_PAT = your-token
    ```

    `.env.local` is in the `.gitignore` file, so this file won't get committed to source code control, reducing the risk of your PAT getting stolen. Replace `your-token` with your PAT token in the preceding code snippet.

That completes the creation of the environment variables.

In the next section, we will start to build the app that will interact with the GitHub GraphQL API.

Using React Query with fetch

In this section, we will build an app containing a form that allows users to search and star GitHub repositories. The app will also have a header containing our name from GitHub. We will use the browser `fetch` function with React Query to interact with the GitHub GraphQL API. Let's get started.

Creating the header

We will create the header for the app, which will contain our GitHub name. We will create a `Header` component containing this, which will be referenced from the `App` component. The `Header` component will use React Query to execute a function that gets our GitHub name calling the GitHub GraphQL API.

Creating a function to get viewer information

Carry out the following steps to create a function that makes a request to the GitHub GraphQL API to get details about the logged-in viewer:

1. We will start by creating a folder for the API calls. Create an `api` folder in the `src` folder.

2. Now, we will create a type that the function will use. Create a file called `types.ts` in the `src/api` folder with the following content:

    ```
    export type ViewerData = {
      name: string;
      avatarUrl: string;
    };
    ```

    This type represents the logged-in viewer.

3. Create a file called `getViewer.ts` in the `api` folder that will contain the function we need to implement. Add an import statement for the type we just created:

    ```
    import { ViewerData } from './types';
    ```

4. Under the import statement, add a constant assigned to the following GraphQL query:

    ```
    export const GET_VIEWER_QUERY = `
      query {
        viewer {
          name
          avatarUrl
        }
      }
    `;
    ```

This is the same query we used earlier in the chapter to get the current viewer's name and avatar URL.

5. Add the following type, which represents the response from the GraphQL API call within this file:

```
type GetViewerResponse = {
  data: {
    viewer: ViewerData;
  };
};
```

6. Start to implement the function as follows:

```
export async function getViewer() {
  const response = await fetch(
    process.env.REACT_APP_GITHUB_URL!
  );
}
```

We use the `fetch` function to make the request to the GraphQL API. We have used the `REACT_APP_GITHUB_URL` environment variable to specify the GraphQL API URL. Environment variable values can be `undefined`, but we know this isn't the case, so we have added a not null assertion (`!`) after it.

7. Specify the GraphQL query in the request body as follows:

```
export async function getViewer() {
  const response = await fetch(
    process.env.REACT_APP_GITHUB_URL!,
    {
      body: JSON.stringify({
        query: GET_VIEWER_QUERY
      }),
      headers: {
        'Content-Type': 'application/json'
      }
    }
  );
}
```

GraphQL queries are specified in the request body in an object structure with a `query` property containing the GraphQL query string, which is `GET_VIEWER_QUERY` in our case. We have also specified that the request is in JSON format using the `Content-Type` HTTP header.

8. The HTTP `POST` method must be used for GraphQL API requests. So, let's specify this in the request:

```
export async function getViewer() {
  const response = await fetch(
    process.env.REACT_APP_GITHUB_URL!,
    {
      method: 'POST',
      body: ...,
      headers: ...,
    }
  );
}
```

9. A PAT protects the GitHub GraphQL API, so let's add this to the request:

```
export async function getViewer() {
  const response = await fetch(
    process.env.REACT_APP_GITHUB_URL!,
    {
      ...,
      headers: {
        'Content-Type': 'application/json',
        Authorization: `bearer ${process.env.REACT_APP_
          GITHUB_PAT}`
      },
    }
  );
}
```

10. The last steps in the function are to get the JSON response body and type it appropriately before returning it:

```
export async function getViewer() {
  const response = await fetch(
    ...
  );
```

```
    const body = (await response.json()) as unknown;
    assertIsGetViewerResponse(body);
    return body.data;
  }
```

11. We narrow the type of body using a type assertion function called assertIsGetViewerResponse. The implementation of this function is lengthy and follows the same pattern as the ones we implemented in *Chapter 9, Interacting with RESTful APIs*, so we won't list it in this step, but see `https://github.com/PacktPublishing/Learn-React-with-TypeScript-2nd-Edition/blob/main/Chapter10/Using-React-Query/src/api/getViewer.ts` for the implementation of this function.

    One difference is that the function's parameter is of the any type rather than unknown. This is due to a known TypeScript issue of not being able to narrow the unknown type when it is an object. For more information on this, see the following link: `https://github.com/microsoft/TypeScript/issues/25720`. Using the any type is fine in this case – the assertIsGetViewerResponse function will work perfectly fine.

That completes the implementation of a function that gets the details of the logged-in GitHub viewer.

Next, we will create the component for the header.

Creating the header component

We will create a component for the app header, which will call the getViewer function we just implemented and show the viewer's name and avatar:

1. We will use React Query to call getViewer and manage the data it returns. So, let's start by installing this package by running the following command in a terminal:

   ```
   npm i @tanstack/react-query
   ```

2. Create a file for the component called Header.tsx in the src folder.

3. Add the following import statements in Header.tsx to import React Query's useQuery hook and our getViewer function:

   ```
   import { useQuery } from '@tanstack/react-query';
   import { getViewer } from './api/getViewer';
   ```

4. Start to implement the Header component as follows:

   ```
   export function Header() {
     const { isLoading, data } = useQuery(['viewer'],
       getViewer);
   }
   ```

We use the `useQuery` hook to call `getViewer`. The data returned from `getViewer` will be in the destructured `data` variable. We have also destructured an `isLoading` variable to implement a loading indicator in the next step.

5. Add a loading indicator as follows:

```
export function Header() {
  const { isLoading, data } = useQuery(['viewer'],
    getViewer);
  if (isLoading || data === undefined) {
    return <div>...</div>;
  }
}
```

6. Finish the component implementation with the following JSX:

```
export function Header() {
  ...
  return (
    <header className="flex flex-col items-center text-
      slate-50 bg-slate-900 h-40 p-5">
      <img
        src={data.viewer.avatarUrl}
        alt="Viewer"
        className="rounded-full w-16 h-16"
      />
      <div>{data.viewer.name}</div>
      <h1 className="text-xl font-bold">GitHub Search</
        h1>
    </header>
  );
}
```

A `header` element with a very dark gray background is rendered. The `header` element contains the viewer's avatar, name, and a heading of **GitHub Search**, all horizontally centered.

That completes the implementation of the header. Next, we will add it to the component tree.

Adding the Header component to the app

Carry out the following steps to add the Header component to the App component:

1. Open App.tsx and remove all the existing content.

2. Add import statements for React Query's provider component and client as well as our Header component:

```
import {
  QueryClient,
  QueryClientProvider,
} from '@tanstack/react-query';
import { Header } from './Header';
```

3. Implement the component by wrapping React Query's provider component around the Header component:

```
const queryClient = new QueryClient();

function App() {
  return (
    <QueryClientProvider client={queryClient}>
      <Header />
    </QueryClientProvider>
  );
}

export default App;
```

4. Now, let's try the app by running npm start in the terminal. A header containing your avatar and name should appear:

Figure 10.10 – Header containing the viewer's avatar and name

That completes the app header. Next, we will start to implement the main part of the app.

Creating the repository page

The main part of the app will be a page that allows a user to search for a GitHub repository and star it. The page component will be called `RepoPage` and will reference three other components, as follows:

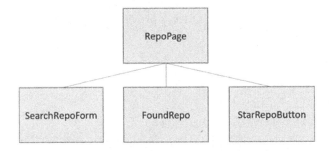

Figure 10.11 – Repository page component structure

Here's an explanation of the components:

- The form that allows users to enter their search criteria will be contained in a `SearchRepoForm` component

- The `FoundRepo` component will render the matched repository after a search

- The `StarRepoButton` component will render the button that the user can click to star a repository

- The `RepoPage` component will use React Query to manage calls to the GitHub GraphQL API and store the returned data

Next, we will make a start on the repository page by implementing a function to do the repository search.

Creating the search function

We will start by implementing the function that calls the GitHub GraphQL API to find a repository. Carry out the following steps:

1. We will start by creating a couple of types that the function will use. Open `src/api/types.ts` and add the following types:

```
export type SearchCriteria = {
  org: string,
  repo: string,
};
export type RepoData = {
  repository: {
```

```
        id: string,
        name: string,
        description: string,
        viewerHasStarred: boolean,
        stargazers: {
          totalCount: number,
        },
      },
    };
```

The `SearchCriteria` type represents the information we need in the GraphQL query parameters to find the GitHub repository. The `RepoData` type represents the data returned from the repository search.

2. Create a file for the function called `getRepo.ts` in the `src/api` folder.

3. Open `getRepo.ts` and start by importing the types just created:

```
import { RepoData, SearchCriteria } from './types';
```

4. Add a constant for the following GraphQL query:

```
export const GET_REPO = `
  query GetRepo($org: String!, $repo: String!) {
    repository(owner: $org, name: $repo) {
      id
      name
      description
      viewerHasStarred
      stargazers {
        totalCount
      }
    }
  }
`;
```

This is the same query we created earlier in the chapter in the GitHub GraphQL API explorer.

5. Add the following type beneath the constant:

```
type GetRepoResponse = {
  data: RepoData;
};
```

The GetRepoResponse type represents the data returned from the GraphQL query – it references the RepoData type we created in *step 1*.

6. Implement the function as follows:

```
export async function getRepo(searchCriteria:
SearchCriteria) {
  const response = await fetch(process.env.REACT_APP_
    GITHUB_URL!, {
    method: 'POST',
    body: JSON.stringify({
      query: GET_REPO,
      variables: {
        org: searchCriteria.org,
        repo: searchCriteria.repo,
      },
    }),
    headers: {
      'Content-Type': 'application/json',
      Authorization: `bearer ${process.env.REACT_APP_
        GITHUB_PAT}`,
    },
  });
  const body = (await response.json()) as unknown;
  assertIsGetRepoResponse(body);
  return body.data;
}
```

This follows the same pattern as the function we created earlier to get the viewer's information. One difference is that we have specified GraphQL query org and repo parameters, which are set to the properties in the searchCriteria function parameter.

7. The assertIsGetRepoResponse type assertion function follows the same pattern as previous type assertion functions. The implementation is lengthy, so it isn't listed here. You can find the implementation here: https://github.com/PacktPublishing/Learn-React-with-TypeScript-2nd-Edition/blob/main/Chapter10/Using-React-Query/src/api/getRepo.ts.

That completes the implementation of a function that finds the GitHub repository.

Next, we will create the component for the repository search form.

Creating the search form component

We will implement a form component that allows the user to search for a repository. The form will contain fields for the organization and repository name. The component won't call the GitHub GraphQL API when the form is submitted; instead, it will pass the submitted search criteria back to a page component to do this.

We will use React Hook Form for implementation, which should already be installed. The pattern for the implementation is very similar to previous forms we have implemented, so the steps to do this implementation aren't listed in detail here. The implemention for the `SearchRepoForm` component can be copied from the book's GitHub repository as follows:

1. Create a new folder called `repoPage` in the `src` folder and then create a new file called `SearchRepoForm.tsx` in this folder.

2. Open `SearchRepoForm.tsx` and copy and paste the contents into it from `https://github.com/PacktPublishing/Learn-React-with-TypeScript-2nd-Edition/blob/main/Chapter10/Using-React-Query/src/repoPage/SearchRepoForm.tsx`.

The implementation for the `SearchRepoForm` component is now in place in our project.

Next, we will implement a component that renders the found repository.

Creating the FoundRepo component

The `FoundRepo` component will display the repository name, description, and number of stars. Carry out the following steps to implement this component:

1. Create a file in the `src/repoPage` folder called `FoundRepo.tsx`.

2. Start the implementation by adding the following type for the component props:

```
type Props = {
  name: string;
  description: string;
  stars: number;
};
```

So, the repository name, description, and the number of stars will be passed into the component.

3. Add the following component implementation:

```
export function FoundRepo({ name, description, stars }:
Props) {
  return (
    <div className="py-4">
```

```
        <div className="flex flex-row items-center justify-
          between mb-2">
          <h2 className="text-xl font-bold">{name}</h2>
          <div className="px-4 py-2 rounded-xl text-
            gray-800 bg-gray-200 font-semibold text-sm flex
            align-center w-max">
            {stars} Stars
          </div>
        </div>
        <p>{description}</p>
      </div>
    );
  }
```

The repository name is rendered as a bold heading. The number of stars is rendered in a gray rounded background to the right of the repository name. The description is rendered underneath the name.

That completes the implementation of the found repository component.

Next, we will implement the function that calls the GitHub GraphQL API to star a repository.

Creating a function to star a repository

We will use the same GraphQL mutation we used earlier in the chapter to star the GitHub repository. The pattern used in the function will be similar to the getViewer function we created earlier. Carry out the following steps:

1. Create a file called starRepo.ts in the src/api folder, with the following GraphQL mutation:

```
export const STAR_REPO = `
  mutation ($repoId: ID!) {
    addStar(input: { starrableId: $repoId }) {
      starrable {
        stargazers {
          totalCount
        }
      }
    }
  }
`;
```

This is the same mutation we created earlier in the chapter in the GitHub GraphQL API explorer.

2. Add the function implementation as follows:

```
export async function starRepo(repoId: string) {
  const response = await fetch(process.env.REACT_APP_
    GITHUB_URL!, {
    method: 'POST',
    body: JSON.stringify({
      query: STAR_REPO,
      variables: {
        repoId,
      },
    }),
    headers: {
      'Content-Type': 'application/json',
      Authorization: `bearer ${process.env.REACT_APP_
        GITHUB_PAT}`,
    },
  });
  await response.json();
}
```

This follows the same pattern as the other functions that call the GitHub GraphQL API.

That completes the function that calls the GitHub GraphQL API to star a repository.

Next, we will implement the component for the star button.

Creating the star button

The star button is a regular button styled to be black with white text.

Create a file called `StarRepoButton.tsx` in the `src/repoPage` folder and add the following implementation to it:

```
type Props = {
  onClick: () => void;
};
export function StarRepoButton({ onClick }: Props) {
  return (
    <button
```

```
        type="button"
        className="mt-2 h-10 px-6 font-semibold bg-black text-
          white"
        onClick={onClick}
    >
        Star
    </button>
  );
}
```

That completes the implementation of the star button.

Next, we will create the main page component for the app.

Creating the repository page

The repository page component will reference the SearchRepoForm, FoundRepo, and StarRepoButton components we just created. This component will also call the getRepo and starRepo functions we created using React Query. To do this, carry out the following steps:

1. Create a file called RepoPage.tsx in the src/repoPage folder with the following import statements:

    ```
    import { useState } from 'react';
    import {
      useQuery,
      useMutation,
      useQueryClient,
    } from '@tanstack/react-query';
    import { getRepo } from '../api/getRepo';
    import { starRepo } from '../api/starRepo';
    import { RepoData, SearchCriteria } from '../api/types';
    import { SearchRepoForm } from './SearchRepoForm';
    import { FoundRepo } from './FoundRepo';
    import { StarRepoButton } from './StarRepoButton';
    ```

    We have imported the components and the data functions we created earlier, along with React Query's hooks and client. We have also imported React's state hook because we need to store a piece of state outside React Query.

2. Start the component implementation as follows:

```
export function RepoPage() {
  const [searchCriteria, setSearchCriteria] = useState<
    SearchCriteria | undefined
  >();
}
```

We store the search criteria in state so that we can feed it into useQuery in the next step. We will set this state when the search repository form is submitted in *step 6*.

3. Next, call the useQuery hook to get the repository for the given search criteria as follows:

```
export function RepoPage() {
  const [searchCriteria, setSearchCriteria] = ...
  const { data } = useQuery(
    ['repo', searchCriteria],
    () => getRepo(searchCriteria as SearchCriteria),
    {
      enabled: searchCriteria !== undefined,
    }
  );
}
```

We don't want the query to execute when the component is mounted, so we use the enabled option to only run the query when searchCriteria is set, which will be when the search repository form is submitted.

We use the search criteria in the query key as well and pass it to the getRepo function. We use a type assertion on the getRepo argument to remove undefined from it. This is safe because we know it can't be undefined when getRepo is called because of the enabled option expression.

4. Define the star mutation as follows:

```
export function RepoPage() {
  const [searchCriteria, setSearchCriteria] = ...
  const { data } = useQuery(...);
  const queryClient = useQueryClient();
  const { mutate } = useMutation(starRepo, {
    onSuccess: () => {
      queryClient.setQueryData<RepoData>(
```

```
          ['repo', searchCriteria],
          (repo) => {
            if (repo === undefined) {
              return undefined;
            }
            return {
              ...repo,
              viewerHasStarred: true,
            };
          }
        );
      }
    });
  }
```

The mutation calls the getRepo function we created earlier. We use the mutation's onSuccess option to update the React Query's cached repository data with the viewerHasStarred property set to true.

5. Return the following JSX from the component:

```
export function RepoPage() {
  ...
  return (
    <main className="max-w-xs ml-auto mr-auto">
      <SearchRepoForm onSearch={handleSearch} />
      {data && (
        <>
          <FoundRepo
            name={data.repository.name}
            description={data.repository.description}
            stars={data.repository.stargazers.totalCount}
          />
          {!data.repository.viewerHasStarred && (
            <StarRepoButton onClick={handleStarClick} />
          )}
        </>
      )}
```

```
      </main>
    );
  }
```

The component is wrapped in a `main` element, which centers its content. The repository search form is placed inside the `main` element. The found repository is rendered (if there is a found repository) along with a star button if the repository hasn't already been starred.

We will implement the `handleSearch` and `handleStarClick` handlers in the following steps.

6. Create the `handleSearch` handler as follows:

```
export function RepoPage() {
  ...
  function handleSearch(search: SearchCriteria) {
    setSearchCriteria(search);
  }
  return ...
}
```

The handler sets the `searchCriteria` state, which triggers a re-render and the `useQuery` hook to call `getRepo` with the search criteria.

7. Create the `handleStarClick` handler as follows:

```
export function RepoPage() {
  ...
  function handleStarClick() {
    if (data) {
      mutate(data.repository.id);
    }
  }
  return ...
}
```

The handler calls the mutation with the found repository's ID, which will call the `starRepo` function.

This completes the implementation of the repository page component.

8. Open `App.tsx` and add the `RepoPage` component we just created under the app header:

```
. . .
import { RepoPage } from './repoPage/RepoPage';
. . .
function App() {
  return (
    <QueryClientProvider client={queryClient}>
      <Header />
      <RepoPage />
    </QueryClientProvider>
  );
}
```

9. Now, let's try the app by running `npm start` in the terminal. The repository search form should appear, as follows:

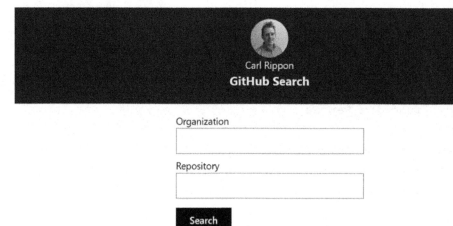

Figure 10.12 – Repository search form

10. Enter a GitHub organization and repository you haven't starred and press **Search**. The found repository will appear with a **Star** button:

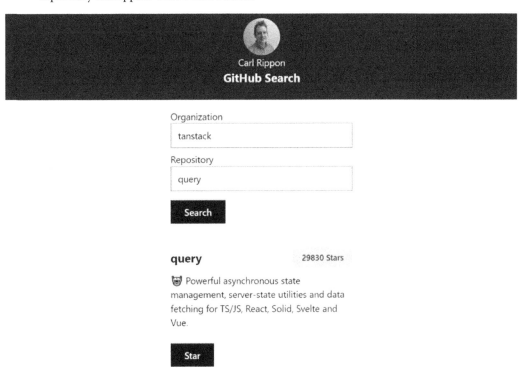

Figure 10.13 – Found repository with a Star button

11. Click the **Star** button to star the repository. The **Star** button will then disappear.

12. Stop the app from running before continuing by pressing *Ctrl* + *C* in the terminal.

That completes the first iteration of the app. Here's a recap of the key points of using fetch and React Query to interact with a GraphQL API:

- The fetch function can call a GraphQL API by putting the query or mutation in the request body and using the HTTP POST method.

- React Query can execute the function containing fetch and manage the response data.

- The enabled option on useQuery and useMutation can execute the function containing fetch when the user interacts with the app. We used this feature to execute a query when the repository search form was submitted.

In the next section, we will refactor the code to use a specialized GraphQL client.

Using Apollo Client

In this section, we will learn about Apollo Client and use it within the app we have built, replacing the use of React Query and `fetch`.

Understanding Apollo Client

Apollo Client is a client library for interacting with GraphQL servers. It has query and mutation hooks called `useQuery` and `useMutation`, like React Query. Apollo Client also stores the data in a client cache like React Query and requires a provider component placed above the components requiring GraphQL data.

One thing that Apollo Client does that React Query doesn't is that it interacts with the GraphQL API directly instead of requiring a function to do this.

Installing Apollo Client

Our first job is to install Apollo Client, which we can do by running the following command in a terminal:

```
npm i @apollo/client graphql
```

This library includes TypeScript types, so no additional package is required to be installed.

Refactoring the App component

The first component we are going to refactor is the `App` component. Carry out the following steps:

1. Open `App.tsx` and replace the React Query import with the following Apollo Client import statement:

   ```
   import {
     ApolloClient,
     InMemoryCache,
     ApolloProvider,
   } from '@apollo/client';
   ```

2. Update the `queryClient` variable assignment as follows:

   ```
   const queryClient = new ApolloClient({
     uri: process.env.REACT_APP_GITHUB_URL!,
     cache: new InMemoryCache(),
     headers: {
   ```

```
        Authorization: `bearer ${process.env.REACT_APP_
    GITHUB_PAT}`,
      }
    });
```

We are now using Apollo Client. We have specified the URL to the API and the PAT because Apollo Client will directly call the API.

3. The last step is to replace `QueryClientProvider` with `ApolloProvider` in the JSX:

```
<ApolloProvider client={queryClient}>
  <Header />
  <RepoPage />
</ApolloProvider>
```

The `App` component is now using Apollo Client.

Next, we will refactor the `Header` component.

Refactoring the Header component

Now, we will refactor the `Header` component to use Apollo Client. Carry out the following steps:

1. Open `getViewer.ts`. The `getViewer` and `assertIsGetViewerResponse` functions and the `GetViewerResponse` type can be removed because Apollo Client doesn't require these. The `ViewerData` import statement can also be removed.

2. Add the following import statement into `getViewer.tsx`:

```
import { gql } from '@apollo/client';
```

`gql` is a function that we will use in the next step to wrap around the GraphQL query string constant.

3. Add the `gql` function in front of the GraphQL query string constant as follows:

```
export const GET_VIEWER_QUERY = gql`
  query {
    viewer {
      name
      avatarUrl
    }
  }
`;
```

So, `GET_VIEWER_QUERY` is now assigned to a tagged template literal rather than a plain string. We covered tagged template literals in *Chapter 5*, when we used Emotion's `css` prop. The `gql` function converts the query string into a query object that Apollo Client can use.

4. Open `Header.tsx` and update the `useQuery` import statement to come from Apollo Client. Also, import the constant we just exported from `getViewer.ts`. We no longer need to import `getViewer`.

```
import { useQuery } from '@apollo/client';
import { GET_VIEWER_QUERY } from './api/getViewer';
```

5. Now update the `useQuery` hook as follows:

```
const { loading: isLoading, data } = useQuery(
  GET_VIEWER_QUERY
);
```

Apollo Client's `useQuery` hook takes in a parameter for the query definition object and returns useful state variables similar to React Query. We have aliased the `loading` state variable as `isLoading` so that the rendering of the loading indicator remains unchanged.

For more information on Apollo Client queries, see the following link: `https://www.apollographql.com/docs/react/data/queries/`.

That completes the `Header` component.

Next, we will refactor the repository page.

Refactoring the repository page

Refactoring the repository page will be a similar process. Carry out the following steps:

1. Open `getRepo.ts` and remove the `getRepo` and `assertIsGetResponse` functions and the `GetRepoReponse` type. Remove the imported `RepoData` and `SearchCriteria` types as well.

2. Import the `gql` function and add it in front of the query string:

```
import { gql } from '@apollo/client';

export const GET_REPO = gql`
  query ...
`;
```

3. Open `starRepo.ts` and remove the `starRepo` function.

4. Import the `gql` function and add it in front of the query string:

    ```
    import { gql } from '@apollo/client';

    export const STAR_REPO = gql`
      mutation ...
    `;
    ```

5. Open `RepoPage.tsx` and replace the React Query import statement with an Apollo Client import statement. Also, import the GraphQL query constants we just changed in the previous two steps:

    ```
    import {
      useLazyQuery,
      useMutation,
      useApolloClient,
    } from '@apollo/client';
    import { GET_REPO } from '../api/getRepo';
    import { STAR_REPO } from '../api/starRepo';
    ```

    We will use the `useLazyQuery` hook rather than `useQuery` because we want to trigger the query during form submission rather than when the component mounts.

6. Replace the call to `useQuery` with the following call to `useLazyQuery`:

    ```
    const [getRepo, { data }] = useLazyQuery(GET_REPO);
    ```

    `useLazyQuery` returns a tuple, with the first element being a function that can be called to trigger the query. We have called this trigger function `getRepo`. The second tuple element is an object containing useful state variables, such as the data from the API response, which we have destructured.

    For more information on `useLazyQuery`, see the following link: https://www.apollographql.com/docs/react/data/queries/#manual-execution-with-uselazyquery.

7. Next, replace the `queryClient` variable assignment and the `useMutation` call with the following:

    ```
    const queryClient = useApolloClient();
    const [starRepo] = useMutation(STAR_REPO, {
      onCompleted: () => {
        queryClient.cache.writeQuery({
    ```

```
      query: GET_REPO,
      data: {
        repository: {
          ...data.repository,
          viewerHasStarred: true,
        },
      },
      variables: searchCriteria,
    });
  },
});
```

The first parameter in Apollo Client's useMutation hook is the mutation definition object, which is STAR_REPO in our case. The second parameter contains options for the mutation. We have specified the onCompleted option, which is a function called after the mutation has been completed. We have used this option to update the data cache to indicate that the viewer has now starred the repository.

For more information on Apollo Client mutations, see the following link: https://www.apollographql.com/docs/react/data/mutations.

8. Update the handleSearch function to call the useLazyQuery trigger function:

```
function handleSearch(search: SearchCriteria) {
  getRepo({
    variables: { ...search },
  });
  setSearchCriteria(search);
}
```

9. Update the handleStarClick function to call the useMutation trigger function:

```
async function handleStarClick() {
  if (data) {
    starRepo({ variables: { repoId: data.repository.id }
  });
  }
}
```

That completes the refactoring of the repository page.

10. Now, try the app by running npm start in the terminal. Try searching for a repository and starring it – it should behave as it previously did.

That completes the second iteration of the app and our use of Apollo Client. Here are the key points on using Apollo Client:

- Apollo Client is a specialized library for interacting with GraphQL APIs

- Unlike React Query, Apollo Client interacts directly with the GraphQL API and, therefore, doesn't require a separate function that uses `fetch`

- Apollo Client's `ApolloProvider` component needs to be placed high in the component tree above where backend data is needed

- Apollo Client's `useQuery` hook allows data to be fetched and cached in state

- Apollo Client's `useMutation` hook allows data to be updated

Next, we will summarize the chapter.

Summary

In this chapter, we started by learning the GraphQL syntax for queries and mutations. A great feature of GraphQL is the ability to request and receive only the required objects and fields. This can really help the performance of our apps.

We used React Query and `fetch` to interact with a GraphQL API. This is very similar to interacting with a REST API, but the HTTP method needs to be `POST`, and the query or mutation needs to be placed in the request body. A new feature we learned about in React Query is the ability to trigger queries when the user interacts with the app using the `enabled` option.

We refactored the app to use Apollo Client, which is a specialized GraphQL client. It is very similar to React Query in that it has `useQuery` and `useMutation` hooks and a provider component. One advantage over React Query is that Apollo Client interacts directly with the GraphQL API, which means we write less code.

In the next chapter, we will cover patterns that help us build reusable components.

Questions

Answer the following questions to check what you have learned in this chapter:

1. The following is an attempt at a GraphQL query to get a GitHub viewer's name and email address:

```
viewer: {
  name,
  email
}
```

The query errors though – what is the problem?

2. What is the mutation that would unstar a GitHub repository? The mutation should have a parameter for the repository ID.

3. The following use of `fetch` is an attempt to call a GraphQL API:

```
const response = await fetch(process.env.REACT_APP_API_
URL!, {
  body: JSON.stringify({
    query: GET_DATA_QUERY,
  }),
});
```

This doesn't work though – what is the problem?

4. Where does the authorization access token in a protected GraphQL API get specified when using Apollo Client?

5. A component uses Apollo Client's `useQuery` hook to fetch data from a GraphQL API, but the component errors with the following error:

Could not find "client" in the context or passed in as an option. Wrap the root component in an <ApolloProvider>, or pass an ApolloClient instance in via options

What do you think the problem is?

6. The following attempts to use Apollo Client's `useQuery` hook to fetch data from a GraphQL API:

```
const { loading, data } = useQuery(`query {
  contact {
    name
    email
  }
}
`);
```

The call errors, though – what do you think the problem is?

7. What state variable can be destructured from Apollo Client's `useMutation` hook to determine whether the request has returned an error?

Answers

1. The query syntax is incorrect – the syntax is like JSON but doesn't have colons and commas. Also, the `query` keyword can be omitted, but it is best practice to include this. Here is the corrected query:

    ```
    query {
      viewer {
        name
        email
      }
    }
    ```

2. The following mutation will unstar a GitHub repository:

    ```
    mutation ($repoId: ID!) {
      removeStar(input: { starrableId: $repoId }) {
        starrable {
          stargazers {
            totalCount
          }
        }
      }
    }
    ```

3. The request is missing the HTTP POST method:

    ```
    const response = await fetch(process.env.REACT_APP_API_
    URL!, {
      method: 'POST',
      body: JSON.stringify({
        query: GET_DATA_QUERY,
      }),
    });
    ```

4. The authorization access token gets specified when Apollo Client is created, which is passed into the provider component:

    ```
    const queryClient = new ApolloClient({
      ...,
      headers: {
    ```

```
      Authorization: `bearer ${process.env.REACT_APP_
ACCESS_TOKEN}`,
    },
  });

function App() {
  return (
    <ApolloProvider
      client={queryClient}
    >

      ...

    </ApolloProvider>
  );
}
```

5. The problem is that Apollo Client's `ApolloProvider` component hasn't been placed above the component using `useQuery` in the component tree.

6. The `gql` function must be applied to the query string to convert it into the object format that Apollo Client expects:

```
const { loading, data } = useQuery(gql`
  query {
    viewer {
      name
      email
    }
  }
`);
```

7. The `error` state variable can be destructured from React Query's `useMutation` hook to determine whether the HTTP request has returned an error.

Part 4:
Advanced React

In this part, we will learn about a number of different patterns to enable us to reuse a high amount of React and TypeScript code. We will also cover how to implement automated tests on React components, giving us the confidence to ship new features of applications quickly.

This part includes the following chapters:

- *Chapter 11, Reusable Components*
- *Chapter 12, Unit Testing with Jest and React Testing Library*

11

Reusable Components

In this chapter, we will build a checklist component and use various patterns to make it highly reusable but still strongly typed.

We will start by using TypeScript **generics** to strongly type the data passed to the component. Then, we will use the **props spreading** pattern to make the component API-flexible, and allow consumers of the component to custom render parts of the component using the **render props** pattern. After that, we will learn how to make custom hooks and use this to extract logic for checked items and how to make the state within a component controllable to change the component's behavior.

We'll cover the following topics:

- Creating the project
- Using generic props
- Using props spreading
- Using render props
- Adding checked functionality
- Creating custom hooks
- Allowing the internal state to be controlled

Technical requirements

We will use the following technologies in this chapter:

- **Node.js** and **npm**: You can install them here: https://nodejs.org/en/download/.
- **Visual Studio Code**: You can install it here: https://code.visualstudio.com/.

All the code snippets in this chapter can be found online at `https://github.com/ PacktPublishing/Learn-React-with-TypeScript-2nd-Edition/tree/main/ Chapter11`.

Creating the project

In this section, we will create the project for the app we will build and its folder structure. The folder structure will be straightforward because it contains a single page with the checklist component we will build.

We will develop the app using Visual Studio Code as in previous chapters, so open Visual Studio Code and carry out the following steps:

1. Create the project using Create React App. See *Chapter 3*, *Setting up React and TypeScript*, if you can't remember the steps for this.

2. We will style the app with Tailwind CSS, so install this into the project and configure it. See *Chapter 5*, *Approaches to Styling Frontends*, if you can't remember the steps for this.

That completes the project setup.

Using generic props

In this section, we'll take some time to understand how to create our own generic types and also learn about the `keyof` TypeScript feature, which is useful for generic types. We will use this knowledge to build the first iteration of the checklist component with a generic type for its props.

Understanding generics

We have used generics throughout this book. For example, the `useState` hook has an optional generic parameter for the type of state variable:

```
const [visible, setVisible] = useState<boolean>()
```

Generic parameters in a function allow that function to be reusable with different types and be strongly typed. The following function returns the first element in an array, or `null` if the array is empty. However, the function only works with a `string` array:

```
function first(array: Array<string>): string | null {
    return array.length === 0 ? null : array[0];
}
```

Generics allows us to make this function usable with any type of array.

Generic functions

Although we have used generic functions throughout this book, we haven't created our own generic function yet. Generic type parameters are defined in angled brackets before the function's parentheses:

```
function someFunc<T1, T2, ...>(...) {
  ...
}
```

The name of a generic type can be anything you like, but it should be meaningful so that it is easy to understand.

Here is a generic version of the function we saw earlier. Now, it can work with arrays containing any type of element:

```
function first<Item>(array: Array<Item>): Item | null {
  return array.length === 0 ? null : array[0];
}
```

The function has a single generic parameter called Item, which is used in the type of the array function parameter, as well as the function's return type.

Generic types

Custom types can be generic as well. For a type alias, its generic parameters are defined in angled brackets after the type name:

```
type TypeName<T1, T2, ...> = {
  ...
}
```

For example, the props of a React component can be generic. An example of a generic props type is as follows:

```
type Props<Item> = {
  items: Item[];
  ...
};
```

The Props type has a single generic parameter called Item, which is used in the type of the items prop.

Generic React components

Generic props can be integrated into a generic function to produce a generic React component. Here's an example of a generic `List` component:

```
type Props<Item> = {
  items: Item[];
};
export function List<Item>({ items }: Props<Item>) {
  ...
}
```

The `items` prop in the `List` component can now have any type, making the component flexible and reusable.

Now that we understand how to create a component with generic props, we will create the first iteration of the checklist component.

Creating a basic list component

We will now start to create our reusable component. In this iteration, it will be a basic list containing some primary and secondary text obtained from an array of data.

Carry out the following steps:

1. Start by creating a folder for the component called `Checklist` in the `src` folder. Then, create a file called `Checklist.tsx` in this folder.

2. Open `Checklist.tsx` and add the following `Props` type:

    ```
    type Props<Data> = {
      data: Data[];
      id: keyof Data;
      primary: keyof Data;
      secondary: keyof Data;
    };
    ```

    Here is an explanation of each prop:

    - The `data` prop is the data that drives the items in the list
    - The `id` prop is the property's name in each data item that uniquely identifies the item
    - The `primary` prop is the property's name in each data item that contains the main text to render in each item
    - The `secondary` prop is the property's name in each data item that includes the supplementary text to render in each item

This is the first time we have encountered the `keyof` operator in a type annotation. It queries the type specified after it for the property names and constructs a union type from them, so the type for id, `primary`, and `secondary` will be a union type of all the property names for each data item.

3. Next, start to implement the component function as follows:

```
export function Checklist<Data>({
  data,
  id,
  primary,
  secondary,
}: Props<Data>) {
  return (
    <ul className="bg-gray-300 rounded p-10">
      {data.map((item) => {
      })}
    </ul>
  );
}
```

The component renders a gray, unordered list element with rounded corners. We also map over the data items where we will eventually render each item.

4. We will start by implementing the function inside `data.map`. The function checks whether the unique identifier (`idValue`) is a string or number, and if not, it won't render anything. The function also checks that the primary text property (`primaryText`) is a string, and again, if not, doesn't render anything:

```
{data.map((item) => {
  const idValue = item[id] as unknown;
  if (
    typeof idValue !== 'string' &&
    typeof idValue !== 'number'
  ) {
    return null;
  }
  const primaryText = item[primary] as unknown;
  if (typeof primaryText !== 'string') {
    return null;
```

```
  }
    const secondaryText = item[secondary] as unknown;
}
```

5. Finish the implementation by rendering the list item as follows:

```
{data.map((item) => {
    ...
    return (
      <li
        key={idValue}
        className="bg-white p-6 shadow rounded mb-4
          last:mb-0"
      >
        <div className="text-xl text-gray-800 pb-1">
          {primaryText}
        </div>
        {typeof secondaryText === 'string' && (
          <div className="text-sm text-gray-500">
            {secondaryText}
          </div>
        )}
      </li>
    );
})}
```

The list items are rendered with a white background and rounded corners. The primary text is rendered as large, gray text with the secondary text rendered much smaller.

6. Create a new file in the Checklist folder called index.ts and export the Checklist component into it:

```
export * from './Checklist';
```

This file will simplify import statements for the Checklist component.

7. The final step before seeing the component in action is to add it to the component tree in the app. Open App.tsx and replace the content within it with the following:

```
import { Checklist } from './Checklist';

function App() {
```

```
    return (
      <div className="p-10">
        <Checklist
          data={[
            { id: 1, name: 'Lucy', role: 'Manager' },
            { id: 2, name: 'Bob', role: 'Developer' },
          ]}
          id="id"
          primary="name"
          secondary="role"
        />
      </div>
    );
  }

  export default App;
```

We reference the `Checklist` component and pass some data into it. Notice how type-safe the `id`, `primary`, and `secondary` attributes are – we are forced to enter a valid property name with the data items.

8. Run the app by entering `npm start` in the terminal. The checklist component appears as shown here:

.Figure 11.1 – Our basic checklist component

Currently, the component renders a basic list – we will add the checked functionality later in this chapter.

That completes this section on generic props.

To recap, here are some key points:

- TypeScript generics allow reusable code to be strongly typed.
- Functions can have generic parameters that are referenced within the implementation.
- Types can also have generic parameters that are referenced within the implementation.
- A React component can be made generic by feeding a generic props type into a generic function component. The component implementation will then be based on generic props.

Next, we will learn about a pattern that allows the prop type to inherit props from an HTML element.

Using props spreading

In this section, we'll learn about a pattern called **props spreading**. This pattern is useful when you want to use all the props from an HTML element in the implementation of a component. In our checklist component, we will use this pattern to add all the props for the `ul` element. This will allow consumers of the component to specify props, such as the height and width of the checklist.

So, carry out the following steps:

1. Open `Checklist.tsx` and import the following type from React:

   ```
   import { ComponentPropsWithoutRef } from 'react';
   ```

   This type allows us to reference the props of an HTML element such as `ul`. It is a generic type that takes the HTML element name as a generic parameter.

2. Add the props from the `ul` element to the component props type as follows:

   ```
   type Props<Data> = {
     data: Data[];
     id: keyof Data;
     primary: keyof Data;
     secondary: keyof Data;
   } & ComponentPropsWithoutRef<'ul'>;
   ```

3. Add a **rest parameter** called `ulProps` to collect all the props for the `ul` element into a single `ulProps` variable:

   ```
   export function Checklist<Data>({
     data,
     id,
   ```

```
    primary,
    secondary,
    ...ulProps
  }: Props<Data>) {
    ...
  }
```

This is the first time we have used rest parameters in this book. They collect multiple arguments that are passed into the function into an array, so any props that aren't called `data`, `id`, `primary`, or `secondary` will be collected into the `ulProps` array. For more information on rest parameters, see `https://developer.mozilla.org/en-US/docs/Web/JavaScript/Reference/Functions/rest_parameters`.

4. Now, we can spread `ulProps` onto the `ul` element using the spread syntax:

```
export function Checklist<Data>({
  data,
  id,
  primary,
  secondary,
  ...ulProps
}: Props<Data>) {
  return (
    <ul
      className="bg-gray-300 rounded p-10"
      {...ulProps}
    >...</ul>
  );
}
```

5. We can use this new feature of `Checklist` to specify the list height and width. Open `App.tsx` and add the following `style` attribute, as well as more data items:

```
<Checklist
  data={[
    { id: 1, name: 'Lucy', role: 'Manager' },
    { id: 2, name: 'Bob', role: 'Developer' },
    { id: 3, name: 'Bill', role: 'Developer' },
    { id: 4, name: 'Tara', role: 'Developer' },
    { id: 5, name: 'Sara', role: 'UX' },
```

```
      { id: 6, name: 'Derik', role: 'QA' }
    ] }
    id="id"
    primary="name"
    secondary="role"
    style={{
      width: '300px',
      maxHeight: '380px',
      overflowY: 'auto'
    }}
  />
```

6. If the app isn't running, run it by entering npm start in the terminal. The checklist component appears sized as we expect:

Figure 11.2 – The sized checklist component

The component now has a fixed height with a vertical scrollbar as a result of the style we passed into the component.

That completes our use of the props spreading pattern. Here's a recap of the key points:

- We intersect the props type with `ComponentPropsWithoutRef` to add props for the HTML element we want to spread onto

- We use a rest parameter in the component props to collect all the HTML element props into an array

- We can then spread the rest parameter onto the HTML element in the JSX

Next, we will learn about a pattern that allows consumers to render parts of a component.

Using render props

In this section, we will learn about the **render props** pattern and use it to allow the consumer of the component to render items within the checklist component.

Understanding the render props pattern

A way of making a component highly reusable is to allow the consumer to render internal elements within it. The `children` prop on a `button` element is an example of this because it allows us to specify any button content we like:

```
<button>We can specify any content here</button>
```

The render props pattern allows us to use a prop other than `children` to provide this capability. This is useful when the `children` prop is already used for something else, as in the following example:

```
<Modal heading={<h3>Enter Details</h3>}>
  Some content
</Modal>
```

Here, `heading` is a render prop in a `Modal` component.

Render props are useful when allowing the consumer to render elements associated with the data passed into the component because the render prop can be a function:

```
<List
  data={[...]}
  renderItem={(item) => <div>{item.text}</div>}
/>
```

The preceding example has a render prop called `renderItem` that renders each list item in a `List` component. The data item is passed into it so it can include its properties in the list item. This is similar to what we will implement next for our checklist component.

Adding a renderItem prop

We will add a prop called `renderItem` to the checklist that allows consumers to take control of the rendering of the list items. Carry out the following steps:

1. Open `Checklist.tsx` and add the `ReactNode` type to the React `import` statement:

    ```
    import { ComponentPropsWithoutRef, ReactNode } from
    'react';
    ```

    `ReactNode` represents an element that React can render. Therefore, we will use `ReactNode` as the return type for our render prop.

2. Add a render prop called `renderItem` to the `Props` type:

    ```
    type Props<Data> = {
      data: Data[];
      id: keyof Data;
      primary: keyof Data;
      secondary: keyof Data;
      renderItem?: (item: Data) => ReactNode;
    } & React.ComponentPropsWithoutRef<'ul'>;
    ```

    The prop is a function that takes in the data item and returns what needs rendering. We have made the prop optional because we will provide a default implementation for list items but also allow consumers to override it.

3. Add `renderItem` to the component function parameters:

    ```
    export function Checklist<Data>({
      data,
      id,
      primary,
      secondary,
      renderItem,
      ...ulProps
    }: Props<Data>) {
      ...
    }
    ```

4. In the JSX, at the top of the mapping function, add an `if` statement to check whether the `renderItem` prop has been specified. If `renderItem` has been specified, call it with the data item, and return its result from the mapping function:

```
<ul ...>
  {data.map((item) => {
    if (renderItem) {
      return renderItem(item);
    }
    const idValue = item[id] as unknown;
    ...
  })}
</ul>
```

So, if `renderItem` has been specified, it will be called to get the element to render as the list item. If `renderItem` hasn't been specified, it will render the list item as it previously did.

5. To try the new prop out, open `App.tsx` and add the following `renderItem` attribute:

```
<Checklist
  ...
  renderItem={(item) => (
    <li key={item.id} className="bg-white p-4
      border-b-2">
      <div className="text-xl text-slate-800 pb-1">
        {item.name}
      </div>
      <div className="text-slate-500">{item.role}</div>
    </li>
  )}
/>
```

The list items are now rendered as flat, white items with a border between them.

6. If the app isn't running, run it by entering npm start in the terminal. The checklist component appears with the overridden list items:

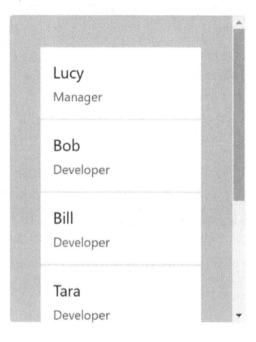

Figure 11.3 – Overridden list items

7. Before continuing to the next section, remove the use of renderItem in the Checklist element in App.tsx. The default rendering of list items should then appear.

That completes this section on the render props pattern. To recap, here are some key points:

- The render props pattern allows a component consumer to override the rendering of parts of the component

- A render prop can either be an element or a function that returns an element

- A common use case for a render prop is a data-driven list in which the rendering of list items can be overridden

Next, we will add checked functionality to our checklist component.

Adding checked functionality

Currently, our checklist component doesn't contain the ability to check items, so we will now add checkboxes to the list of items, giving users the ability to check them. We will track the checked items using a React state.

So, carry out the following steps to add this functionality to our component:

1. Open `Checklist.tsx` and add `useState` to the React `import` statement:

```
import {
  ComponentPropsWithoutRef,
  ReactNode,
  useState
} from 'react';
```

We will use the state to store the IDs of the checked items.

2. At the top of the component implementation, add the state for the IDs of the checked items:

```
const [checkedIds, setCheckedIds] =
useState<IdValue[]>([]);
```

We have referenced an `IdValue` type that we haven't defined yet – we'll define this after we have finished the component implementation in *step 6*.

3. Add checkboxes to the list of items as follows:

```
<li
  key={idValue}
  className="bg-white p-6 shadow rounded mb-4 last:mb-0"
>
  <label className="flex items-center">
    <input
      type="checkbox"
      checked={checkedIds.includes(idValue)}
      onChange={handleCheckChange(idValue)}
    />
    <div className="ml-2">
      <div className="text-xl text-gray-800 pb-1">
        {primaryText}
      </div>
      {typeof secondaryText === 'string' && (
```

```
            <div className="text-sm text-gray-500">
              {secondaryText}
            </div>
          )}
        </div>                    ,
      </label>
    </li>
```

The `checkedIds` state powers the `checked` attribute of the checkbox by checking whether the list item's ID is contained within it.

We will implement the referenced `handleCheckChange` function in the next step. Notice that the reference calls the function passing the ID of the list item that has been checked.

4. Start to implement the `handleCheckChange` function in the component as follows:

```
const [checkedIds, setCheckedIds] =
useState<IdValue[]>([]);
const handleCheckChange = (checkedId: IdValue) => () =>
{};
return ...
```

This is a function that returns the handler function. This complexity is because a basic checked handler doesn't pass in the list item's ID. This approach is called **currying**, and more information on it can be found at the following link: `https://javascript.info/currying-partials`.

5. Complete the handler implementation as follows:

```
const handleCheckChange = (checkedId: IdValue) => () => {
  const isChecked = checkedIds.includes(checkedId);
  let newCheckedIds = isChecked
    ? checkedIds.filter(
        (itemCheckedid) => itemCheckedid !== checkedId
      )
    : checkedIds.concat(checkedId);
  setCheckedIds(newCheckedIds);
};
```

The implementation updates the list item's ID to the `checkedIds` state if the list item has been checked and removes it if it is unchecked.

6. Next, let's define the `IdValue` type. Create a new file in the `Checklist` folder called `types.ts` with the definition of `IdValue`:

```
export type IdValue = string | number;
```

Here, the list item's ID can be a `string` or `number` value.

7. Move back to `Checklist.tsx` and import `IdValue`:

```
import { IdValue } from './types';
```

The compilation errors should now be resolved.

8. If the app isn't running, run it by entering `npm start` in the terminal. The checklist component appears with checkboxes for each list item:

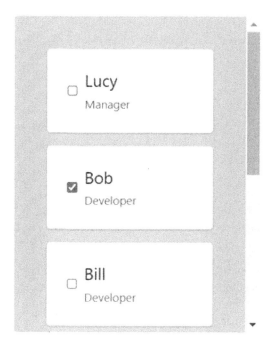

Figure 11.4 – Checkboxes for list items

The checklist component now includes checkboxes. However, there is an opportunity to make the checked logic reusable – we'll cover this in the next section.

Creating custom hooks

In this section, we'll learn about custom React hooks. Then, we will use this knowledge to extract the checked logic from the checklist component into a reusable custom hook.

Understanding custom hooks

As well as standard hooks such as `useState`, React allows us to create our own custom hooks. Custom hooks allow logic to be isolated and reused across multiple components.

A custom hook is defined using a function with a name that starts with the word *use*. This naming convention helps ESLint check for problems with the use of the custom hook. Here's a custom hook that provides toggling logic:

```
export function useToggle() {
  const [toggleValue, setToggleValue] = useState(false);

  function toggle() {
    setToggleValue(!toggleValue);
  }

  return {toggleValue, toggle};
};
```

The custom hook contains the state of the current toggle value, which is either `true` or `false`. It also includes a function called `toggle`, which toggles the current value. The current toggle value and the `toggle` function are returned from the custom hook in an object structure.

Note that an object structure doesn't have to be returned. If the custom hook only returns a single item, then that item can be returned directly. If the custom hook returns two things (as in the preceding example), it can return a tuple (as `useState` does). An object structure is better for more than two items because the object keys make it clear what each item is.

Another trait of a custom hook is that it uses other standard React hooks. For example, the `useToggle` custom hook uses `useState`. If the custom hook doesn't call a React hook or another custom hook, it's just a regular function rather than a custom hook.

This custom hook can then be used in the implementation of a component as follows:

```
const { toggleValue, toggle } = useToggle();
return (
  <div className="App">
    <button onClick={toggle}>{toggleValue ? 'ON' : 'OFF'}</
```

```
button>
  </div>
);
```

The toggle value (`toggleValue`) and the `toggle` function are destructed from the return value of the custom hook. The toggle value is used to render text **ON** or **OFF** inside the button content depending on whether it is `true` or `false`. The `toggle` function is also assigned to the click handler of the button.

Custom hooks can take in parameters as well. In the example here, we have added a default value in the `useToggle` hook:

```
type Params = {
  defaultToggleValue?: boolean;
};
export function useToggle({ defaultToggleValue }: Params) {
  const [toggleValue, setToggleValue] = useState(
    defaultToggleValue
  );
  ...
}
```

In the preceding example, the parameters are in an object structure. An object structure is nice when there are multiple parameters and nothing breaks when new parameters are added.

Arguments are passed into the custom hook in an object. Here's an example of using `useToggle` with its value initially being `true`:

```
const { toggleValue, toggle } = useToggle({
  defaultToggleValue: true
});
```

Now that we understand how to create and use custom hooks, we will put this into practice in our checklist component.

Extracting checked logic into a custom hook

We will extract the logic for checked items into a custom hook. This will allow potential future components to use the logic and clean up the code a little.

The custom hook will be called `useChecked` and will contain the state for the checked list item IDs. The hook will also include a handler that can be attached to the checkboxes, updating the checked list item ID's state.

To do this, carry out the following steps:

1. In the Checklist folder, create a file for the custom hook called useChecked.ts.

2. Open useChecked.ts and add the following import statements:

    ```
    import { useState } from 'react';
    import { IdValue } from './types';
    ```

    The hook will use React state that is typed using IdValue.

3. Start to implement the function for the custom hook by initializing the state:

    ```
    export function useChecked() {
      const [checkedIds, setCheckedIds] =
        useState<IdValue[]>([]);
    }
    ```

    The hook doesn't have any parameters. The useState call is exactly the same as the one currently in the Checklist component – this could be copied and pasted into the custom hook.

4. Add a checked handler to the custom hook. This can be copied from the implementation of the Checklist component:

    ```
    export function useChecked() {
      const [checkedIds, setCheckedIds] =
        useState<IdValue[]>([]);

      const handleCheckChange = (checkedId: IdValue) => () =>
    {
        const isChecked = checkedIds.includes(checkedId);
        let newCheckedIds = isChecked
          ? checkedIds.filter(
              (itemCheckedid) => itemCheckedid !== checkedId
            )
          : checkedIds.concat(checkedId);
        setCheckedIds(newCheckedIds);
      };
    }
    ```

5. The last task in the custom hook implementation is to return the checked IDs and the handler function:

```
export function useChecked() {
    ...
    return { handleCheckChange, checkedIds };
}
```

6. Next, open `Checklist.tsx` and remove the state definition and the `handleCheckChange` handler function. Also, remove `useState` and `IdValue` from the `import` statements, as they are redundant.

7. Still in `Checklist.tsx`, import the `useChecked` hook we just created:

```
import { useChecked } from './useChecked';
```

8. Add a call to `useChecked` and destructure the checked IDs and the handler function:

```
export function Checklist<Data>({ ... }: Props<Data>) {
    const { checkedIds, handleCheckChange } = useChecked();
    return ...
}
```

9. If the app isn't running, run it by entering `npm start` in the terminal. The checklist component will appear and behave as it did before we made these changes.

That completes the implementation and use of the custom hook. To recap, here are some key points:

- Custom hooks make code a little cleaner and are reusable because they isolate logic, which can be complex.

- Custom hooks must start with `use`.

- Custom hooks must use a standard React hook or another custom hook.

- A custom hook is just a function that returns useful things for components to use. Using an object structure for the returned items is ideal when returning many items because the object keys make it clear what each item is.

- A custom hook can have parameters. Using an object structure for the parameters is ideal for many items and doesn't break anything when new parameters are added.

Next, we will cover a pattern that will allow the consumer of a component to control some of its behavior with the state.

Allowing the internal state to be controlled

In this section, we'll learn how to allow consumers of a component to control its internal state. We will use this pattern in the checklist component so that users can check just a single item.

Understanding how the internal state can be controlled

Allowing consumers of a component to control the state allows the behavior of a component to be tweaked if that behavior is driven by the state. Let's go through an example using the useToggle custom hook we covered in the last section when learning about custom hooks.

Two additional props are required to allow the internal state to be controlled – one for the current state value and one for a change handler. These additional props are toggleValue and onToggleValueChange in useToggle:

```
type Params = {
  defaultToggleValue?: boolean;
  toggleValue?: boolean;
  onToggleValueChange?: (toggleValue: boolean) => void;
};

export function useToggle({
  defaultToggleValue,
  toggleValue,
  onToggleValueChange,
}: Params) {

  ...

}
```

These props are marked as optional because this pattern doesn't force the consumer of the component to control the state – it's a feature they can opt in to.

> **Note**
> The consumer of the component will never specify both defaultToggleValue and toggleValue. defaultToggleValue should only be used when the consumer doesn't want to control toggleValue with the state. When the consumer does want to control toggleValue with the state, they can set the initial value of their state.

The toggleValue prop now clashes with the toggleValue state because they have the same name, so the state needs to be renamed:

```
const [resolvedToggleValue, setResolvedToggleValue] =
  useState(defaultToggleValue);

function toggle() {
  setResolvedToggleValue(!resolvedToggleValue);
}


return { resolvedToggleValue, toggle };
```

The default value of the internal state now needs to consider that there might be a prop controlling the state:

```
const [resolvedToggleValue, setResolvedToggleValue] =
  useState(defaultToggleValue || toggleValue);
```

When the state is changed, the change handler is called, if it has been defined:

```
function toggle() {
  if (onToggleValueChange) {
    onToggleValueChange(!resolvedToggleValue);
  } else {
    setResolvedToggleValue(!resolvedToggleValue);
  }
}
```

Again, it's important that we still update the internal state in case the consumer isn't controlling the state.

The last step in implementing this pattern is to update the internal state when the controlled state is updated. We can do this with useEffect as follows:

```
useEffect(() => {
  const isControlled = toggleValue !== undefined;
  if (isControlled) {
    setResolvedToggleValue(toggleValue);
  }
}, [toggleValue]);
```

The effect is triggered when the state prop changes. We check whether the state prop is being controlled; if so, the internal state is updated with its value.

Here's an example of controlling `toggleValue` in `useToggle`:

```
const [toggleValue, setToggleValue] = useState(false);
const onCount = useRef(0);
const { resolvedToggleValue, toggle } = useToggle({
  toggleValue,
  onToggleValueChange: (value) => {
    if (onCount.current >= 3) {
      setToggleValue(false);
    } else {
      setToggleValue(value);
      if (value) {
        onCount.current++;
      }
    }
  },
});
```

This example stores the toggle value in its own state and passes it to `useToggle`. `onToggleValueChange` is handled by updating the state value. The logic for setting the state value only allows it to be `true` up to three times.

So, this use case has overridden the default behavior of the toggle so that it can only be set to `true` up to three times.

Now that we understand how to allow the internal state to be controlled, we will use it in our checklist component.

Allowing checkedIds to be controlled

At the moment, our checklist component allows many items to be selected. If we allow the `checkedIds` state to be controlled by the consumer, they can change the checklist component so that they can select just a single item.

So, carry out the following steps:

1. We will start in `useChecked.ts`. Add `useEffect` to the React `import` statement:

    ```
    import { useState, useEffect } from 'react';
    ```

2. Add new parameters for the controlled checked IDs and the change handler:

```
type Params = {
  checkedIds?: IdValue[];
  onCheckedIdsChange?: (checkedIds: IdValue[]) => void;
};
export function useChecked({
  checkedIds,
  onCheckedIdsChange,
}: Params) {
  ...
}
```

3. Update the internal state name to `resolvedCheckedIds` and default it to the passed-in `checkedIds` parameter if defined:

```
export function useChecked({
  checkedIds,
  onCheckedIdsChange,
}: Params) {
  const [resolvedCheckedIds, setResolvedCheckedIds] =
    useState<IdValue[]>(checkedIds || []);
  const handleCheckChange = (checkedId: IdValue) => () =>
  {
    const isChecked = resolvedCheckedIds.
      includes(checkedId);
    let newCheckedIds = isChecked
      ? resolvedCheckedIds.filter(
          (itemCheckedid) => itemCheckedid !== checkedId
        )
      : resolvedCheckedIds.concat(checkedId);
    setResolvedCheckedIds(newCheckedIds);
  };
  return { handleCheckChange, resolvedCheckedIds };
}
```

4. Update the `handleCheckChange` handler to call the passed-in change handler if defined:

```
const handleCheckChange = (checkedId: IdValue) => () => {
  const isChecked = resolvedCheckedIds.
    includes(checkedId);
  let newCheckedIds = isChecked
    ? resolvedCheckedIds.filter(
        (itemCheckedid) => itemCheckedid !== checkedId
      )
    : resolvedCheckedIds.concat(checkedId);
  if (onCheckedIdsChange) {
    onCheckedIdsChange(newCheckedIds);
  } else {
    setResolvedCheckedIds(newCheckedIds);
  }
};
```

5. The last task in `useCheck.ts` is to synchronize the controlled checked IDs with the internal state. Add the following `useEffect` hook to achieve this:

```
useEffect(() => {
  const isControlled = checkedIds !== undefined;
  if (isControlled) {
    setResolvedCheckedIds(checkedIds);
  }
}, [checkedIds]);
```

6. Now, open `Checklist.tsx` and import the `IdValue` type:

```
import { IdValue } from './types';
```

7. Add the new props for the controlled checked IDs and the change handler:

```
type Props<Data> = {
  data: Data[];
  id: keyof Data;
  primary: keyof Data;
  secondary: keyof Data;
  renderItem?: (item: Data) => ReactNode;
  checkedIds?: IdValue[];
```

```
    onCheckedIdsChange?: (checkedIds: IdValue[]) => void;
  } & ComponentPropsWithoutRef<'ul'>;

  export function Checklist<Data>({
    data,
    id,
    primary,
    secondary,
    renderItem,
    checkedIds,
    onCheckedIdsChange,
    ...ulProps
  }: Props<Data>) {}
```

8. Pass these props to useChecked and rename the destructured checkedIds variable resolvedCheckedIds:

```
  const { resolvedCheckedIds, handleCheckChange } =
  useChecked({
    checkedIds,
    onCheckedIdsChange,
  });
  return (
    <ul className="bg-gray-300 rounded p-10" {...ulProps}>
      {data.map((item) => {
        ...
        return (
          <li ... >
            <label className="flex items-center">
              <input
                type="checkbox"
                checked={resolvedCheckedIds.
                  includes(idValue)}
                onChange={handleCheckChange(idValue)}
              />
              ...
            </label>
          </li>
```

```
        );
      })}
    </ul>
  );
```

9. Open `index.ts` in the `Checklist` folder. Export the `IdValue` type because consumers of the component can now pass in `checkedIds`, which is an array of this type:

```
export type { IdValue } from './types';
```

The `type` keyword after the `export` statement is required by TypeScript when exporting a named type already exported from the referenced file.

10. Now, open `App.tsx` and import `useState` from React, as well as the `IdValue` type:

```
import { useState } from 'react';
import {
  Checklist,
  IdValue
} from './Checklist';
```

11. Define the state in the `App` component for the single checked ID:

```
function App() {
  const [checkedId, setCheckedId] = useState<IdValue |
    null>(
    null
  );

  ...

}
```

The state is `null` when there is no checked item. This can't be set to `undefined` because `Checklist` will think `checkedIds` is uncontrolled.

12. Create a handler for when an item is checked:

```
function handleCheckedIdsChange(newCheckedIds: IdValue[])
{
  const newCheckedIdArr = newCheckedIds.filter(
    (id) => id !== checkedId
  );
  if (newCheckedIdArr.length === 1) {
    setCheckedId(newCheckedIdArr[0]);
```

```
    } else {
      setCheckedId(null);
    }
  }
```

The handler stores the checked ID in the state or sets the state to `null` if the checked item has been unchecked.

13. Pass the checked ID and the change handler to the `Checklist` element as follows:

```
<Checklist
  ...
  checkedIds={checkedId === null ? [] : [checkedId]}
  onCheckedIdsChange={handleCheckedIdsChange}
/>;
```

14. Let's give this a try. If the app isn't running, run it by entering `npm start` in the terminal. You will find that only a single list item can be checked.

That completes this section on allowing the internal state to be controlled. Here's a recap:

- This pattern is useful because it changes the component's behavior

- The component must expose a prop to control the state value and another for its change handler

- Internally, the component still manages the state and synchronizes it with the consumer's using `useEffect`

- If the state is controlled, the consumer's change handler is called in the internal change handler

Summary

In this chapter, we created a reusable checklist component and used many useful patterns along the way.

We started by learning how to implement generic props, which allow a component to be used with varying data types but still be strongly typed. We used this to allow varying data to be passed into the checklist component without sacrificing type safety.

We learned how to allow consumers of a component to spread props onto an internal element. A common use case is spreading props onto the internal container element to allow the consumer to size it, which is what we did with the checklist component.

The render prop pattern is one of the most useful patterns when developing reusable components. We learned that it allows the consumer to take responsibility for rendering parts of the component. We used this pattern to override the rendering of list items in our checklist component.

Custom hooks isolate logic and are useful for sharing logic across components and keeping the code within a component clean. Custom hooks must call a standard React hook directly or indirectly. We extracted the checked logic from our checklist component into a custom hook.

The last pattern we learned about was allowing a component's internal state to be controlled. This powerful pattern allows the consumer of the component to tweak its behavior. We used this to only allow a single list item to be checked in our checklist component.

In the next chapter, we will learn how to write automated tests for React components.

Questions

Answer the following questions to check what you have learned in this chapter:

1. The snippet of the following component renders options and one can be selected:

```
type Props<TOption> = {
  options: TOption[];
  value: string;
  label: string;
};
export function Select({
  options,
  value,
  label,
}: Props<TOption>) {
  return ...
}
```

The following TypeScript error is raised on the component props parameter though: **Cannot find name 'TOption'**. What is the problem?

2. The value and label props from the component in *question 1* should only be set to a property name in the options value. What type can we give value and label so that TypeScript includes them in its type checking?

3. A prop called option has been added to the Select component from the previous question as follows:

```
type Props<TOption> = {
  ...,
  option: ReactNode;
```

```
    };

    export function Select<TOption>({
      ...,
      option
    }: Props<TOption>) {
      return (
        <div>
          <input />
          {options.map((option) => {
            if (option) {
              return option;
            }
            return ...
          })}
        </div>
      );
    }
```

option is supposed to allow the consumer of the component to override the rendering of the options. Can you spot the flaw in the implementation?

4. The following is a Field component that renders a label element and an input element:

```
    type Props = {
      label: string;
    } & ComponentPropsWithoutRef<'input'>;

    export function Field({ ...inputProps, label }: Props) {
      return (
        <>
          <label>{label}</label>
          <input {...inputProps} />
        </>
      );
    }
```

There is a problem with the implementation though – can you spot it?

5. How could the consumer specify props to spread onto the `label` element in the `Field` component from the previous question? Note that we still want the consumer to spread props onto the `input` element.

6. A custom hook has been added to the `Field` component from the previous question. The custom hook is called `useValid`, which validates that the field has been filled in with something:

```
export function useValid() {
  function validate(value: string) {
    return (
      value !== undefined && value !== null && value !==
        ''
    );
  }
  return validate;
}

export function Field({ ... }: Props) {
  const [valid, setValid] = useState(true);
  const validate = useValid();
  return (
    <>
      <label {...labelProps}>{label}</label>
      <input
        {...inputProps}
        onBlur={(e) => {
          setValid(validate(e.target.value));
        }}
      />
      {!valid && <span>Please enter something</span>}
    </>
  );
}
```

What is wrong with the implementation?

7. How many render props can a function component have?

Answers

1. The generic type must be defined in the component function as well as the prop:

    ```
    export function Select<TOption>({
      options,
      value,
      label,
    }: Props<TOption>) {
      return ...
    }
    ```

2. The keyof operator can be used to ensure value and label are keys in options:

    ```
    type Props<TOption> = {
      options: TOption[];
      value: keyof TOption;
      label: keyof TOption;
    };
    ```

3. The consumer is likely to need the data for the option, so the prop should be a function containing the data as a parameter:

    ```
    type Props<TOption> = {
      ...,
      renderOption: (option: TOption) => ReactNode;
    };

    export function Select<TOption>({
      options,
      value,
      label,
      renderOption,
    }: Props<TOption>) {
      return (
        <div>
          <input />
          {options.map((option) => {
            if (renderOption) {
    ```

```
            return renderOption(option);
        }
        return ...
      </div>
    );
}
```

4. There is a syntax error because the rest parameter is the first parameter. The rest parameter must be the last one:

```
export function Field({ label, ...inputProps }: Props) {
  ...
}
```

5. A labelProps prop could be added using the ComponentPropsWithoutRef type. This could then be spread onto the label element:

```
type Props = {
  label: string;
  labelProps: ComponentPropsWithoutRef<'label'>;
} & ComponentPropsWithoutRef<'input'>;

export function Field({
  label,
  labelProps,
  ...inputProps
}: Props) {
  return (
    <>
      <label {...labelProps}>{label}</label>
      <input {...inputProps} />
    </>
  );
}
```

6. useValid doesn't call a standard React hook. A better implementation would be to extract the state into the custom hook as well:

```
export function useValid() {
  const [valid, setValid] = useState(true);
  function validate(value: string) {
    setValid(
      value !== undefined && value !== null && value !==
''
    );
  }
  return { valid, validate };
}


export function Field({ ... }: Props) {
  const { valid, validate } = useValid();
  return (
    <>
      <label {...labelProps}>{label}</label>
      <input
        {...inputProps}
        onBlur={(e) => {
          validate(e.target.value);
        }}
      />
      {!valid && <span>Please enter something</span>}
    </>
  );
}
```

7. There is no limit on the number of render props a component can have.

12

Unit Testing with Jest and React Testing Library

In this chapter, we learn how to use Jest and React Testing Library, two popular automated testing tools that can be used together in React applications. We will create tests on the checklist component we created in *Chapter 11, Reusable Components*.

We will start by focusing on Jest and using it to test simple functions, learning about Jest's common **matcher** functions for writing expectations, and how to execute tests to check whether they pass.

We will then move on to learning about component testing using React Testing Library. We'll understand the different query types and variants and how they help us create robust tests.

After that, we will learn the most accurate way to simulate user interactions using a React Testing Library companion package. We will use this to create tests for items being checked in the checklist component.

At the end of the chapter, we will learn how to determine which code is covered by tests and, more importantly, which code is uncovered. We use Jest's code coverage tool to do this and understand all the different coverage stats it gives us.

So, in this chapter, we'll cover the following topics:

- Testing pure functions
- Testing components
- Simulating user interactions
- Getting code coverage

Technical requirements

We will use the following technologies in this chapter:

- **Node.js** and **npm**: You can install them from `https://nodejs.org/en/download/`
- **Visual Studio Code**: You can install it from `https://code.visualstudio.com/`

We will start with a modified version of the code we finished in the last chapter. The modified code contains logic extracted into pure functions, which will be ideal to use in the first tests we write. This code can be found online at `https://github.com/PacktPublishing/Learn-React-with-TypeScript-2nd-Edition/tree/main/Chapter12/start`.

Carry out the following steps to download this to your local computer:

1. Go to `https://download-directory.github.io/` in a browser.
2. In the textbox on the web page, enter the following URL: `https://github.com/PacktPublishing/Learn-React-with-TypeScript-2nd-Edition/tree/main/Chapter12/start`.
3. Press the *Enter* key. A ZIP file containing the `start` folder will now be downloaded.
4. Extract the ZIP file to a folder of your choice and open that folder in Visual Studio Code.
5. In Visual Studio Code's terminal, execute the following command to install all the dependencies:

```
npm i
```

You are now ready to start writing tests for the checklist component.

Testing pure functions

In this section, we will start by understanding the fundamental parts of a Jest test. Then, we will put this into practice by implementing tests on a pure function in the checklist component.

A pure function has a consistent output value for a given set of parameter values. These functions depend only on the function parameters and nothing outside the function, and also don't change any argument values passed into them. So, pure functions are nice for learning how to write tests because there are no tricky side effects to deal with.

In this section, we will also cover how to test exceptions, which is useful for testing type assertion functions. Finally, at the end of this section, we will learn how to run the tests in a test suite.

Understanding a Jest test

Jest is preinstalled in a Create React App project and configured to look for tests in files with particular extensions. These file extensions are `.test.ts` for tests on pure functions and `.test.tsx` for tests on components. Alternatively, a `.spec.*` file extension could be used.

A test is defined using Jest's `test` function:

```
test('your test name', () => {
  // your test implementation
});
```

The `test` function has two parameters for the test name and implementation. It is common practice for the test implementation to be an anonymous function. The test implementation can be asynchronous by placing the `async` keyword in front of the anonymous function:

```
test('your test name', async () => {
  // your test implementation
});
```

The test implementation will consist of calling the function with arguments being tested and checking the result is as we expect:

```
test('your test name', async () => {
  const someResult = yourFunction('someArgument');
  expect(someResult).toBe('something');
});
```

Jest's `expect` function is used to define our expectations. The result of the function call is passed into `expect`, and it returns an object containing methods we can use to define specific expectations for the result. These methods are referred to as **matchers**. If the expectation fails, Jest will fail the test.

The preceding test uses the `toBe` matcher. The `toBe` matcher checks that primitive values are equal, and the preceding test uses it to check that the `someResults` variable is equal to `"something"`. Other common matchers are as follows:

- `toStrictEqual` for checking the values in an object or array. This recursively checks every property in the object or array. Here's an example:

  ```
  expect(someResult).toStrictEqual({
    field1: 'something',
    field2: 'something else'
  });
  ```

- `not` for checking the opposite of a matcher. Here's an example:

  ```
  expect(someResult).not.toBe('something');
  ```

- `toMatch` for checking strings against **regular expressions** (**regexes**). Here's an example:

  ```
  expect(someResult).toMatch(/error/);
  ```

- `toContain` for checking if an element is in an array. Here's an example:

  ```
  expect(someResult).toContain(99);
  ```

A complete list of all the standard matchers can be found in the Jest documentation at `https://jestjs.io/docs/expect`.

Now that we understand the basics of a Jest test, we will create our first Jest test.

Testing isChecked

The first function we will test is `isChecked`. This function has two parameters:

- `checkedIds`: This is an array of IDs that are currently checked
- `idValue`: This is the ID to determine whether it is checked

We will write a test for when the list item is checked and another for when it isn't checked:

1. Create a file called `isChecked.test.ts` in the `src/Checklist` folder that will contain the tests.

> **Note**
>
> It is best practice to place test files adjacent to the source file being tested. This allows the developers to navigate to the test for a function quickly.

2. Open `isChecked.test.ts` and import the `isChecked` function:

   ```
   import { isChecked } from './isChecked';
   ```

3. Start to create the first test as follows:

   ```
   test('', () => {
   });
   ```

   Jest puts the `test` function in the global scope, so there is no need to import it.

4. Add the test name as follows:

   ```
   test('should return true when in checkedIds', () => {
   });
   ```

Forming a naming convention for test names is good practice so that they are consistent and easy to understand. Here, we have used the following naming structure:

should {expected output / behaviour} when {input / state condition}

5. Now, let's start to implement the logic inside the test. The first step in the test is to call the function being tested with the arguments we want to test:

```
test('should return true when in checkedIds', () => {
    const result = isChecked([1, 2, 3], 2);
});
```

6. The second (and last) step in the test is to check that the result is what we expect, which is `true` for this test:

```
test('should return true when in checkedIds', () => {
    const result = isChecked([1, 2, 3], 2);
    expect(result).toBe(true);
});
```

Since the result is a primitive value (a Boolean), we use the `toBe` matcher to verify the result.

7. Add a second test to cover the case when the ID isn't in the checked IDs:

```
test('should return false when not in checkedIds', () =>
{
    const result = isChecked([1, 2, 3], 4);
    expect(result).toBe(false);
});
```

That completes the tests on the `isChecked` function. Next, we will learn how to test exceptions that are raised. We will check that our tests work after that.

Testing exceptions

We are going to test the `assertValueCanBeRendered` type assertion function. This is a little different from the last function we tested because we want to test whether an exception is raised rather than the returned value.

Jest has a `toThrow` matcher that can be used to check whether an exception has been raised. For this to catch exceptions, the function being tested has to be executed inside the expectation, as follows:

```
test('some test', () => {
  expect(() => {
    someAssertionFunction(someValue);
```

```
    }).toThrow('some error message');
});
```

We will use this approach to add three tests on the `assertValueCanBeRendered` type assertion function. Carry out the following steps:

1.   Create a file called `assertValueCanBeRendered.test.ts` in the `src/Checklist` folder for the tests and import the `assertValueCanBeRendered` type assertion function:

     ```
     import { assertValueCanBeRendered } from './
     assertValueCanBeRendered';
     ```

2.   The first test we will add is to check whether an exception is raised when the value isn't a string or number:

     ```
     test('should raise exception when not a string or
     number', () => {
       expect((() => {
         assertValueCanBeRendered(
           true
         );
       }).toThrow(
         'value is not a string or a number'
       );
     });
     ```

     We pass the `true` Boolean value, which should cause an error.

3.   Next, we will test whether an exception isn't raised when the value is a string:

     ```
     test('should not raise exception when string', () => {
       expect((() => {
         assertValueCanBeRendered(
           'something'
         );
       }).not.toThrow();
     });
     ```

     We use the `not` matcher with `toThrow` to check that an exception is not raised.

4.   The last test will test an exception isn't raised when the value is a number:

     ```
     test('should not raise exception when number', () => {
       expect((() => {
     ```

```
assertValueCanBeRendered(
    99
);
}).not.toThrow();
});
```

That completes the tests for the `assertValueCanBeRendered` type assertion function.

Now that we have implemented some tests, we will learn how to run them next.

Running tests

Create React App has an npm script called `test` that runs the tests. After the tests are run, a watcher will rerun the tests when the source code or test code changes.

Carry out the following steps to run all the tests and experiment with the test watcher options:

1. Open the terminal and execute the following command:

    ```
    npm run test
    ```

    `test` is a very common npm script, so the `run` keyword can be omitted. In addition, `test` can be shortened to `t`. So, a shortened version of the previous command is as follows:

    ```
    npm t
    ```

    The tests will be run, and the following summary will appear in the terminal:

```
PASS  src/Checklist/assertValueCanBeRendered.test.ts
PASS  src/Checklist/isChecked.test.ts

Test Suites: 2 passed, 2 total
Tests:       5 passed, 5 total
Snapshots:   0 total
Time:        9.409 s
Ran all test suites.

Watch Usage
 › Press f to run only failed tests.
 › Press o to only run tests related to changed files.
 › Press q to quit watch mode.
 › Press p to filter by a filename regex pattern.
 › Press t to filter by a test name regex pattern.
 › Press Enter to trigger a test run.
```

Figure 12.1 – First test run

Notice that there is no Command Prompt in the terminal like there usually is after a command has finished executing. This is because the command hasn't fully completed as the test watcher is running—this is called **watch mode**. The command won't complete until watch mode is exited using the *q* key. Leave the terminal in watch mode and carry on to the next step.

2. All the tests pass at the moment. Now, we will deliberately make a test fail so that we can see the information Jest provides us. So, open `assertValueCanBeRendered.ts` and change the expected error message on the first test as follows:

```
test('should raise exception when not a string or
number', () => {
  expect(() => {
    assertValueCanBeRendered(true);
  }).toThrow('value is not a string or a numberX');
});
```

As soon as the test file is saved, the tests are rerun, and a failing test is reported as follows:

```
FAIL  src/Checklist/assertValueCanBeRendered.test.ts
  ● should raise exception when not a string or number

  expect(received).toThrow(expected)

  Expected substring: "value is not a string or a numberX"
  Received message:   "value is not a string or a number"

       5 | ): asserts value is IdValue {
       6 |   if (typeof value !== "string" && typeof value !== "number") {
    >  7 |     throw new Error("value is not a string or a number");
         |           ^
       8 |   }
       9 | }
      10 |
```

Figure 12.2 – Failing test

Jest provides valuable information about the failure that helps us quickly resolve test failures. It tells us this:

- Which test failed

- What the expected result was, in comparison to the actual result

- The line in our code where the failure occurred

Resolve the test failure by reverting the test to check for the correct error message. The test should be as follows now:

```
test('should raise exception when not a string or
number', () => {
  expect(() => {
    assertValueCanBeRendered(true);
  }).toThrow('value is not a string or a number');
});
```

3. We will now start to explore some of the options on the test watcher. Press the *w* key in the terminal, where the test watcher is still running. The test watcher options will be listed as follows:

```
Watch Usage
 › Press a to run all tests.
 › Press f to run only failed tests.
 › Press q to quit watch mode.
 › Press i to run failing tests interactively.
 › Press p to filter by a filename regex pattern.
 › Press t to filter by a test name regex pattern.
 › Press Enter to trigger a test run.
```

Figure 12.3 – Test watcher options

4. We can filter the test files that Jest executes by using the *p* watch option. Press the *p* key and enter isChecked when prompted for the pattern. The pattern can be any regex. Jest will search for test files that match the regex pattern and execute them. So, Jest runs the tests in isChecked.test.ts in our test suite:

```
PASS  src/Checklist/isChecked.test.ts
  √ should return true when in checkedIds (1 ms)
  √ should return false when not in checkedIds

Test Suites: 1 passed, 1 total
Tests:       2 passed, 2 total
Snapshots:   0 total
Time:        6.234 s
Ran all test suites matching /isChecked/i.

Watch Usage: Press w to show more.
```

Figure 12.4 – Jest running a test file checking for a matching pattern

5. To clear the filename filter, press the *c* key.

6. We can also filter the tests that Jest executes by the test name using the *t* watch option. Press *t* and enter `should return false when not in checkedIds` when prompted for the test name. Jest will search for test names that match the regex pattern and execute them. So, Jest runs the `should return false when not in checkedIds` test in our test suite:

```
 PASS  src/Checklist/isChecked.test.ts

Test Suites: 1 skipped, 1 passed, 1 of 2 total
Tests:       4 skipped, 1 passed, 5 total
Snapshots:   0 total
Time:        8.05 s
Ran all test suites with tests matching "should return false when not in checkedIds".

Watch Usage: Press w to show more.▮
```

Figure 12.5 – Jest running test name matching a pattern

7. Press the *c* key to clear the test name filter and then press the *q* key to exit the test watcher.

That completes our exploration of running Jest tests and this section on testing pure functions. Here's a quick recap of the key points:

- Tests are defined using Jest's `test` function.

- Expectations within the test are defined using Jest's `expect` function in combination with one or more matchers.

- The `expect` function argument can be a function that executes the function being tested. This is useful for testing exceptions with the `toThrow` matcher.

- Jest's test runner has a comprehensive set of options for running tests. The test watcher is particularly useful on large code bases because it only runs tests impacted by changes by default.

Next, we will learn how to test React components.

Testing components

Testing components is important because this is what the user interacts with. Having automated tests on components gives us confidence that the app is working correctly and helps prevent regressions when we change code.

In this section, we will learn how to test components with Jest and React Testing Library. Then, we will create some tests on the checklist component we developed in the last chapter.

Understanding React Testing Library

React Testing Library is a popular companion library for testing React components. It provides functions to render components and then select internal elements. Those internal elements can then be checked using special matchers provided by another companion library called `jest-dom`.

A basic component test

Here's an example of a component test:

```
test('should render heading when content specified', () => {
  render(<Heading>Some heading</Heading>);
  const heading = screen.getByText('Some heading');
  expect(heading).toBeInTheDocument();
});
```

Let's explain the test:

- React Testing Library's `render` function renders the component we want to test. We pass in all the appropriate attributes and content so that the component is in the required state for the checks. In this test, we have specified some text in the content.

- The next line selects an internal element of the component. There are lots of methods on React Testing Library's `screen` object that allow the selection of elements. These methods are referred to as **queries**. `getByText` selects an element by matching the text content specified. In this test, an element with `Some heading` text content will be selected and assigned to the `heading` variable.

- The last line in the test is the expectation. The `toBeInTheDocument` matcher is a special matcher from `jest-dom` that checks whether the element in the expectation is in the DOM.

Understanding queries

A React Testing Library query is a method that selects a DOM element within the component being rendered. There are many different queries that find the element in different ways:

- `ByRole`: Queries elements by their role.

> **Note**
>
> DOM elements have a `role` attribute that allows assistive technologies such as screen readers to understand what they are. Many DOM elements have this attribute preset—for example, the `button` element automatically has the role of `'button'`. For more information on roles, see `https://developer.mozilla.org/en-US/docs/Web/Accessibility/ARIA/Roles`.

- `ByLabelText`: Queries elements by their associated label. See this page in the React Testing Library documentation for the different ways elements can be associated with a label: `https://testing-library.com/docs/queries/bylabeltext`.

- `ByPlaceholderText`: Queries elements by their placeholder text.

- `ByText`: Queries elements by their text content.

- `ByDisplayValue`: Queries `input`, `textarea`, and `select` elements by their value.

- `ByAltText`: Queries `img` elements by their `alt` attribute.

- `ByTitle`: Queries elements by their `title` attribute.

- `ByTestId`: Queries elements by their test ID (the `data-testid` attribute).

There are also different types of queries that behave slightly differently on the found element. Each query type has a particular prefix on the query method name:

- `getBy`: Throws an error if a single element is not found. This is ideal for synchronously getting a single element.

- `getAllBy`: Throws an error if at least one element is not found. This is ideal for synchronously getting multiple elements.

- `findBy`: Throws an error if a single element is not found. The check for an element is repeated for a certain amount of time (1 second by default). So, this is ideal for asynchronously getting a single element that might not be immediately in the DOM.

- `findAllBy`: Throws an error if at least one element is not found within a certain time (1 second by default). This is ideal for asynchronously getting multiple elements that might not be immediately in the DOM.

- `queryBy`: This returns `null` if an element is not found. This is ideal for checking that an element does *not* exist.

- `queryAllBy`: This is the same as `queryBy`, but returns an array of elements. This is ideal for checking multiple elements do *not* exist.

So, the `getByText` query we used in the preceding test finds the element by the text content specified and raises an error if no elements are found.

For more information on queries, see the following page in the React Testing Library documentation: `https://testing-library.com/docs/queries/about/`.

Notice that none of these queries references implementation details such as an element name, ID, or CSS class. If those implementation details change due to code refactoring, the tests shouldn't break, which is precisely what we want.

Now that we understand React Testing Library, we will use it to write our first component test.

Implementing checklist component tests

The first component test we will write is to check that list items are rendered correctly. The second component test will check list items are rendered correctly when custom rendered.

React Testing Library and jest-dom are preinstalled in a Create React App project, which means we can get straight to writing the test. Carry out the following steps:

1. Create a new file in the src/Checklist folder called Checklist.test.tsx and add the following import statements:

```
import { render, screen } from '@testing-library/react';
import { Checklist } from './Checklist';
```

2. Start to create the test as follows:

```
test('should render correct list items when data
specified', () => {
});
```

3. In the test, render Checklist with some data:

```
test('should render correct list items when data
specified', () => {
  render(
    <Checklist
      data={[{ id: 1, name: 'Lucy', role: 'Manager' }]}
      id="id"
      primary="name"
      secondary="role"
    />
  );
});
```

We've rendered a single list item that should have primary text Lucy and secondary text Manager.

4. Let's check Lucy has been rendered:

```
test('should render correct list items when data
specified', () => {
  render(
    <Checklist
      data={[{ id: 1, name: 'Lucy', role: 'Manager' }]}
```

```
        id="id"
        primary="name"
        secondary="role"
      />
    );
    expect(screen.getByText('Lucy')).toBeInTheDocument();
  });
```

We have selected the element using the getByText query and fed that directly into the expectation. We use the toBeInTheDocument matcher to check that the found element is in the DOM.

5. Complete the test by adding a similar expectation for checking for Manager:

```
test('should render correct list items when data
specified', () => {
  render(
    <Checklist
      data={[{ id: 1, name: 'Lucy', role: 'Manager' }]}
      id="id"
      primary="name"
      secondary="role"
    />
  );
  expect(screen.getByText('Lucy')).toBeInTheDocument();
  expect(screen.getByText('Manager')).
    toBeInTheDocument();
});
```

That completes our first component test.

6. We will add the second test in one go, as follows:

```
test('should render correct list items when renderItem
specified', () => {
  render(
    <Checklist
      data={[{ id: 1, name: 'Lucy', role: 'Manager' }]}
      id="id"
      primary="name"
      secondary="role"
```

```
        renderItem={(item) => (
          <li key={item.id}>
            {item.name}-{item.role}
          </li>
        )}
      />
    );
    expect(
      screen.getByText('Lucy-Manager')
    ).toBeInTheDocument();
  });
```

We render a single list item with the same data as the previous test. However, this test custom renders the list items with a hyphen between the name and role. We use the same getByText query to check that the list item with the correct text is found in the DOM.

7. If the tests aren't automatically running, run them by running npm test in the terminal. Use the *p* option to run these two new tests—they should both pass:

```
PASS  src/Checklist/Checklist.test.tsx
  √ should render correct list items when data specified (37 ms)
  √ should render correct list items when renderItem specified (5 ms)

Test Suites: 1 passed, 1 total
Tests:       2 passed, 2 total
Snapshots:   0 total
Time:        6.593 s
Ran all test suites matching /Checklist\.test/i.

Watch Usage: Press w to show more.
```

Figure 12.6 – Component tests passing

That completes our first two component tests. See how easy React Testing Library makes this!

Using test IDs

The next test we will implement is to check that a list item is checked when specified. This test will be slightly trickier and requires a test ID on the checkboxes. Carry out the following steps:

1. Start by opening Checklist.tsx and notice the following test ID on the input element:

```
<input
  ...
```

```
        data-testid={`Checklist__input__${idValue.toString()}`}
  />
```

Test IDs are added to elements using a `data-testid` attribute. We can concatenate the list item ID so that the test ID is unique for each list item.

2. Now, return to the `Checklist.test.tsx` file and begin to write the test:

```
test('should render correct checked items when
specified', () => {
  render(
    <Checklist
      data={[{ id: 1, name: 'Lucy', role: 'Manager' }]}
      id="id"
      primary="name"
      secondary="role"
      checkedIds={[1]}
    />
  );
});
```

We have rendered the checklist with the same data as the previous tests. However, we have specified that the list item is checked using the `checkedIds` prop.

3. Now, on to the expectation for the test:

```
test('should render correct checked items when
specified', () => {
  render(
    <Checklist
      data={[{ id: 1, name: 'Lucy', role: 'Manager' }]}
      id="id"
      primary="name"
      secondary="role"
      checkedIds={[1]}
    />
  );
  expect(
    screen.getByTestId('Checklist__input__1')
  ).toBeChecked();
});
```

We select the checkbox by its test ID using the `getByTestId` query. We then use the `toBeChecked` matcher to verify the checkbox is checked. `toBeChecked` is another special matcher from the `jest-dom` package.

This new test should pass, leaving us with three passing tests on `Checklist`:

```
PASS  src/Checklist/Checklist.test.tsx
  √ should render correct list items when data specified (37 ms)
  √ should render correct list items when renderItem specified (4 ms)
  √ should render correct checked items when specified (7 ms)

Test Suites: 1 passed, 1 total
Tests:       3 passed, 3 total
Snapshots:   0 total
Time:        7.07 s
Ran all test suites matching /Checklist\.test/i.

Watch Usage: Press w to show more.
```

Figure 12.7 – All three component tests passing

4. Stop the test runner by pressing the *q* key.

That completes this section on testing components. Here's a quick recap:

- React Testing Library contains lots of useful queries for selecting DOM elements. Different query types will find single or many elements and will or won't error if an element isn't found. There is even a query type for repeatedly searching for elements rendered asynchronously.

- `jest-dom` contains lots of useful matchers for checking DOM elements. A common matcher is `toBeInTheDocument`, which verifies an element is in the DOM. However, `jest-dom` contains many other useful matchers, such as `toBeChecked` for checking whether an element is checked or not.

Next, we will learn how to simulate user interactions in tests.

Simulating user interactions

So far, our tests have simply rendered the checklist component with various props set. Users can interact with the checklist component by checking and unchecking items. In this section, we will first learn how to simulate user interactions in tests. We will then use this knowledge to test whether list items are checked when clicked and that `onCheckedIdsChange` is raised.

Understanding fireEvent and user-event

React Testing Library has a `fireEvent` function that can raise events on DOM elements. The following example raises a `click` event on a **Save** button:

```
render(<button>Save</button>);
fireEvent.click(screen.getByText('Save'));
```

This is okay, but what if logic was implemented using a `mousedown` event rather than `click`? The test would then need to be as follows:

```
render(<button>Save</button>);
fireEvent.mouseDown(screen.getByText('Save'));
```

Fortunately, there is an alternative approach to performing user interactions in tests. The alternative approach is to use the `user-event` package, which is a React Testing Library companion package that simulates user interactions rather than specific events. The same test using `user-event` looks like this:

```
const user = userEvent.setup();
render(<button>Save</button>);
await user.click(screen.getByText('Save'));
```

The test would cover logic implemented using a `click` event or `mousedown` event. So, it is less coupled to implementation details, which is good. For this reason, we'll use the `user-event` package to write interactive tests on our checklist component.

The `user-event` package can simulate interactions other than clicks. See the documentation at the following link for more information: `https://testing-library.com/docs/user-event/intro`.

Implementing checklist tests for checking items

We will now write two interactive tests on the checklist component. The first test will check items are checked when clicked. The second test will check `onCheckedIdsChange` is called when items are clicked. Carry out the following steps:

1. Create React App does preinstall the `user-event` package, but it may be a version before version 14, which has a different API. Open `package.json`, and then find the `@testing-library/user-event` dependency and check the version. If the version isn't 14 or above, then run the following command in the terminal to update it:

    ```
    npm i @testing-library/user-event@latest
    ```

2. We will add the interactive tests in the same test file as the other component tests. So, open Checklist.test.tsx and add an import statement for user-event:

```
import userEvent from '@testing-library/user-event';
```

3. The first test will test that items are checked when clicked. Start to implement this as follows:

```
test('should check items when clicked', async () => {
});
```

We have marked the test as asynchronous because the simulated user interactions in user-event are asynchronous.

4. Next, initialize the user simulation as follows:

```
test('should check items when clicked', async () => {
  const user = userEvent.setup();
});
```

5. We can now render a list item as we have done in previous tests. We will also get a reference to the checkbox in the rendered list item and check that it isn't checked:

```
test('should check items when clicked', async () => {
  const user = userEvent.setup();
  render(
    <Checklist
      data={[{ id: 1, name: 'Lucy', role: 'Manager' }]}
      id="id"
      primary="name"
      secondary="role"
    />
  );
  const lucyCheckbox = screen.getByTestId(
    'Checklist__input__1'
  );
  expect(lucyCheckbox).not.toBeChecked();
});
```

6. Now, on to the user interaction. Simulate the user clicking the list item by calling the `click` method on the `user` object; the checkbox to be clicked needs to be passed into the `click` argument:

```
test('should check items when clicked', async () => {
  const user = userEvent.setup();
  render(
    <Checklist
      data={[{ id: 1, name: 'Lucy', role: 'Manager' }]}
      id="id"
      primary="name"
      secondary="role"
    />
  );

  const lucyCheckbox = screen.getByTestId(
    'Checklist__input__1'
  );
  expect(lucyCheckbox).not.toBeChecked();
  await user.click(lucyCheckbox);
});
```

7. The last step in the test is to check that the checkbox is now checked:

```
test('should check items when clicked', async () => {
  const user = userEvent.setup();
  render(
    <Checklist
      data={[{ id: 1, name: 'Lucy', role: 'Manager' }]}
      id="id"
      primary="name"
      secondary="role"
    />
  );
  const lucyCheckbox = screen.getByTestId(
    'Checklist__input__1'
  );
```

```
    expect(lucyCheckbox).not.toBeChecked();
    await user.click(lucyCheckbox);
    expect(lucyCheckbox).toBeChecked();
  });
```

8. The next test will test that the function assigned to the onCheckedIdsChange prop is called when a list item is clicked. Here is the test:

```
test('should call onCheckedIdsChange when clicked', async
() => {
  const user = userEvent.setup();
  let calledWith: IdValue[] | undefined = undefined;
  render(
    <Checklist
      data={[{ id: 1, name: 'Lucy', role: 'Manager' }]}
      id="id"
      primary="name"
      secondary="role"
      onCheckedIdsChange={(checkedIds) =>
        (calledWith = checkedIds)
      }
    />
  );
  await user.click(screen.getByTestId('Checklist__
input__1'));
  expect(calledWith).toStrictEqual([1]);
});
```

We set a calledWith variable to the value of the onCheckedIdsChange parameter. After the list item is clicked, we check the value of the calledWith variable using the toStrictEqual matcher. The toStrictEqual matcher is a standard Jest matcher that is ideal for checking arrays and objects.

9. The second test references the IdValue type, so add an import statement for this:

```
import { IdValue } from './types';
```

10. Run the tests by running npm test in the terminal. Press the *p* key to run all the tests in the Checklist.test.tsx file. We should now have five passing component tests:

```
PASS  src/Checklist/Checklist.test.tsx
  √ should render correct list items when data specified (61 ms)
  √ should render correct list items when renderItem specified (10 ms)
  √ should render correct checked items when specified (11 ms)
  √ should check items when clicked (125 ms)
  √ should call onCheckedIdsChange when clicked (63 ms)

Test Suites: 1 passed, 1 total
Tests:       5 passed, 5 total
Snapshots:   0 total
Time:        7.958 s
Ran all test suites matching /Checklist\.test/i.

Watch Usage: Press w to show more.▉
```

Figure 12.8 – Five passing component tests

11. Stop the test runner by pressing the *q* key.

That completes the tests for clicking items and this section on simulating user interactions. We learned that React Testing Library's fireAction function raises a particular event that couples tests to implementation details. A better approach is to use the user-event package to simulate user interactions, potentially raising several events in the process.

Next, we will learn how to quickly determine any code that isn't covered by tests.

Getting code coverage

Code coverage is how we refer to how much of our app code is covered by unit tests. As we write our unit tests, we'll have a fair idea of what code is covered and not covered, but as the app grows and time passes, we'll lose track of this.

In this section, we'll learn how to use Jest's code coverage option so that we don't have to keep what is covered in our heads. We will use the code coverage option to determine the code coverage on the checklist component and understand all the different statistics in the report. We will use the code coverage report to find some uncovered code in our checklist component. We will then extend the tests on the checklist component to achieve full code coverage.

Running code coverage

To get code coverage, we run the `test` command with a `--coverage` option. We also include a `--watchAll=false` option that tells Jest not to run in watch mode. So, run the following command in a terminal to determine code coverage on our app:

```
npm run test -- --coverage --watchAll=false
```

The tests take a little longer to run because of the code coverage calculations. When the tests have finished, a code coverage report is output in the terminal with the test results:

```
----------------------------|---------|----------|---------|---------|-------------------
File                        | % Stmts | % Branch | % Funcs | % Lines | Uncovered Line #s
----------------------------|---------|----------|---------|---------|-------------------
All files                   |   57.44 |    62.5  |    60   |   57.77 |
 src                        |       0 |       0  |     0   |       0 |
  App.tsx                   |       0 |       0  |     0   |       0 | 5-14
  index.tsx                 |       0 |     100  |   100   |       0 | 7-19
  reportWebVitals.ts        |       0 |       0  |     0   |       0 | 3-10
 src/Checklist              |    93.1 |   93.75  |    90   |   92.85 |
  Checklist.tsx             |     100 |     100  |   100   |     100 |
  assertValueCanBeRendered.ts |   100 |     100  |   100   |     100 |
  getNewCheckedIds.ts       |      50 |      50  |    50   |      50 | 9-10
  index.ts                  |       0 |       0  |     0   |       0 |
  isChecked.ts              |     100 |     100  |   100   |     100 |
  types.ts                  |       0 |       0  |     0   |       0 |
  useChecked.ts             |     100 |     100  |   100   |     100 |
----------------------------|---------|----------|---------|---------|-------------------
```

Figure 12.9 – Terminal code coverage report

Next, we will take some time to understand this code coverage report.

Understanding the code coverage report

The coverage report lists the coverage for each file and aggregates coverage in a folder for all the files in the project. So, the whole app has between 57.44% and 62.5% code coverage, depending on which statistic we take.

Here's an explanation of all the statistic columns:

- **% Stmts**: This is **statement coverage**, which is how many source code statements have been executed during test execution
- **% Branch**: This is **branch coverage**, which is how many of the branches of conditional logic have been executed during test execution
- **% Funcs**: This is **function coverage**, which is how many functions have been called during test execution
- **% Lines**: This is **line coverage**, which is how many lines of source code have been executed during test execution

The rightmost column in the report is very useful. It gives the lines of source code that aren't covered by tests. For example, the getNewCheckedIds.ts file in the checklist component has lines 9 and 10, which are uncovered.

There is another version of the report that is generated in HTML format. This file is automatically generated every time a test is run with the --coverage option. So, this report has already been generated because we have just run the tests with the --coverage option. Carry out the following steps to explore the HTML report:

1. The report can be found in an index.html file in the coverage\lcov-report folder. Double-click on the file so that it opens in a browser:

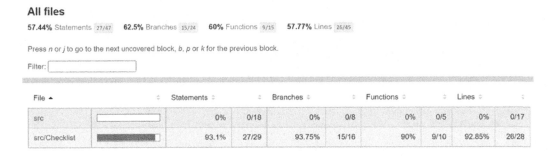

All files

57.44% Statements 27/47   **62.5%** Branches 15/24   **60%** Functions 9/15   **57.77%** Lines 26/45

Press *n* or *j* to go to the next uncovered block, *b, p* or *k* for the previous block.

Filter:

File ▲		Statements		Branches		Functions		Lines	
src		0%	0/18	0%	0/8	0%	0/5	0%	0/17
src/Checklist		93.1%	27/29	93.75%	15/16	90%	9/10	92.85%	26/28

Figure 12.10 – HTML coverage report

The report contains the same data as the terminal report, but this one is interactive.

2. Click on the **src/Checklist** link in the second row of the report. The page now shows the coverage for the files in the checklist component:

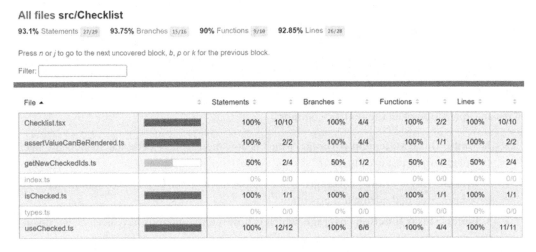

All files src/Checklist

93.1% Statements 27/29   **93.75%** Branches 15/16   **90%** Functions 9/10   **92.85%** Lines 26/28

Press *n* or *j* to go to the next uncovered block, *b, p* or *k* for the previous block.

Filter:

File ▲		Statements		Branches		Functions		Lines	
Checklist.tsx		100%	10/10	100%	4/4	100%	2/2	100%	10/10
assertValueCanBeRendered.ts		100%	2/2	100%	4/4	100%	1/1	100%	2/2
getNewCheckedIds.ts		50%	2/4	50%	1/2	50%	1/2	50%	2/4
index.ts		0%	0/0	0%	0/0	0%	0/0	0%	0/0
isChecked.ts		100%	1/1	100%	0/0	100%	1/1	100%	1/1
types.ts		0%	0/0	0%	0/0	0%	0/0	0%	0/0
useChecked.ts		100%	12/12	100%	6/6	100%	4/4	100%	11/11

Figure 12.11 – Coverage report for checklist component files

3. Click on the `getNewCheckedIds.ts` link to drill into the coverage for that file:

All files / src/Checklist **getNewCheckedIds.ts**

50% Statements 2/4   **50%** Branches 1/2   **50%** Functions 1/2   **50%** Lines 2/4

Press *n* or *j* to go to the next uncovered block, *b, p* or *k* for the previous block.

```
 1      import { isChecked } from "./isChecked";
 2      import { IdValue } from "./types";
 3
 4      export function getNewCheckedIds(
 5        currentCheckedIds: IdValue[],
 6        checkedId: IdValue
 7      ) {
 8  2x    I if (isChecked(currentCheckedIds, checkedId)) {
 9         return currentCheckedIds.filter(
10           (itemCheckedid) => itemCheckedid !== checkedId
11         );
12        } else {
13  2x     return currentCheckedIds.concat(checkedId);
14        }
15      }
```

Figure 12.12 – Coverage report for getNewCheckedIds.ts

We can see that the uncovered lines 9 and 10 are very clearly highlighted in the `getNewCheckedIds.ts` file.

So, the HTML coverage report is useful in a large code base because it starts with high-level coverage and allows you to drill into coverage on specific folders and files. When viewing a file in the report, we can quickly determine where the uncovered code is because it is clearly highlighted.

Next, we will update our tests so that lines 9 and 10 in `getNewCheckedIds.ts` are covered.

Gaining full coverage on the checklist component

The logic not currently being checked by tests is the logic used when a list item is clicked but has already been checked. We will extend the `'should check items when clicked'` test to cover this logic. Carry out the following steps:

1. Open `Checklist.test.tsx` and rename the `'should check items when clicked'` test as follows:

    ```
    test('should check and uncheck items when clicked', async
    () => {
      ...
    });
    ```

2. Add the following highlighted lines at the end of the test to click the checkbox for a second time and check it is unchecked:

    ```
    test('should check and uncheck items when clicked', async
    () => {
      const user = userEvent.setup();
      render(
        <Checklist
          data={[{ id: 1, name: 'Lucy', role: 'Manager' }]}
          id="id"
          primary="name"
          secondary="role"
        />
      );
      const lucyCheckbox = screen.getByTestId(
        'Checklist__input__1'
      );
      expect(lucyCheckbox).not.toBeChecked();
      await user.click(lucyCheckbox);
      expect(lucyCheckbox).toBeChecked();
      await user.click(lucyCheckbox);
      expect(lucyCheckbox).not.toBeChecked();
    });
    ```

3. In the terminal, rerun the tests with coverage:

```
npm run test -- --coverage --watchAll=false
```

All the tests still pass, and the coverage on the checklist component is now reported as 100% on all the statistics:

```
-------------------------------|---------|----------|---------|---------|-------------------
File                           | % Stmts | % Branch | % Funcs | % Lines | Uncovered Line #s
-------------------------------|---------|----------|---------|---------|-------------------
All files                      |   61.7  |   66.66  |   66.66 |  62.22  |
 src                           |     0   |     0    |     0   |    0    |
  App.tsx                      |     0   |     0    |     0   |    0    | 5-14
  index.tsx                    |     0   |   100    |   100   |    0    | 7-19
  reportWebVitals.ts           |     0   |     0    |     0   |    0    | 3-10
 src/Checklist                 |   100   |   100    |   100   |  100    |
  Checklist.tsx                |   100   |   100    |   100   |  100    |
  assertValueCanBeRendered.ts  |   100   |   100    |   100   |  100    |
  getNewCheckedIds.ts          |   100   |   100    |   100   |  100    |
  index.ts                     |     0   |     0    |     0   |    0    |
  isChecked.ts                 |   100   |   100    |   100   |  100    |
  types.ts                     |     0   |     0    |     0   |    0    |
  useChecked.ts                |   100   |   100    |   100   |  100    |
-------------------------------|---------|----------|---------|---------|-------------------
```

Figure 12.13 – 100% coverage on the checklist component

The checklist component is now well covered. However, it is a little annoying that index.ts and types.ts appear in the report with zero coverage. We'll resolve this next.

Ignoring files in the coverage report

We will remove index.ts and types.ts from the coverage report because they don't contain any logic and create unnecessary noise. Carry out the following steps:

1. Open the package.json file. We can configure Jest in the package.json file in a jest field, and there is a coveragePathIgnorePatterns configuration option for removing files from the coverage report. Add the following Jest configuration to package.json to ignore the types.ts and index.ts files:

```
{
  ...,
  "jest": {
    "coveragePathIgnorePatterns": [
      "types.ts",
      "index.ts"
    ]
  }
}
```

2. In the terminal, rerun the tests with coverage:

```
npm run test -- --coverage --watchAll=false
```

The types.ts and index.ts files are removed from the coverage report:

```
----------------------------------|---------|----------|---------|---------|----------------------
File                              | % Stmts | % Branch | % Funcs | % Lines | Uncovered Line #s
----------------------------------|---------|----------|---------|---------|----------------------
All files                         |   65.9  |   66.66  |   66.66 |   66.66 |
 src                              |     0   |     0    |     0   |     0   |
  App.tsx                         |     0   |     0    |     0   |     0   | 5-14
  reportWebVitals.ts              |     0   |     0    |     0   |     0   | 3-10
 src/Checklist                    |   100   |   100    |   100   |   100   |
  Checklist.tsx                   |   100   |   100    |   100   |   100   |
  assertValueCanBeRendered.ts     |   100   |   100    |   100   |   100   |
  getNewCheckedIds.ts             |   100   |   100    |   100   |   100   |
  isChecked.ts                    |   100   |   100    |   100   |   100   |
  useChecked.ts                   |   100   |   100    |   100   |   100   |
----------------------------------|---------|----------|---------|---------|----------------------
```

Figure 12.14 – types.ts and index.ts files removed from the coverage report

That completes this section on code coverage. Here's a quick recap:

- The --coverage option outputs a code coverage report after the tests have run.
- An interactive HTML code coverage report is generated in addition to the one in the terminal. This is useful on a large test suite to drill into uncovered code.
- Both report formats highlight uncovered code, giving us valuable information to improve our test suite.

Summary

In this chapter, we created tests on a checklist component using Jest and React Testing Library. In addition, we learned about common Jest matchers in Jest's core package and useful matchers for component testing in a companion package called jest-dom.

We used Jest's test runner and used options to run certain tests. This is particularly useful on large code bases.

We learned about the wide variety of queries available in React Testing Library to select elements in different ways. We used the getByText query extensively in the checklist tests. We also created a test ID on list item checkboxes so that the getByTestId query could be used to select them uniquely.

We learned that the user-event package is an excellent way of simulating user interactions that are decoupled from the implementation. We used this to simulate a user clicking a list item checkbox.

We learned how to produce code coverage reports and understood all the statistics in the report. The report included information about uncovered code, which we used to gain 100% coverage on the checklist component.

So, we have reached the end of this book. You are now comfortable with both React and TypeScript and have excellent knowledge in areas outside React core, such as styling, client-side routing, forms, and web APIs. You will be able to develop components that are reusable across different pages and even different apps. On top of that, you will now be able to write a robust test suite so that you can ship new features with confidence.

In summary, the knowledge from this book will allow you to efficiently build the frontend of large and complex apps with React and TypeScript. I hope you have enjoyed reading this book as much as I did writing it!

Questions

Answer the following questions to check what you have learned in this chapter:

1. We have written some tests for a `HomePage` component and placed them in a file called `HomePage.tests.tsx`. However, the tests aren't run when the `npm test` command is executed—not even when the *a* key is pressed to run all the tests. What do you think the problem might be?

2. Why doesn't the following expectation pass? How could this be resolved?

   ```
   expect({ name: 'Bob' }).toBe({ name: 'Bob' });
   ```

3. Which matcher can be used to check that a variable isn't `null`?

4. Here's an expectation that checks whether a **Save** button is disabled:

   ```
   expect(
     screen.getByText('Save').hasAttribute('disabled')
   ).toBe(true);
   ```

   The expectation passes as expected, but is there a different matcher that can be used to simplify this?

5. Write a test for the `getNewCheckedIds` function we used in this chapter. The test should check if an ID is removed from the array of checked IDs if it is already in the array.

6. We have a `form` element containing a **Save** button only when data has been loaded into fields from a server API. We have used the `findBy` query type so that the query retries until the data has been fetched:

   ```
   expect(screen.findByText('Save')).toBeInTheDocument();
   ```

   However, the expectation doesn't work—can you spot the problem?

7. The following expectation attempts to check that a **Save** button isn't in the DOM:

```
expect(screen.getByText('Save')).toBe(null);
```

This doesn't work as expected, though. Instead, an error is raised because the **Save** button can't be found. How can this be resolved?

Answers

1. The problem is that the file extension is `tests.tsx` rather than `test.tsx`.

2. The `toBe` matcher should only be used for checking primitive values such as numbers and strings—this is an object. The `toStrictEqual` matcher should be used to check objects because it checks the values of all its properties instead of the object reference:

```
expect({ name: 'Bob' }).toStrictEqual({ name: 'Bob' });
```

3. The `not` and `toBeNull` matchers can be combined to check a variable isn't `null`:

```
expect(something).not.toBeNull();
```

4. The `toBeDisabled` matcher can be used from `jest-dom`:

```
expect(screen.getByText('Save')).toBeDisabled();
```

5. Here's a test:

```
test('should remove id when already in checked ids', ()
=> {
  const result = getNewCheckedIds([1, 2, 3], 2);
  expect(result).toStrictEqual([1, 3]);
});
```

6. The `findBy` query type requires awaiting because it is asynchronous:

```
expect(await screen.findByText('Save')).
toBeInTheDocument();
```

7. The `queryBy` query type can be used because it doesn't throw an exception when an element isn't found. In addition, the `not` and `toBeInTheDocument` matchers can be used to check that the element isn't in the DOM:

```
expect(screen.queryByText('Save')).not.
toBeInTheDocument();
```

Index

Other Books You May Enjoy

If you enjoyed this book, you may be interested in these other books by Packt:

React and React Native

Adam Boduch, Roy Derks, Mikhail Sakhniuk

ISBN: 978-1-80323-128-0

- Explore React architecture, component properties, state, and context
- Work with React Hooks for handling functions and components
- Implement code splitting using lazy components and Suspense
- Build robust user interfaces for mobile and desktop apps using Material-UI
- Write shared components for Android and iOS apps using React Native
- Simplify layout design for React Native apps using NativeBase
- Write GraphQL schemas to power web and mobile apps
- Implement Apollo-driven components

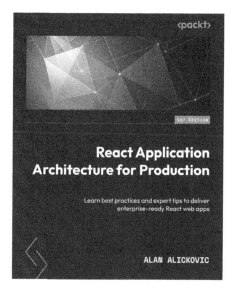

React Application Architecture for Production

Alan Alickovic

ISBN: 978-1-80107-053-9

- Use a good project structure that scales well with your application
- Create beautiful UIs with Chakra UI and emotion
- Configure a base Next.js app with static code analysis and Git hooks
- Learn to mock API endpoints for prototyping, local development and testing
- Choose an optimal rendering strategy in Next.js based on the page needs
- Learn to choose the best state management solution for given problem
- Write unit tests, integration tests and e2e tests in your React Application
- Deploy your React applications on Vercel

Packt is searching for authors like you

If you're interested in becoming an author for Packt, please visit `authors.packtpub.com` and apply today. We have worked with thousands of developers and tech professionals, just like you, to help them share their insight with the global tech community. You can make a general application, apply for a specific hot topic that we are recruiting an author for, or submit your own idea.

Share Your Thoughts

Now you've finished *Learn React with TypeScript (Second Edition)*, we'd love to hear your thoughts! Scan the QR code below to go straight to the Amazon review page for this book and share your feedback or leave a review on the site that you purchased it from.

`https://packt.link/r/1-804-61420-3`

Your review is important to us and the tech community and will help us make sure we're delivering excellent quality content.

Download a free PDF copy of this book

Thanks for purchasing this book!

Do you like to read on the go but are unable to carry your print books everywhere? Is your eBook purchase not compatible with the device of your choice?

Don't worry, now with every Packt book you get a DRM-free PDF version of that book at no cost.

Read anywhere, any place, on any device. Search, copy, and paste code from your favorite technical books directly into your application.

The perks don't stop there, you can get exclusive access to discounts, newsletters, and great free content in your inbox daily

Follow these simple steps to get the benefits:

1. Scan the QR code or visit the link below

https://packt.link/free-ebook/9781804614204

2. Submit your proof of purchase
3. That's it! We'll send your free PDF and other benefits to your email directly

Made in the USA
Middletown, DE
25 May 2023